The Source® for Reading Comprehension Strategies

by Regina G. Richards, M.A.

| Skill Area: | Reading Comprehension | Age Level: | 6 to 18 |
| | | Grades: | 1 to 12 |

Evidence-Based Practice

The strategies in this book incorporate components identified by the National Reading Panel (NRP) as having a solid evidence base and match the mandates of No Child Left Behind and Reading First. Studies supporting these techniques are referenced in Appendix A, Chapter 3 of *Vocabulary Instruction Methods: A Summary Of Vocabulary Instruction Methods* (National Reading Panel, 1999, pp. 3-33 to 3-35). These are some of the evidence-based strategies and approaches presented in the book:

- Association method
- Cognitive strategies
- Concept method
- Decoding strategies
- Graphic organizers
- Key word
- Mental imagery
- Multiple strategies approach
- Prior knowledge
- Roots/affix analysis
- Summarization
- Visual mapping
- Basic mnemonic techniques
- Comprehension monitoring
- Cooperative learning
- Elaborate and rich instruction
- Interactive vocabulary techniques
- Listening actively
- Mnemonics
- Pre-instruction of vocabulary words
- Question answering
- Semantic mapping
- Text structure
- Wide reading & background exposure

LinguiSystems®

LinguiSystems, Inc.
3100 4th Avenue
East Moline, IL 61244-9700
800-776-4332

FAX: 800-577-4555
E-mail: service@linguisystems.com
Web: linguisystems.com

Printed in the U.S.A.

ISBN 0-7606-0659-5

About the Author

Regina G. Richards, M.A., is a Director and President of Richards Educational Therapy Center, Inc. and RET Center Press. She founded and was Director of Big Springs School for 27 years. Her professional emphasis has been in developing and providing multidisciplinary programs for students with language-learning disabilities, especially dyslexia and dysgraphia. Regina began her career in bilingual education, working on curriculum development and test design.

A practicing educational therapist in Riverside, California since 1975, Regina has authored a variety of journal articles and books on reading, dyslexia, dysgraphia, learning/memory, and visual development. She is an active member of her local branch of the International Dyslexia Association, the Inland Empire Branch, where she has served as president numerous times. She presents workshops and classes at the University of California Extension programs at both the Riverside and San Diego campuses. She is an accomplished speaker and presents at numerous conferences and workshops nationally.

Regina is also the author of *The Source for Dyslexia and Dysgraphia* and *The Source for Learning and Memory Strategies*.

A note about the CD included with this book

The CD attached to the inside back cover of this book contains an Appendix of materials in Adobe Acrobat .pdf document format that you will find invaluable in your reading comprehension instruction. These materials, including many graphic organizer templates, are referred to specifically throughout the text of the book. Simply insert the CD into your computer and you will be able to easily view and print the pages.

Table of Contents

Table of Contents

The Source for Reading Comprehension Strategies

Table of Contents

Table of Contents

Table of Contents

Preface

Comprehension is only a four-syllable word, but it implies a cornucopia of meanings. On the surface, reading comprehension means understanding what you read. However, full understanding of print involves so much more than just the words and phrases on the page. Our job as teachers, therapists, and parents is to facilitate the learner's journey to full comprehension — leading our students to use efficient strategies and to celebrate their successes and their gifts. What we do, how we model strategies, and how we deal with our students all matter to a highly significant degree. As stated by Haim Ginott,

> "I have come to a frightening conclusion that I am the decisive element in the classroom. It is my personal approach that creates the climate. It's my daily mood that makes the weather. As a teacher, I possess a tremendous power to make a student's life miserable or joyous. I can be a tool of torture or an instrument of inspiration. I can humiliate or humor, hurt or heal. In all situations, it is my response that decides whether a situation will be escalated or de-escalated and a student humanized or dehumanized[1]."

The purpose of this book is to contribute to the vast collection of tools used by dedicated teachers, therapists, and parents who are working to help our students enhance their skills and reach their potential. Best wishes to all of you.

I wish to sincerely thank a large number of researchers and clinicians who have presented at various conferences, sponsored by The International Dyslexia Association and other groups. Their discussions and examples, as well as my association with them, triggered ideas for many of the strategies developed within these pages.

- Rich Allen, Ph.D.
- Susan Carraker, Ph.D.
- Louisa Cook-Moats, Ed.D.
- Peter Fisher
- Melvin D. Levine, M.D.
- Margaret Richek, Ph.D.
- Andrew Stetkevich
- Camille I. Z., Blachowicz
- Thomas Conn
- Nancy Cushen-White, Ph.D.
- Marcia Henry, Ph.D.
- Michael C. McKenna
- Steven A. Stahl, Ph.D.

To those creative minds and many more with whom I've associated and interacted, thank you for your inspirations. I value your professionalism and commitment. And, thank you for valuing our children.

I dedicate this book to the following people who hold special places in my heart:
- My best friend and lifelong companion — my husband, Irv: thanks for all of your support and encouragement
- Our son, Eli: thank you for your spirit and your courage and for teaching me about learning issues from the inside out
- The memory of our son, Dovid: forever in my heart. Thank you for your love of life.

— Regina

---

[1]Ginott, Haim. (1985). *Between teacher and child.* New York: Avon Books.

CHAPTER 1

Readers comprehend texts by extracting and creating meaning. Successful comprehension entails a variety of prerequisite skills, abilities, and knowledge. A reader must be motivated and engaged with the text and must have a purpose or a goal for reading. Readers use a variety of cognitive and metacognitive strategies to draw on their knowledge to arrive at a meaning:

- word knowledge
- linguistic knowledge
- discourse knowledge
- vocabulary

In addition, readers have to process many non-print sources of information, including pictures, tables, and charts, to fully comprehend text. Fluency is also an important element in comprehending text. That is, in order to orchestrate the components of comprehension, a reader should be able to do oral reading with reasonable speed, accuracy, and expression (Snow, 2001).

| All teachers are reading teachers. |

The goal of this book is to present reading comprehension strategies that contribute to our professional knowledge base and will, ultimately, improve the lives of all children. The selected strategies are based upon current research standards and exemplify a range of techniques. You are encouraged to use these strategies as models as you develop additional strategies related to your own students' needs and curriculum.

How the Brain Reads

Reading comprehension is an extremely complex process involving accurate decoding and attaching meaning to the written word, while doing so with ease and speed. Reading First Legislation defines the term *reading* as "a complex system of deriving meaning from print that requires all of the following:

- the skills and knowledge to understand how phonemes, or speech sounds, are connected to print
- the ability to decode unfamiliar words
- the ability to read fluently
- sufficient background information and vocabulary to foster reading comprehension
- the development of appropriate active strategies to construct meaning from print
- the development and maintenance of the motivation to read" (U.S. Dept. of Education, 2002, title I, part B, subpart 1, section 1208)

The integration of many brain processes is required to enable us to perform reading comprehension skills efficiently. (See pages 23-24 for a more thorough discussion of brain processes and reading.) Good readers typically activate brain areas in the anterior, temporal parietal, and occipital temporal portions

(Shaywitz 2003; Sandak 2005). In contrast, studies of brain activation patterns in students with dyslexia continue to indicate a characteristic activation. One of the researchers, Fletcher, concludes that the dyslexic students in his studies have not recruited and trained the language areas in their brain. To compensate, these children use more right hemisphere processing; however, the right hemisphere is not as proficient at reading. Additional findings reveal that children who are not at risk for reading problems demonstrate very little right hemispheric activation (Fletcher, 2004).

Intervention studies with these children generated changes in network activation of many of the dyslexic children. Fletcher found that after intervention, the students were beginning to demonstrate activation in the left hemisphere that had not been there previously. He concludes that appropriate instruction is able to develop a systematic shift regarding hemispheric specialization: the student begins to recruit left hemisphere temporal areas for use in reading. Consequently, he states that development of reading skills is dependent on establishing neural networks in the left hemisphere and the brain needs to recruit these language areas for efficient reading to occur.

> **With appropriate instruction, students begin to recruit left hemisphere language areas of the brain for use in reading.**

Decades of careful research related to literacy have yielded findings (such as those mentioned in the previous paragraph) that allow description of these and other physiological processes. Research has also contributed evidence that provides a solid foundation for building our instructional practices. The combination of understanding physiological causes and designing instructional intervention is awesome and provides us with opportunities for individualizing reading instruction on a more precise basis. As an example of the power of research-based methods, a study where a first-grade classrooms used high-quality reading instruction over the course of the year resulted in just 3% of the students exhibiting literacy problems compared to a typical 10-20% (Fletcher, 2004).

Sandak (2005) concluded from her research at Haskins Laboratories at Yale University School of Medicine, that attention to both the phonological and semantic features of new words resulted in better learning than attention to either of the features alone. She states, "The phonological and semantic processes are driven by different underlying brain mechanisms and these react in different ways." Better and more effective learning and processing is achieved by integrating sounds and meaning.

Teaching Reading

Teaching a child to read was once a complicated and confusing process, with individual schools and teachers using their own "favorite" methods. Today our substantial knowledge about how children learn has eliminated much of the confusion regarding how to teach a child to read. To learn to read, children require a systematic and well-planned process — one that is based upon philosophies and procedures grounded in science. The Reading First Legislation defines the essential components of reading instruction as explicit and systematic instruction in these areas:

- **Phonemic awareness:** the ability to hear, identify, and manipulate the individual sounds and spoken words
- **Phonics:** the relationship between the letters of the written language and the sounds of spoken language
- **Vocabulary development:** the words students must know to read effectively
- **Reading fluency (including oral reading skills):** the capacity to read text accurately and quickly
- **Reading comprehension strategies:** the ability to understand and gain meaning from what has been read (U.S. Dept. of Education, 2002, title I, part B, subpart 1, section 1208)

> We need to incorporate instruction in reading comprehension strategies into all content area instruction.

All teachers are teachers of reading, and because of that, we need to incorporate instruction in reading comprehension strategies into all content area instruction. Although strategies will not be implemented identically in all content areas, we need to help students modify the appropriate strategies so they are most effective in each area.

Some children will learn to read by any method. It almost seems as though these students absorb the information and skills through osmosis. Our concern is to provide a methodology that will allow *all* children to learn to read. We can dream of a future where standard classroom instruction will be so effective that the majority of children develop the necessary language and literacy skills for success. Then we will be able to gear our specialized intervention and remediation programs to those children with the most significant processing problems. When that occurs, we will have sufficient time to provide the special students with the intensive instruction that they require.

This book is intended to provide foundational knowledge and reading comprehension strategies that teachers and therapists can incorporate within general education classrooms, small group intervention, remedial assistance, or special education. Most of these techniques can be readily integrated within the existing classroom curriculum, thus providing relevant contextual base. That also means you won't have to gather additional reading materials to use these strategies. Well-chosen strategy implementation can enhance teaching the existing curriculum and provide students with greater opportunity to meet grade level standards.

Reduced Literacy Development Is Not Just a School Problem

The National Institutes of Health (NIH) is greatly concerned with literacy. One might wonder why a Health Institute would worry about reading. The answer is that poor literacy greatly affects society in countless ways.

> Reading instruction is seldom effectively integrated with content area instruction. Children need to read well if they are to learn what is expected of them in school beyond grade three (Snow, 2001, section 1.1.3).

The National Institute of Child Health and Human Development (NICHD) considers poor literacy to be a major public health concern for many reasons, among which are multiple longitudinal studies substantiating devastating consequences of school failure. Some of these consequences include poor self-esteem, impaired social development, and interference with future employment. Consider these statistics reported at the Hearing on Measuring Success: Using Assessments and Accountability (McCardle, 2004, p. 39):

- Of the 10-15% of children who will eventually drop out of school, over 75% will report difficulties learning to read.
- Only 2% of students receiving special or compensatory education for difficulty in learning to read will complete a four-year college program.
- Surveys of adolescents and young adults with criminal records indicate that at least half of them have reading difficulties.
- Approximately half of the children and adolescents with a history of substance abuse have reading problems.

The NICHD, one of many Institutes within the NIH, funded high-quality research related to many aspects of the reading process throughout the last quarter of the 20th century. Under the leadership of visionaries such as its director, Dr. Duane Alexander, and Dr. G. Reid Lyon, former Chief of the Child

> "Current difficulties in reading largely originate from rising demands for literacy, not from declining absolute levels of literacy" (Snow, et al., 1998, p. 4). Increasing demands for higher levels of literacy in the workforce require that we do better than we have ever done before in teaching all children to read.

Development and Behavioral Branch, this agency continues to have a profound impact on public policy and educational practice. The convergence of research indicates that solid, systematic techniques, based on processes grounded in science, are essential but not sufficient: Programs do not teach — teachers teach.

The Premise Underlying This Book

Many students in our schools struggle to understand what they read beyond a surface level. They often must reread passages to grasp the content, misinterpret the author's message, and/or become frustrated with the overall task of reading. While frustration is not inherently bad, excess and/or persistent frustration during the process of reading leads to avoidance and cascades into additional problems.

Our schools classify a large number of students as "learning disabled" because of poor literacy skills. Many of these students may not truly be disabled. They may simply be "casualties of an instructional system that has not relied on scientifically-based instructional strategies. [Researchers feel] many could have learned to read if they had been taught by highly qualified, well-trained teachers using scientifically-based instructional strategies" (Pasternak, 2004, p. xxviii).

A tool bag of efficient strategies is valuable for all students, regardless of their reading level. Competently using such strategies will enhance a reader's overall effectiveness and efficiency in reading tasks while providing tools to aid in systematically progressing through text. These advantages decrease frustration and increase confidence and enjoyment.

> "There should never be any excuse for a child to be in special education and not demonstrate literacy growth acceleration" (Torgesen, 2004).

Poor readers frequently do not approach material systematically or strategically. They rarely use what they already know as a vehicle to determine what they do not know. Similarly, they don't consistently chunk or divide a task into more manageable parts.

Important metacognitive concepts exist as an overlay to the majority of literacy issues. For example, readers need to learn both *how* to use each strategy and *when* to do so. Besides analyzing the how and when of strategy use, struggling readers often fail to attribute their success or failure on a task to their own efforts regarding whether or not their approach to the task was effective. While these children do not take ownership of their successes, they *do* take terrible ownership of their failures.

For a long time, our educational models have been similar to a medical model, which suggests the student has a "problem" that needs to be fixed (Ruddell, 2001). The following three models have been especially prevalent in reading education, special education, and compensatory programs:

1. **Defect Model**
   - Something is wrong with the child.
   - The teacher's role is to find the problem and fix it.

2. **Deficit Model**
   - Something is missing in the child's development.
   - The teacher's role is to discover what is missing and teach it.

3. **Disruption Model**
   - Some trauma is interfering with learning.
   - The teacher's role is to remove or reduce the trauma.

Ruddell recommends a shift to a model she calls the **Difference Model**, which is an approach that avoids the issue of a "problem." This author agrees with Ruddell that the Difference Model provides a more appropriate way of viewing student involvement in literacy education.

⚑ **Difference Model**
- There is a difference between student performance and expected achievement.
- The teacher's role is to locate the difference and adjust instruction and materials to achieve a closer match.

"It is important to expose learners to exceptional instructors who have a gift for making the diagnosis, a talent for precise observation, and excellent judgment in making difficult management decisions" (Sackett, 1992).

The Difference Model is appropriate for all learners who have experienced an instructional mismatch. The focus for change is placed on the educational process, as guided by the teacher, who identifies appropriate strategies and materials and applies them as necessary.

This book provides strategy recommendations and suggestions for explicit instruction related to reading comprehension within a variety of situations. The reader's task is to identify and select strategies to match both the needs of the student and requirements of the curriculum.

Sally Shaywitz, in a discussion of the "Evolution of Evidence-Based Education," emphasizes the value and role of the educator. She states, "Taken as a whole, evidence-based practice seeks to integrate evidence along with clinical expertise and client choice, and still maintain a high level and consistency of the application of different treatments" (Shaywitz, 2004). In her discussion, she also shares related quotes, such as the following by David Sackett:

"External clinical evidence can inform but never replace individual clinical expertise. It is the clinician who decides whether external evidence applies to the individual patient at all, and if so, how it should be integrated into a clinical decision. It is important to expose learners to exceptional clinicians who have a gift for intuitive diagnosis, a talent for precise observation, and excellent judgment in making difficult management decisions" (Sackett, 1992).

All Teachers Are Reading Comprehension Teachers

Many curriculum developers appear to adopt the perspective that reading instruction takes place in elementary school and thereafter the focus is on content. Many of today's teachers received their training based on that perspective. It is critical to realize that reading instruction today no longer takes place in isolation. Throughout school, students' needs change: they need strategies that will enable them to analyze and comprehend the more difficult words and passages they encounter in content area textbooks and literature. They need to realize the following truths about reading:
- ⚑ Reading involves complex processes.
- ⚑ The reader must be purposeful, and flexibly and critically integrate a variety of skills and strategies.
- ⚑ Readers need to construct meaning in different texts within a variety of contexts.

Even students who feel that they "read okay" often struggle to interpret or analyze text in more than superficial ways. If they use strategies, they may not adjust them to different styles of text. One study found that 60% of 12th graders were unable to make inferences or understand figurative language (Langer, 2001). Teachers who recognize how essential it is for students to adjust reading strategies to a specific content learning task are much more likely to teach content and process concurrently.

> Teachers who recognize how essential it is for students to adjust reading strategies to a specific content learning task are much more likely to teach content and process concurrently.

Reading efficiency requires competencies in the basic components of decoding, fluency, and comprehension. The key, as identified by the National Reading Council, is to integrate explicit instruction and alphabetic principles (necessary for word accuracy), reading for meaning (critical for comprehension), and active engagement (critical for fluency) (Fletcher, 2004). Achieving competencies in these areas frees the reader to reach for the primary goal of reading — deriving meaning from the printed text and interacting with the writer, especially if the reader applies the gained competencies efficiently and effectively.

➤ Literacy for Life

Literacy development is a lifelong endeavor. Even as adults, we are constantly learning to read and reading to learn. For example, you decide you want to do your own taxes for the first time. You buy the software and begin to follow the steps for installation and use; however, the language of tax forms is new to you and some of the software instructions don't seem to make sense. It takes you a while to get comfortable with this new vocabulary and style. You find that after you have read a while, you fall into the rhythm of the language and adjust to its vocabulary and patterns. Thus, you are learning to read while you are reading to learn.

The Value of Practice

Our educational system helps beginning readers and writers develop phonological awareness, concepts about print, and an understanding of the alphabetic principle. We want students to instantly and easily recognize words so focus on fluency needs to start at the beginning of instruction. Beginning readers require a great deal of practice and need to reinforce and enhance their skills by reading manageable texts and being exposed to a variety of literature. Interaction and discussion intensify reading fluency skill building, regardless of the format: pictorial, verbal, or written.

The issue of practice is critical but teachers do not always provide practice equitably. Studies indicate that teachers tend to provide higher performing students with more opportunities for higher quality practice. For example, such students experienced these advantages:

- more instructional time related to comprehension
- more opportunities to engage in higher levels of thinking and strategic learning, and more independent research and synthesis projects
- questioning requiring higher levels of thinking followed by more wait time
- richer, comprehensive, grade-level text and supplemental materials (Stanovich, 1986; Vogt, 1989)

> The Matthew Effect applies to all aspects of literacy development.

The types of discrepant opportunities outlined above led Stanovich to describe a phenomenon he termed the "Matthew Effect," a concept that applies to all stages of literacy development. As applied to reading comprehension, the Matthew Effect suggests that more instructional time and more opportunity to read lead to greater skill, which then encourages more practice. The opposite leads to less practice, poor skill development, and eventually, avoidance. Consider the effect as it applies to the development of phonological awareness. Some children begin school with a rich background of listening to words and perhaps even playing with and manipulating sounds within words. Words are transparent for these students — they gain much from instruction, and they develop basic reading skills. Those experiences lead to greater practice and even more skill development. In contrast, when children begin school without the same background, they do not gain skills as rapidly and miss much of the practice which would have led to greater development. In both situations, the gap between the groups enlarges: the rich get richer and the poor get poorer.

Students who do not come from literacy enriching backgrounds do not have experiences that enable cognitive strategy development. Research indicates that "the true discrimination that comes out of poverty is the lack of cognitive strategies." Students who lack these unseen attributes are handicapped in every aspect of life (Payne, 1998, p. 139).

Learning language, including written language, is a social activity. That notion has been accepted since the 1930s when Vygotsky described his sociocultural framework. He suggested that learning occurs "within an environment in which both [a teacher and student] can participate in thoughtful examination and discourse about language in content" (Langer, 2001, p. 839).

Extending Vygotsky's framework, we realize that true literacy as a social activity occurs through interactions with others. Each child brings a different background and perspective to the situation. As educators, it is useful to consider the learner and to value each learner's uniqueness. Consider questions such as the following:

- In what unique ways does this child engage in language-related tasks and interactions?
- How can I use this information to provide appropriate literacy instruction for this child?

➤ About Vygotsky

Lev Vygotsky was a Russian psychologist. His most productive years were at the Institute of Psychology in Moscow (1924-34), where he expanded his ideas on cognitive development, particularly the relationship between language and thinking. His writings emphasized the roles of historical, cultural, and social factors in cognition and argued that language was the most important symbolic tool provided by society. His *Thought and Language* (1934) is a classic text in psycholinguistics.

We constantly need to strive to enhance our students' opportunities for practice. Here are some suggestions for increasing practice opportunities:

- Provide appropriate materials.
- Encourage engagement with these materials.
- Structure opportunities so that students use academic language in a meaningful way (reflections, pair-share).
- Maintain consistent awareness of each student's uniqueness.
- Help students pull in, value, and relate to their existing knowledge.

Attending to those features will allow us to help each student achieve relevant skills and avoid unnecessary frustration with reading.

Specific Needs of the Adolescent Reader

Adolescent readers with poor skills usually have struggled with reading since the beginning of their schooling. Consequently, they adopt complex strategies to avoid potentially embarrassing situations (such as reading aloud). Some students act out or withdraw during literacy-related activities. The majority have poor grades, low self-esteem, and little interest in school. By middle school, many students have given up hope of ever improving their reading ability and they openly proclaim distaste for reading. These and similar findings have been reported by many investigators (Kos, 1991; Meek, 1983; Vogt, 1997; Shearer, Ruddell, & Vogt, 2001).

A symbiotic relationship exists between reading and writing. When efficient, students read for pleasure and knowledge, and they write to develop their ideas and have their thoughts and ideas read by others. When poor literacy skills, especially comprehension, disrupt this relationship between reading and writing, the poor skills disturb the entire learning continuum with devastating long-term effects on life skills.

➤ Steps Needed to Reverse Negative Effects

Older students acquire literacy skills in ways that are broader than their younger peers. For them, the *context* of the learning is much more important. For example, when a teenager reads a science text, it is generally only for an assignment. However, she may often exhibit more interest when reading a driver's manual, as this activity relates to learning to drive, which is an important social goal for many.

Provide adolescents with instruction that build skills as well as the desire to read increasingly complex material.

Students of all ages bring their life experiences with them to school, which is especially true for adolescents. Consequently, many experts in adolescent literacy describe the concept of *connectedness*: the linking of new information to personal experience. Connectedness is an essential element for the construction of meaning during reading and is an especially critical component for adolescents (Rudell, 2001).

Among the recommendations of the Commission on Adolescent Literacy of The International Reading Association is the recommendation to provide adolescents with instruction that builds skills as well as the desire to read increasingly complex material. The Commission recommends encouraging students to critically use their knowledge, values, and questions to search for ways to make meaningful connections between reading material and personal experiences (including peer interaction). This approach requires a socially mediated literacy across media, genres, cultural systems, and affinity groups, and involves new, explicit methods of preparing students to read (Moore, Bean, Birdyshaw, & Rycik, 1999).

Scientifically-Based Strategies

➤ Defining What Is Scientifically-Based

Effective reading instruction requires approaches and strategies based on scientific evidence that has shown them to be successful. Using scientific research to teach children to read and write efficiently is essential for ensuring the best academic and life opportunities for our children. As emphasized by many, including Dr. G. Reid Lyon, if children do not learn to read, they will have difficulty succeeding in life (McCardle, 2001, p. 3). Lyon states, "The downstream consequences [of poor reading] are so much greater than the reading failure itself" (Lyon, 2004).

Lyon has been among the scientists who have served as a catalyst for progress in reading research and promoting the implementation of research-based methods in reading instruction. In a portion of his testimony to the House Committee on Education and The Workforce, Subcommittee on Education Reform (2001), he proclaimed the following:

> "Through scientific inquiry, we have identified elements of an optimal reading program. We know how to measure a child's progress towards reading with fluency and comprehension" (McCardle, 2004, p. 8).

Scientifically-based reading research (SBRR) was first defined in the Reading Excellence Act in 1998:

(A) SBRR means the application of rigorous, systematic, and objective procedures to obtain valid knowledge relevant to reading development, reading instruction, and reading difficulties; and

(B) SBRR shall include research that
  i. Employs systematic, empirical methods that draw on observation or experiment;
  ii. Involves rigorous data analyses that are adequate to test the stated hypothesis and justify the general conclusions drawn;
  iii. Relies on measurement or observational methods that provide valid data across evaluators and observers and across multiple measurement and observation;
  iv. Has been accepted by a peer-reviewed journal or approved by a panel of independent experts through a comparably rigorous, objective, and scientific review (National Reading Panel, 1999; McCardle, 2004).

While this Act was only funded for three years, the definition continues to be agreed upon and included in legislation that followed, including No Child Left Behind (NCLB).

In 1997, Congress asked Lyon, then Chief of The Child Development and Behavioral Branch of the NICHD, in consultation with the Secretary Of Education, to convene a national panel to assess the status of research-based knowledge, including the effectiveness of various approaches to teaching children to read (McCardle, 2004, p. 23). Among the many important actions of the panel, it developed a set of rigorous methodological standards to screen the research literature relevant to each topic. These standards provided consistency and scientific rigor among the various reviewers (McCardle, 2004, p. 24).

Susan B. Neuman, Assistant Secretary for Elementary and Secondary Education, U.S. Department of Education and Former Director, the Center for the Improvement of Early Reading Achievement, states, "our understanding of 'what works' in reading is dynamic and fluid, subject to ongoing review and assessment through quality research . . . We encourage all teachers to explore the research, open their minds to changes in their instructional practice, and take up the challenge of helping all children become successful readers." She encourages teachers to use the guide, *Put Reading First: The Research Building Blocks for Teaching Children to Read. Kindergarten Through Grade 3*, which compiles the findings from scientifically-based research in reading instruction (Armbruster, Lehr, & Osborn, 2003).

➤ Seeking Converging Evidence

Another value of the National Reading Panel was that it considered multiple studies regarding each topic. Researchers and educators know that one size never fits all, and that is certainly true for children learning to read. Consequently, a large number of children need to be studied, and the studies need to take place in many different places and with many different schools and teachers. When multiple studies obtain highly similar results over time with a wide cross-section of children, researchers become more confident that the findings reflect the true picture of reading development, reading difficulties, and the effects of different types of instruction. Findings that converge provide greater indication that the results will be transferable.

It is critical for policy and instructional decisions to have a strong foundation in converging evidence. There is now such convergence for early reading instruction and literacy development throughout the learning continuum (McCardell, 2004, p. 6). Although scientific evidence is an important factor to consider when making educational decisions regarding programs, it is important to realize that such evidence, while critical, is not the sole criteria. Teachers' values, skills, and explicit teaching of strategies are all essential.

Research is the only defensible foundation for sound educational practice. Here are some common alternatives and why they avoid scientific evidence:

- *Tradition:* It's the way we've always done things, but continued use alone isn't evidence of success.
- *Philosophy:* The rhetoric is appealing, but this approach often lacks evidence.
- *Superstition:* It's the illusion of correlation.
- *Anecdote:* It is not representative.
- *Intuition:* It is unreliable without additional study (McCardle, 2004, p. 48).

In the design of scientific research, there must be a clear set of answerable questions. These questions then motivate the design. Here are the six guiding principles of scientific research commonly used to establish instructional design:

- Pose the significant questions that can be investigated empirically.
- Link research to relevant theory.
- Use methods that permit direct investigation of the question.
- Provide a coherent and explicit chain of reasoning.
- Replicate and generalize across studies.
- Disclose research to encourage professional scrutiny and critique (McCardle, 2004, p. 62).

➤ Challenges

Research studies need to have strong internal and external validity to indicate that the study is measuring what it proposes to measure. Any research involving humans presents a unique set of considerations that are not present in the natural sciences.

Several design and implementation challenges exist for education studies: humans are involved, the phenomena concerned are multiply determined, and the phenomena differ widely across human participants. These challenges present threats to both internal and external validity, and as a result, the level of certainty of the research conclusions is often lower than in the physical sciences.

18 *The Source for Reading Comprehension Strategies*

Consequently, research on humans often requires more observations with larger samples to reach certainty.

Practitioners and researchers alike consider these challenges worth dealing with because of the great value in obtaining replicable data that is translated into evidence. We need to know the long-term, not just the immediate or transitory, effects of various instructional programs and methodology. The need for long-term data underscores the importance of longitudinal research and highlights the impressive value of the many longitudinal studies sponsored by NICHD.

➤ Longitudinal Evidence

By definition, longitudinal or follow-up studies require multiple data collection points over a period of time (often years). As a result, the longitudinal researcher encounters real and continuing needs for resources and research support, including personnel. In spite of these and other challenges to long-term research, the data gathered from longitudinal designs provide unique and powerful evidence about development and experience, including the efficacy of early intervention programs.

> When evaluating reading research or programs, the most important outcome measure is how well the students derive meaning from extended text because this relates to the high stakes accountability (i.e., national and state testing) of reading comprehension. Furthermore, it translates more directly to real-life situations (Torgesen, 2005).

We have learned quite a bit from follow-up studies of early intervention because such ongoing studies provide solid data, which translate to evidence of efficacy. Individual differences among children have been widely documented and are one part of the equation that describes intervention effects. Two of the major researchers, Foorman and Torgesen (2001), have identified what they believe are critical features of instructional programs for young children at risk for reading failure. These two critical features are consistent with converging instructional literature (Jenkins & O'Connor, 2002) and point the way to reducing reading failure:

- Instruction is phonemically explicit, comprehensive, and intensive.
- Instruction provides both cognitive and emotional support.

The NRP, and subsequently, Reading First Legislation, indicate that a total reading program should include instruction in phonemic awareness, vocabulary development, fluency and comprehension (U.S. Department of Education, 2002). Instruction for beginning readers needs to include the following components:

- Phonological awareness
- Visual perception of letters
- Word recognition
- Syntax
- Phonemic awareness
- Alphabetic principal
- Orthographic awareness
- Fluency in oral reading

Each of these components is a necessary — but by itself not sufficient — factor for reading success, which is especially true with phonemic awareness. Furthermore, there are differences in how individual children interact with or respond to particular programs. Some do not respond positively to well-planned and carefully implemented interventions, and the reasons behind that add to the complexity of determining program efficacy. Torgesen (2000) has found that about 2 to 6% of children are "treatment resistors."

The most critical factors for reading success differ at varying age levels. The top factors that statistically differentiated unsuccessful from successful readers are listed below. Torgesen's study defined unsuccessful readers as those who scored at Levels 1 and 2 from among five Levels on the Florida State testing (FCAT).

- Critical factors at third grade:
  - Fluency
  - Verbal knowledge and reasoning
  - Working memory (how many things the student can think of at one time)

- Critical factors at seventh grade:
  - Fluency
  - Verbal knowledge and reasoning
  - Phonemic decoding

- Critical factors at tenth grade:
  - Verbal knowledge and reasoning
  - Fluency (Torgesen, 2005)

In general, fluency and automaticity are most critical at the earlier levels. Later on, a lack of vocabulary knowledge and reasoning are shown to be more of a deterrent to reading success. Because ongoing skill-building is important to overall success it is easy to see the impact of early reading impairment on all further academic skills.

Three specific quotations from the National Reading Panel summarize other important findings (National Reading Panel, 1999, p. 4-46):
- "The best way to pursue meaning is through conscious, controlled use of strategies" (Duffy, 1993, p. 223).
- "Becoming an effective transactional strategies instruction teacher takes several years" (Brown et al., 1996, p. 20).
- "The data suggests that students at all skill levels would benefit from being taught the strategies" (Rosenshine, Meister, & Chapman, 1996, p. 201).

Recent converging research indicates the value of using a multifaceted approach. For example, Lovett initially gathered data from sites in Toronto, Atlanta, and Boston. She designed her multifaceted approach to get at the core deficits in phonological awareness, fluency, and strategy learning. She found that students with poor literacy demonstrate inefficient strategies for new learning that then develops into a more global impairment. Her design provided 70 hours of remedial instruction in small groups. She found that students maintained their advantage and gains on follow-up assessment performed one year after conclusion of the remediation (Lovett et al., 2005).

Defining Reading Comprehension

Developmental theories about reading comprehension since the 1970s have emphasized that reading comprehension is not a passive, receptive process. It is an active process that needs to engage the reader. Meaning is derived from intentional, problem-solving, thinking processes used by the reader. Those processes occur during an interchange with the text. An important implication of this definition is that the reader's prior knowledge, when brought to the reading activity, greatly influences understanding of the meaning.

"Reading comprehension is intentional thinking during which meaning is constructed through interactions between text and reader" (Durkin, 1993 in NRP introduction).

The theoretical idea of comprehension is that readers construct meaning representations of the text as they read, and that those representations are essential to enable the reader to recall and use what was read and understood. Therefore, reading must be purposeful and active. A reader can read a text to learn, derive information, or be entertained. While different purposes require a different set of strategies, in all situations the reader reads the text using these three processes:

- The reader reads to understand what is read.
- The reader constructs memory representations of what is understood.
- The reader uses this understanding to become engaged with the material.

➤ A Reflection By G. Reid Lyon

Education is at a crossroads. We can choose to be part of the modern scientific community and base our work with children on converging evidence of what works, or we can continue to bring instruction to our youngsters based upon untested assumptions and philosophical beliefs.

The first path leads to successful readers with far better prospects. The second will invariably lead to failure and wasted lives (G. Reid Lyon, 2004, pp. 480-81).

Reflections

Effective reading needs to be an active process; therefore, it is useful to reflect on a few of the key points within this chapter. Some suggestions for your reflections follow. Feel free to create your own and add other notes.

1. In what ways can you help your students achieve greater connectedness with your current curricular reading materials?

   _____

   _____

   _____

   _____

   _____

2. How can you ensure that your students are using active processing when reading?

   _____

   _____

   _____

   _____

   _____

Reading is to the mind what exercise is to the body.

3. Explore what, if anything, your school site is doing in connection with Reading First and/or NCLB standards.

   _____

   _____

   _____

   _____

   _____

Appendix/Notes

How the Brain Reads

The process of reading requires use of the language system: at a neural level this means that reading relies on the brain circuits already in place for language. "In the condition of developmental dyslexia, where reading fails to develop normally, something has gone awry right from the beginning. Consequently, we would not necessarily expect to find a distinct lesion, a cut in the wiring; instead, the wiring may not have been laid down correctly in the first place, a glitch having taken place during fetal life, when the brain is hard-wired for language. As a result, the tens of thousands of neurons carrying the phonological messages necessary for language do not appropriately connect to form the resonating networks that make skilled reading possible" (Shaywitz, 2003, p. 67).

➤ Results of Studies Using Functional MRI

Shaywitz's study presented a task that required adults to judge whether two nonsense words rhymed. Resulting brain images revealed that men activated the left inferior frontal gyrus as they completed the task, while women activated the right as well as the left. "This represented the first demonstration of a visible sex difference in brain organization for language" (Shaywitz, 2003, p. 77).

The studies identified specific neural sites for sounding out words: the inferior frontal gyrus. Studies over the last decade have continued to map the neural systems for reading, and have identified at least two neural pathways for reading:

1. A pathway for beginning reading — for slowly sounding out the words

2. A pathway for speedier, skilled reading

Shaywitz states, "Studies from around the world leave no doubt that dyslexic readers use different brain pathways than do good readers." Good readers activate highly interconnected neural systems that encompass regions in the back and front of the left side of the brain. "The reading circuitry includes brain regions dedicated to processing the visual features, lines and curves that make up letters, and to transforming the letters into the sounds of language and to getting to the meaning of words" (Shaywitz, 2003, p. 78).

Most of the reading part of the brain is in the back and involves two different pathways. The two sub-systems have different roles in reading, and their functions make sense regarding the changing needs of a reader: beginning readers must first analyze a word; skilled readers identify a word instantaneously:

1. The *parieto-temporal system* works for the novice reader. It is a slow, step-by-step process that helps to analyze a word by pulling it apart and linking letters to sounds.

2. The *occipito-temporal region* is the express pathway to reading and is the one used by skilled readers. The more skilled the reader, the more she activates this region. It responds very rapidly (less than 150 milliseconds) when seeing a word. This region is referred to as the *word form system*.

Imaging studies revealed very different brain activation patterns in dyslexic readers (see the next page). Poor readers reveal underactivation of neural pathways in the back of the brain. Consequently, poor readers have initial trouble analyzing words and transforming letters into sounds, and even as these students mature, their reading remains slow and not fluent. Struggling readers use systems in front of the brain as they try to compensate for the disruption in the back of the brain (Shaywitz, 2003, p. 79).

Appendix/Notes

Typical Neural Activation Pattern of Normal Readers

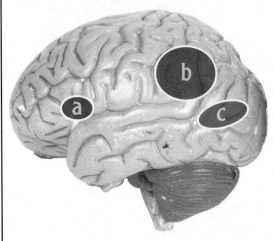

Typical Neural Activation Pattern of Poor Readers

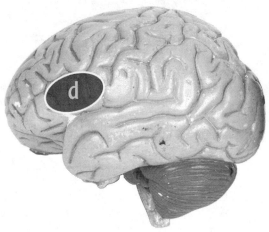

a *Broca's area: inferior gyrus* — takes charge of articulation and word analysis

b *parietal-temporal area* — takes charge of word analysis; the area Shaywitz calls the "slow area" for novice readers

c *occipital-temporal area* — the word form or orthographic area; Shaywitz calls it the "express pathway"

d *neural activation pattern in dyslexic readers* — underactivation of neural pathways in the back of brain, and compensation by using systems in the front of the brain

 The Source for Reading Comprehension Strategies

CHAPTER 2

TEACHING OF STRATEGIES

The comprehension strategies in this book are based on the extensive work provided by the National Reading Panel (NRP); a large number of other current, well-designed studies; and the mandates in No Child Left Behind and Reading First Legislation*. Strong evidence supports combining reading strategies in natural learning situations as well as integrating skills and strategies with metacognitive awareness. The strategies in this book particularly reflect three of the six instructional components in the mandates from Reading First (U.S. Dept. of Education, 2002, title I, part B, subpart 1, section 1208):

1. Sufficient background information and vocabulary to foster reading comprehension

2. Development of appropriate strategies to construct meaning from print

3. Development and maintenance of the motivation to read

The goal of individual and multiple strategies instruction is to enhance motivation to actively read more text. To achieve that goal, students need exposure to and practice with multiple strategies. Students need to be flexible in selecting the strategies to use in a given situation and also need to be able to discuss valid reasons for their choices. Throughout discussion of the strategies, components are discussed in relationship to scientifically-based information on how the brain processes information most efficiently.

Four basic premises underlie the strategies in this book:

1. Reading comprehension is a complex cognitive process.

2. Reading comprehension significantly interacts with vocabulary development.

3. Reading comprehension is an active process that requires an intentional and thoughtful interaction between the reader and the text.

4. Explicit teaching of a variety of strategies is critical.

This volume organizes the strategies into two specific sections: activities for vocabulary development and activities for text comprehension.

- **Vocabulary and Prereading Strategies**
  - associative strategies
  - structural strategies
  - contextual strategies

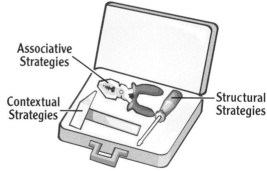

Associative Strategies

Contextual Strategies

Structural Strategies

---

*Chapters 3 through 9 focus on reading comprehension strategies. It is beyond the function of this book to elaborate upon those elements that are prerequisites for reading comprehension, but the reader is cautioned to be aware of their impact on overall reading efficiency.

✦ Text Comprehension Strategies
- organizational strategies
- questioning strategies
- summarization strategies

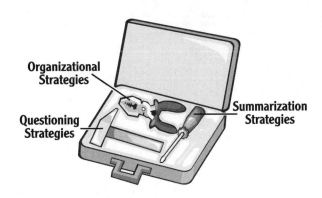

The goal of each section is to enable teachers and therapists to develop a tool bag of effective strategies while understanding which strategy best matches a given situation and specific student style. The last two chapters (Chapters 8 and 9) of this book discuss helping students implement strategies after reading the text, while preparing for retention and retrieval of the information and concepts. Chapter 9 also emphasizes generalization and answers the question, "How we can best help our students transfer and generalize the use of strategies so that they apply the strategies in other situations?"

The Function of Fluency

Fluency is the ability to read a text accurately and quickly. When fluent readers read silently, they recognize words automatically. They group words quickly to help them gain meaning from what they read. Fluent readers read aloud effortlessly and with expression. Their reading sounds natural, as if they are speaking. Readers who have not yet developed fluency read slowly, word by word. Their oral reading is choppy and plodding.

An efficient reader is required to "perform at least two interdependent tasks: the reader must determine what words constitute the text while simultaneously constructing meaning. As such, the greater the amount of attention expended on decoding, the less there is available for comprehension" (Kuhn & Stahl, 2004, p. 3).

Fluency is important because it provides a bridge between word recognition and comprehension. Because fluent readers do not have to concentrate on decoding the words, they can focus their attention on what the text means. They can make connections among the ideas in the text and between the text and their background knowledge. In other words, fluent readers recognize words and comprehend at the same time. Less fluent readers, however, must focus their attention on figuring out the words, which leaves them little attention for understanding the text (Armbruster, Lehr, & Osborn, 2003).

Fluent reading contributes substantially to our ability to construct meaning from what we read. A reciprocal relationship exists between fluency and comprehension. Effortless reading aids comprehension.

Fluency helps the student cross an important bridge. The developmental process of building decoding and automatic vocabulary skills leads to successful reading comprehension. When a reader has built a solid foundation of these skills, he is then able to cross this bridge by reading with speed, accuracy, and proper expression (Pikulski & Chard, 2005).

All skills need to be automatic in order to facilitate our reaction time as we read and integrate sentence structure, decoding, and semantics. Consequently, a major consideration of using vocabulary strategies is to provide enough repetition so that students are able to read the word(s) with ease and accuracy. Even though the strategy descriptions may seem to imply a single experience with the word, it is important to help students become fluent with the target words through varied practice. The goal is for students to develop fluency with key target words prior to reading the passage. They can then transfer this fluency into their reading experiences.

Fluency is different from *automaticity*. "Automaticity is the fast, effortless word recognition that comes with a great deal of reading practice. In the early stages of learning to read, readers may be accurate but slow and inefficient at recognizing words. Continued reading practice helps word recognition become more automatic, rapid, and effortless. Automaticity refers only to accurate, speedy word recognition, not to reading with expression. Therefore, automaticity (or automatic word recognition) is necessary, but not sufficient, for fluency" (Armbruster, Lehr, & Osborn, 2003).

These are the components of reading fluency:

- Ability to attend to prosody (patterns of stress and intonation)
- Anticipation of what comes next in text
- A feeling of anticipation you get by looking ahead as you read

The Value of Visualization

Visualization and imagery provide mental pegs for memory storage and retrieval and serve as repositories of deeper meanings derived from text information. Visualization impacts many aspects of reading comprehension. "School age readers instructed to image while reading recalled more and made significantly more predictive inferences about story events than did the control group subjects" (Gambrel, 1982, in Bell, 1991, p. 17).

Sadosky conducted studies with students of varying ages. With younger students (1984), he found that certain images evoked by stories and stored in memory served as conceptual pegs for the storage and retrieval of story information. In discussing later studies with college students, he stated, "the prediction that imagery in reading stories may serve as a unifying comprehension strategy and serve thematic purposes is consistent with the results of our earlier studies" (Sadosky, Goetz, & Kangiser, 1988). These findings also support Paivio's Dual Coding Theory indicating a parallel nonverbal dimension to discourse processing that can be analyzed, and which contributes to the overall comprehension, integration, and appreciation of text (Paivio, A. 1986). "Dual coding theory explains human behavior and experience in terms of dynamic, associative processes that operate on a rich network of modality-specific verbal and nonverbal (or imagery) representations" (Clark & Paivio, 1991).

> Good readers often form mental pictures, or images, as they read. Readers (especially younger readers) who visualize during reading understand and remember what they read better than readers who do not visualize. Help your students learn to form visual images of what they are reading. For example, urge them to picture a setting, character, or event described in the text (Armbruster, Lehr, & Osborn, 2003).

The strength of these and other findings emphasize the importance of teaching our students to activate their mental imagery skills. Too often students view images passively (as when watching TV). Continually emphasizing the value of imagery will help our students develop automatic and active habits for actively imaging information. Therefore, use your creativity to add visual images and visualization to any of the strategies because doing so enhances a strategy's value.

A Mention of Metacognitive Skills

Metacognition is a person's ability to think about his or her own cognitive processes and performances. It is cognition about cognition, with cognition defined as "the psychological results of perception and learning and reasoning" (Paragon Software). Researchers consistently suggest that metacognition plays an important role in reading. It has been defined as "having knowledge (cognition) and having understanding, control over, and appropriate use of that knowledge" (Tei & Stewart, 1985). It involves both the conscious awareness and the conscious control of one's learning. Good readers use metacognitive strategies to think about and have control over their reading (Armbruster, Lehr, & Osborn, 2003).

What does metacognition mean for us as we strive to enhance our students' reading comprehension skills? We need to ensure that students not only learn *how* to use the strategies, but that they are aware of *when* to use given strategies. They need to be aware of the relationship between their efforts, strategy use, and the resulting success or failure.

When students achieve metacognitive awareness, they will be much more efficient at generalizing and efficiently using strategies. "Integration of executive processes and motivational beliefs are essential for producing generalization . . . Students require insights about the importance of effort and personal causality in leading to successful learning, memory, and problem-solving performances" (Borkowski & Burke, 1996, p. 252).

➤ Cognitive/Metacognitive Strategies in Reading

Strategies are processes and procedures that readers use in comprehending text. Some of these strategies reflect conscious awareness whereas others are acquired without conscious effort or become automatic with practice. A strategy is regarded as metacognitive if its use is triggered by the reader's assessment of his or own cognitive state; for example, the reader slows down when reading text on an unfamiliar topic or rereads a sentence that contradicts previously held beliefs.

> Strategies are processes and procedures that readers use in comprehending text.

Cognitive and metacognitive strategies have been extensively investigated in the fields of cognitive psychology, cognitive science, and education during the last four decades, so there is an abundance of mature theories that are grounded in empirical research. Some individual strategies have proven to be effective in laboratory, group, and classroom environments, including comprehension monitoring, question generation, and the construction of both explanations and story structures (Snow, C., 2001, section 1.4.4).

There are specific steps we can take with our students to enhance metacognition related to reading comprehension strategies (adapted from Borkowski & Burke, 1996).

Step 1: Present a strategy by modeling how to use it in a relevant situation. Have the students repeat its appropriate use so that they learn the various steps and are able to apply each step easily and automatically. Continue with repeated practice until students effectively use each step in the strategy.

Step 2: Teach other strategies similarly and have the students repeat their use in multiple contexts. Using a variety of contexts is important in both enlarging and enriching the students' specific strategy knowledge.

Step 3: Using modeling and scaffolding, teach students how to select an appropriate strategy for a given task. Model the appropriate self-talk that takes place when deciding to select a strategy that matches a specific task. Help students learn to identify when a certain strategy may be efficient for a task, as well as when a particular strategy would not work as well in that situation.

This step is important because it requires students to initiate higher order executive processes such as self-regulation. This process forms the basis for adaptive learning and thinking, as well as generalization.

Step 4: As your students become efficient in using and selecting strategies, help them form positive beliefs about their abilities to use strategies. Also, help them recognize the overall importance of being strategic.

This step is especially critical because students need to learn to associate successful and unsuccessful learning outcomes with how much effort they expended in strategy use instead of attributing success or failure to luck. Help your students realize that they have the capability to enhance their own competencies through self-directed actions.

Feedback is important to help students understand their own capabilities: explain how successful a performance was and its causes. Guide them in progressing to a level where they can use self-feedback about their own successes and the causes of those outcomes.

Metacognition in reading relates to students' awareness of their own personal characteristics — background knowledge, degree of interest, and reading skills and deficiencies — and how they affect learning. Each student needs to take that awareness and translate it into a change in reading behavior. For example, research indicates that less successful students show little tendency to use previous knowledge to clarify text.

There is a significant relationship between a person's cognitive level, executive functioning, and metacognitive level. Butterfield and Albertson (1995, p. 241) represent this interconnection using a visual model. The *cognitive* level is the knowledge and strategies that exist in long-term memory. The *metacognitive* level is the awareness of these strategies and knowing how and when to implement specific strategies. *Executive functioning* coordinates the two levels by monitoring and controlling the use of the knowledge and strategies in accordance with the metacognitive level.

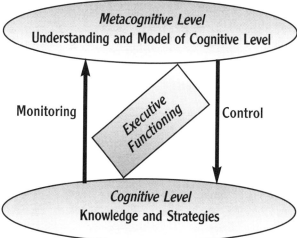

Vocabulary and Varied Prereading Strategies

A large body of research converges on the importance of vocabulary knowledge for fluency and comprehension. Word knowledge develops from our experiences in the world as well as from reading. Our challenge today is that children come to school with wide variability in their language experiences and discrepancies in cultural and language backgrounds. Children gain substantial experience with speaking and listening vocabularies prior to entering school. The development of these vocabularies is dependent upon oral language experiences and conversations; therefore, teachers need to consider and continually deal with the wide variability in students' backgrounds.

The four types of vocabularies — listening, speaking, reading, and writing — are organized and accessed in the brain in various ways. In some situations, there is integration between the types. For other situations, the brain organizes and accesses the vocabularies separately. Because memory is reconstructive and involves a variety of components related to a given word, concept, or experience, the brain needs to be prompted to sort, combine, and organize information for recall from several areas (Richards, 2001, p. 32). The integration of varied information is the primary focus of Chapter 3: Associative Strategies.

As children advance in school, they primarily expand their active vocabularies by developing reading and writing skills, which both occur through classroom experiences and leisure reading activities. Other criteria essential for development of vocabularies include reading aloud, listening to stories, explicit vocabulary instruction, and especially, having fun with words. Furthermore, efficient vocabulary development requires interpersonal interaction, as discussion encourages greater depth of exploration.

➤ How Children Learn New Words

As children encounter new information, they unconsciously access their long-term memory systems to search for previous, similar experiences. They bring the new information, along with previous similar experiences, to their working memory. They make sense of the new information by considering, using, and connecting the new with the familiar.

> Children's brains make new neural connections as they store information from classroom instruction, their experiences, and the environment in which they live (Wolfe, 2004, p. 121).

Children from working class and/or ethnic minority families often come to school with specific knowledge related to their own cultural and community backgrounds. It is important that we take advantage of students' world knowledge while explicitly focusing on increasing the relevancy of new vocabulary words. Vocabulary development and overall reading comprehension are at risk when readers do not tap into their world knowledge.

Good instruction for vocabulary building matches the way children's brains are organized. To learn vocabulary from reading, the teacher must draw the students' attention to the word or words to be learned. Students say the word, spell the word, and learn its meaning before they encounter the word during reading. The best practice is for them to be exposed to the word again in many ways and many places after they read (Wolfe, 2004, p. 126).

Guidelines for implementing the Reading First Legislation indicate that students learn vocabulary directly when they are explicitly taught both individual words and word-learning strategies. Specific word instruction deepens students' knowledge and enhances reading comprehension efficiency. Specific teaching components include the following:

- "Teaching specific words before reading helps both vocabulary learning and reading comprehension;
- Extended instruction that promotes active engagement with vocabulary improves word learning; and
- Repeated exposure to vocabulary in many contexts aids word learning" (Armbruster, Lehr, & Osborn, 2003).

➤ The Importance of Experience on Vocabulary Development

Because the size of children's vocabulary and their comprehension of what they read are highly dependent upon their experiences, we must provide thorough pre-exposure experiences to our students and not depend on having them gain vocabulary knowledge solely by reading. Therefore, the vocabulary chapters (3, 4, and 5) are more extensive than the text chapters.

Wolfe (2004, p. 128) discusses three levels of word knowledge that enable us to determine when a child "owns" a word and has stored it for automatic recall and long-term memory.

Level	Description
Unknown	A child has no previous experience with the word.
Acquainted	A child has some understanding of the word.
Established	A child is able to identify the word and provide its meaning.

A word at the *unknown* level carries the risk that the student will readily drop the word from his working memory. *Acquainted* words are those that the student holds in working memory but has not yet moved into long-term, automatic storage. Without elaborate rehearsal, these too will be lost. Words that are *established* are "owned" by the student and firmly attached to a network of words, ideas, and concepts that the brain can easily access. These words are more likely to be available for the student's use.

The *Reading First Guide* extends a similar discussion by reiterating the four different kinds of word learning that research has identified (Armbruster, Lehr, & Osborn, 2003):

- Learning a new meaning for a known word
- Learning the meaning for a new word representing a known concept
- Learning the meaning of a new word representing an unknown concept
- Clarifying and enriching the meaning of a known word

> The amount of exposure that a child needs to move a target word into long-term memory for automatic recall depends on whether previous neural networks are available or if they need to be developed to attach the word (Wolfe, 2004, p. 129).

Our goal is to help students build elaborate networks of meaning by providing sufficient repetition, encouraging interactions, and involving movement and visual models to both enhance the learning experience and consolidate memory patterns. With any of the strategies in the following chapters, you may incorporate (as appropriate) interactions, drawing, visualizing (mental imagery), and/or body movements (acting out and role-playing the meaning).

Vocabulary Strategies

The three vocabulary chapters (3, 4, and 5) present a variety of strategies that are excellent models you can adapt to fit the age level of your students and your curriculum. Use the activities from any chapter in the sequence that best integrates with your curriculum.

Consider each chapter as a guide. Select a strategy appropriate to your content and use it with your students until they develop proficiency. Then select a related strategy to expand your students' use of it as you bring them towards a level of independent strategy selection.

Text Comprehension Strategies

Good readers are purposeful: they have a purpose for reading. Good readers are active: they think as they read and integrate the new information with their background knowledge. Good readers use strategies before, during, and after reading. Chapters 6, 7, and 8 describe strategies that students can use during their reading process. Almost all of these may be adapted for use after the student has completed the reading to help him organize the information for review, study, or writing preparation.

All students benefit from using strategies, especially those who have learning challenges. Students with learning disabilities "possess the necessary cognitive tools to process information but they do so inefficiently. Researchers suspect that the breakdowns occur in the domain of strategic processing and metacognition" (Gersten, Fuchs, Williams, & Baker, 2001). Three issues contribute to this problem for students with learning challenges:

- They may not possess appropriate strategies.
- They may not realize they need to monitor their comprehension.
- They may not know when to use a strategy they do possess.

The text strategies are discussed individually to increase clarity; however, in a natural context, we often use more than one strategy with a reading passage. For example, while reading a *National Geographic* story, "Mummies Unmasked," I might first use KWL (see page 107) to pull in my background knowledge about mummies. As I read, I monitor my comprehension by asking myself questions and creating a visual graphic of the information. Afterwards, I complete my KWL chart (adding "What" I learned to the "W" column) and I summarize the information using one of my summarization strategies. This procedure combined several strategies: KWL, visual graphic, questioning, monitoring, and summarizing.

As our students gain confidence in their abilities to use strategies, we slowly need to begin to combine the strategies and emphasize the value of using multiple strategies in a situation. "There is very strong empirical, scientific evidence that the instruction of more than one strategy in a natural context leads to the acquisition and use of these reading strategies and transfers to standard and comprehension tests" (National Reading Panel, 1999, p. 4-107). The combination of multiple strategies with metacognitive awareness is the most powerful of all (Lovett, 2005).

➤ Why Teach Text Comprehension Strategies?

Our overall goal is the development of competent, self-regulated readers. We explicitly teach text comprehension strategies to encourage students to interact more actively with the content and to begin to use specific cognitive strategies and reason strategically when they encounter barriers during the process of reading. These text strategies will guide our students as they read.

Some effective readers may acquire strategies for active comprehension informally. Research indicates that explicit or formal instruction of strategies leads to improvement in understanding text and using the information, which helps more students become more effective readers. The research also identifies that some students who do not receive explicit instruction in these strategies are unlikely to learn, develop, or use them spontaneously. Therefore, teaching strategy use to *all* students has multiple benefits. Using strategies effectively will enable students to interact meaningfully with the text without assistance. Strategies break through our students' passivity and involve them in their own learning. The text comprehension procedures guide students to become aware of how well they understand as they are in the process of reading.

A Brief History of Teaching Strategies

"The past 30 years of the scientific study of instruction of text comprehension reveal a distinct trend. The initial investigations focused on the training of particular individual strategies such as comprehension monitoring or identifying main ideas. Here the question was whether readers could learn to use an individual strategy. Then the focus was on whether particular strategies could be learned and whether they could facilitate comprehension. This was an important advance because it validated the teaching of text comprehension strategies. Next, researchers began to study whether the teaching of combinations of different strategies lead to their acquisition and improvement of text comprehension. The success of these 'multiple' strategy teaching methods led to study of the preparation of teachers to teach strategies in natural classroom contexts. This historical development from the instruction of individual strategies to the preparation of teachers to implement them in interaction with readers in the classroom is an important contribution of the scientific approach to the study of reading instruction" (National Reading Panel, 1999, p. 4-40).

➤ Sequencing the Instruction

Some important foundations are especially critical in presenting text comprehension strategies:

1. Help your students develop awareness and understanding that their own cognitive processes can be adapted and modified through instruction and learning.
2. Set up a frame: establish a reason, purpose, and value for using the particular strategy.
3. Demonstrate and model use of the strategy.
4. Guide your students to understand and use the strategy automatically. Lead them in achieving a gradual internalization of the necessary processes.
5. When students attain efficiency with the strategy, encourage them to use it with peers and in smaller groups. The value of cooperative learning is student interaction: discussions help students learn and practice using the strategy while also enhancing their understanding and depth of their explorations. It also provides a more natural context for discussing the content and the strategy.
6. When students are skilled in using the strategy in small groups and pairs, then they are ready to use the strategy independently.

➤ The Text Chapters

Chapters 6, 7, and 8 present a variety of strategies. Use these as suggestions and models while adapting them to fit the age level of your students and your curriculum. Consider each chapter as a guide: select a strategy appropriate to your task and use it with your students until they develop proficiency. Then select a related strategy to expand their strategy use as you bring them towards an automatic level of strategy selection.

Overview

While using these strategies, keep in mind the following aspects that you can incorporate within almost any strategy.

- Movement
- Repetition (including "Think-Pair-Share")
- Visualization

- Novelty
- Interaction
- Metacognition

And, most importantly, strive to build your students' *established* level of word knowledge and encourage your students to have *fun* with words!

Chapter
2

Reflections

Since effective reading needs to be an active process, it is useful to reflect on a few of the key points within this chapter.

1. What are three ways you can help your students build their established word knowledge?

   ❶ _____

   _____

   _____

   ❷ _____

   _____

   _____

   ❸ _____

   _____

   _____

2. How have you been incorporating metacognitive strategies into your classroom environment?

   _____

   _____

   _____

   _____

   What, if anything, will you change? _____

   _____

   _____

   _____

   _____

 Copyright 2006 © LinguiSystems, Inc. *The Source for Reading Comprehension Strategies*

CHAPTER 3

ASSOCIATIVE STRATEGIES

Associative strategies provide us with skills to take a word or object that is familiar and connect it to something we are trying to remember. Associations may take many forms, such as a key word used as a hook or tag, or a visual image. The working memory functions within our brain allow us to hold on to information long enough to manipulate and rehearse it. This process is *active*, and for that reason, Mel Levine refers to it as *active working memory* (Levine, 1998, p. 66; Levine, 2001, p. 75).

> Our brains are meaning-making machines, searching for matches to previous experiences.

Working memory greatly affects comprehension because of the complexity of the process that must occur during reading: written strings of letters must be mapped onto words in long-term memory, and these must be held in working memory so that the meaning of the phrases and sentences can be constructed. When this process breaks down, comprehension is impeded.

Our active working memory has its limitations: it is unable to hold too many components at a time, and generally, it only retains one new component at a time. Consequently, using a tag or a hook based on an associative strategy greatly facilitates the efficiency of active working memory. The old-fashioned idea of tying a string around a finger as a reminder is an example of an associative strategy: it is a cue or a tag. Its function is to be a reminder to remember something. There are times while driving that I think of something important I need to remember. Since I can't make a note, I switch my watch to the "wrong" hand. Consequently, my watch is "out of place," which provides a cue to encourage me to think about what I wanted to remember. Generally, the technique is successful.

As discussed in Chapter 1, neural circuitry is necessary, but not sufficient, for creating a reading brain. Specific kinds of experiences in the environment are also necessary to hook up the circuits so that they function efficiently. Teaching a brain to read requires the application of instructional design principles (Berninger & Richards, 2002, p. 217).

Evidence Base

The strategies in this chapter incorporate components identified by the National Reading Panel (NRP) as having a solid evidence base and matches the mandates of NCLB and Reading First. Studies supporting these techniques are referenced in Appendix A, Chapter 3 of *Vocabulary Instruction Methods: A Summary Of Vocabulary Instruction Methods* (National Reading Panel, 1999, pp. 3-33 to 3-35). These are the evidence-based strategies presented in the chapter:

- Basic mnemonic techniques
- Interactive vocabulary techniques
- Pre-instruction of vocabulary words
- Semantic mapping
- Wide reading & background exposure
- Specific methods: Key word, Concept, Association

General Considerations

The techniques presented in this chapter help students develop cues to focus on and remember new vocabulary, and to encourage them to attend to patterns — both within word categories and patterns that contrast meanings of different words. The goal is for students to enhance both the breadth and depth of their vocabulary knowledge, because a rich vocabulary is the true base of comprehension.

- Enhancing the **breadth** of word knowledge:
  Knowing the meanings of *many* words greatly increases both the oral language base and the general fund of world knowledge.

- Enhancing the **depth** of word knowledge:
  It is important to understand, at a deep level, all of the meanings of a given word, including multiple meanings and connotations.

When incorporating any of this chapter's strategies into your lessons, keep in mind that learning language is a social activity. There is real power in discussion, as it helps children generate connections between new and previously known information. Students learn from each other, and as they contribute to the discussion, they become active thinkers. Therefore, it is important that the classroom or group environment be a safe one in which students can generate ideas. Using review strategies such as Think-Pair-Share allows you to incorporate rehearsal as well as language interaction in an activity.

Think — Pair — Share

Have your students follow these steps to share their thoughts with others and facilitate meaningful discussion (Jensen, 2003, p. 137):

Think: Stand and mentally reflect on your topic for moment.

Pair: Move to find a partner.

Share: Share your prior learning with your partner.
Listen to your partner's prior learning.
Thank your partner and return to your seat.

In addition to interaction and rehearsal with other students, the way you present new vocabulary is also important. One technique is to incorporate physical movements with associations for your initial introduction of the word(s). As you explain the new word or concept, let your hands "do the talking," by pairing hand gestures with new vocabulary. Showing a related gesture as you are explaining new information provides a hook to enhance your students' comprehension and retention. For example, while saying the sentence, "Vocabulary is learned best *contextually* with *interactive* follow-up," show hand gestures for *contextually* (make a large square with your hands) and *interactive* (make a circle with the thumb and forefinger of each hand and interlace them).

> **Vocabulary is learned best contextually and with interactive follow-up.**

Another important consideration is to remember to teach strategies at the same time you are teaching content. This involves students more directly from the beginning of the lesson while they also develop the strategies for learning how to learn.

We know that learning discipline-specific vocabulary words, text structures, methods, and perspectives involves acquiring both content and reading skills simultaneously. The relatively poor performance of U.S. middle school and secondary school students in international math and science comparisons likely reflects in part their poor performances as readers (Snow, 2001, section 1.1.4). Providing students with strategies for remembering new vocabulary will increase their retention of new word meanings and increase their reading performance.

The prereading stage (activities performed before beginning to read a text) is the most important phase of instruction, especially for poor readers. Rather than approaching a reading task with little enthusiasm and without clear goals, prereading activities help students clarify their goals and develop enthusiasm for the task and content.

Some students might not have an adequate body of domain-specific content knowledge upon which to draw as they read. This limitation compounds the difficulty they will have with comprehending informational text. Prereading activities should address these main goals:

- Help students think about what they already know.
- Focus students' attention on the purpose for the reading.
- Spark students' interest and curiosity.
- Enhance students' familiarity with and knowledge about key vocabulary that will be used in the text.

A student's prior knowledge plays a critical role in reading comprehension. Prior knowledge refers to content and to knowledge of the procedures and strategies needed while reading. Understanding of individual words, as well as concepts, depends upon a student's world or background knowledge, which then provides a framework for understanding ideas and information. When engaging students with word meanings, it is important to provide student-friendly explanations and/or scaffolding to enable them to derive word meaning from instructional contexts and your explanations. At the same time, students need to actually deal with the meanings, and associative strategies can play a critical role in achieving that goal.

Connecting Words Strategies

Students learn the meanings of new words by first developing and remembering a clue that they use as a hint to the word's meaning. These hints create hooks or tags, which are critical and necessary components of memory development, because they link that clue with the word or concept. Having a tag helps students access information and once they do, they are able to focus on developing a deeper understanding of the word or concept.

> The brain's cross-indexing puts the best library to shame (Begley, 1986).

Our memory system stores the same item in multiple ways; therefore, retrieval memory is a complex process. It involves reconstructing or reactivating elements of experiences that reside in many parts within the brain. We use an index process to aid in this reconstruction, and the hooks or tags that students develop greatly enhance the efficiency of the brain indexing system. Different aspects of words (the orthographic, the phonological, and the semantic/morphological) are "in separate, but partially overlapping, neural networks, mostly distributed throughout the left side of the cortex, but there also appear to be circuits for forging connections among them" (Berninger & Todd, 2002, p. 223). Our task is to help students form multiple connections by providing redundant representations and teaching strategies that encourage reflection.

At the conclusion of any of the following activities, help students solidify their associations with questions such as these:
- Which word goes with "crook"? (*accomplice*)
- Which word goes with "gift to build a new hospital"? (*philanthropist*)
- Which word goes with "piano"? (*virtuoso*)

Show-Me Strategy

The Show-Me Strategy encourages students to activate background knowledge as they approach a new target word and decide what they need to know about it. They associate the target word with a movement that represents something familiar. For example, students might simulate a frog hop to illustrate the word *leap*. This approach integrates muscle and visual cues by simultaneously using mental imagery and movement. Students might move only their arms and/or make facial expressions — full body movements aren't necessary. Muscle memory is valuable in helping students develop and retain vocabulary understanding because it uses the brain's primary neural pathways (visual, auditory, kinesthetic, and tactual) to establish the memory. The technique associates these pathways within a conceptual framework.

The steps for presenting the technique are essentially the same for all ages:

1. Present a movement to your students that provides a clue to the basic meaning for a new word and have them mimic it. You model the movement initially, but as students progress in using the technique, they may come up with their own. Using a student's suggested movement provides ownership, which further enhances the memory process.

2. Present three to six words at a time, depending upon the students' skill level. Move through the list rapidly and have students repeat each word and its related movement.

3. Repeat the words and movements, in random order.

4. Present the movement and have the students say the corresponding word.

5. Present the word and have the students perform the corresponding movement.

6. Students practice the words and movements with partners, encouraging further rehearsal of the connections. Use Pair-Share to provide opportunities for social interaction and rehearsal.

This strategy allows you to easily check for understanding by either saying a word and having students respond with the corresponding gesture or providing the gesture and having students say the word. By looking around the group, you get immediate feedback regarding students' involvement and comprehension.

The Show-Me Strategy may be enhanced by adding a visualization component. For example, after performing the activity as described below, ask the students to close their eyes and visually imagine the corresponding gesture as you say a word. As an alternative, students may draw a picture of their gesture and corresponding word.

➤ Show-Me Strategy for Elementary Students

Word list: **rotors, helicopter, soar**

Vocabulary words and sample movements to accompany them are listed below. As you introduce each word, provide a simple explanation before modeling the movement.

- *Explanation:* **Rotors** are big blades that go around and tilt forward or backward.
  Movement: Raise arms above head and simultaneously move each in a circle towards the center, repeating several times.

- *Explanation:* A **helicopter** is a machine that flies. It can go straight up and straight down.
  Movement: Crouch down toward the floor and lift your body upward while using your arms to make rotary movements above your head.

- *Explanation:* To **soar** is to fly in the air like an airplane. *Movement:* Hold arms out to the side and move them up and down like an airplane. If space permits, students may move around while they "soar." Students will enjoy adding sound effects to these movements.

soar

➤ Show-Me Strategy for Middle School Students

Word list: **right angle, acute angle, obtuse angle**

Students frequently confuse these terms; therefore, a motor memory hook is extremely valuable. Here are some sample explanations and movements:

- *Explanation:* A **right angle** is a 90° angle whose sides are perpendicular to each other. *Movement:* Make a right angle with your first finger and thumb. Use exaggerated movements (moving your hand/angle back and forth) and say, "Right on! Right angle!"

- *Explanation:* An **acute angle** is an angle that is less than 90°. *Movement:* Make an acute angle using two fingers, such as your pointer and thumb. Using exaggerated movement and voice, say, "Oh, what a cute angle! Acute angle!"

- *Explanation:* An **obtuse angle** is an angle that is more than 90° but less than 180°. *Movement:* Make an obtuse angle using your pinky and thumb. With an exaggerated "high five" movement with your hand, say, "Hang loose, obtuse!"

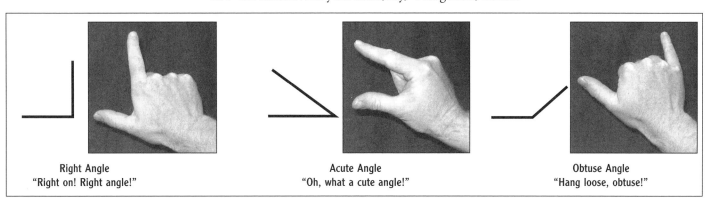

Right Angle
"Right on! Right angle!"

Acute Angle
"Oh, what a cute angle!"

Obtuse Angle
"Hang loose, obtuse!"

➤ Show-Me Strategy for High School Students

Word list: **infallible, resolute, extolling**

These words are from *Beowulf* in a high school senior literature anthology. Initially, present students with basic gestures to signal the words, as in the following example explanations and movements. After the gestures become familiar, expand the explanations to involve deeper content.

- *Explanation:* When you are **resolute**, you are very determined in your purpose. It means being very stubborn. *Movement:* Cross your arms in front of your body and take a stance that shows determination. Include the appropriate facial gesture.

- *Explanation:* Someone who is very sure and certain believes they are **infallible** or incapable of making a mistake.

Movement: Point to yourself. Have fun with this gesture, as if implying, "Oh sure, I don't make mistakes."

- *Explanation:* When you praise someone very highly, you are **extolling** or glorifying them. *Movement:* Put your hands together as in a prayer position and bow down, making appropriate head movements and facial gestures to suggest you are glorifying, or extolling, someone.

Anything Goes Strategy   *Connecting Words*

This activity encourages students to connect vocabulary words with meaning, structure, and/or function (Richek, 2001). You may play the Anything Goes game at any time, as it only requires a few minutes. It may function as a perfect "filler" when there are only a few minutes before lunch or recess.

➤ Anything Goes for Elementary Students

Select several key words from an upcoming reading selection and display them on the board. Choose words that carry meaning important for the story, as in the following list of words from a fiction selection for elementary students:

playground	*castle*	*night*
princess	*prince*	*dragon*
sleep	*marry*	*carry*

Here are some procedural variations (you will probably develop your own as you become more familiar with the strategy):

Variation 1: The teacher points to a word and asks a question:
- Who can pronounce this word?
- Who can put this word in a sentence?
- What is the definition of this word?
- Which word is a compound word?
- How many syllables does this word have?
- Which word can be changed to past tense?
  - Who can use that word in a sentence referring to the past?
  - Who can spell that word as a past tense word?
- How are this word and this word related? (pointing to two words)

Variation 2: The teacher asks a question and a student answers while pointing to a specific word or words:
- Who can point to and read a word that has two syllables?
- What word tells where a prince or princess usually lives?
- Which word or words refers to people?
- Which word or words refers to a mythical animal?
- Who can point to and read a word that is a verb?
- How many syllables does *dragon* have?
- What is the difference between a prince and a princess?

Variation 3: Students work in pairs to develop a single sentence that uses at least two of the words from the list. Working with a peer encourages the students to discuss the words and in doing so they usually create more complex sentences. Have the students share their sentences verbally.

➤ *Anything Goes for Older Students*

Use this activity with older students to help them access more conceptually loaded vocabulary. Here are some sample earth science words you might use:

biome	*climate*	*spruce*
pine	*fir*	*moose*
	bears	

Possible questions:
- Who can tell me two or more words that relate, explaining why?
  - What other words fit within this category?
- Which word refers to a large region of land that has its own climate, plants, and animals?
- Who can find a word that has an open syllable? (*bi-* in biome)
- Which word relates to the concept of community? How?
- Which word or words relate(s) to *desert*?
- Which word or words relate(s) to *grasslands*?
- Which word or words relate(s) to *swamps*?
- Which word or words relate(s) to *forest*?
- Which word or words relate(s) to *coniferous*?

Connecting Words Strategy

Connecting Words

Begin the activity by displaying two lists of words from upcoming reading material. The students work in pairs to encourage greater discussion of the words. Working in pairs also increases interaction and the likelihood of students learning from each other's background knowledge.

Challenge students to think of something that a word in the first list has in common with a word in the second list. When a pair of students thinks it has found a connection, both members come to the board and draw a line to connect the words while explaining what they have in common.

As students explain word connections to their peers, they verbalize higher level thinking that helps increase their depth of understanding regarding the words. Since personal and group interaction is so important to this task, it is more valuable as a discussion activity rather than an independent homework assignment. Here are two sample lists of words from Lynne Cherry's *The Great Kapok Tree* (4th grade).

List 1	List 2
generations	*ancestors*
pollinate	*jaguar*
Kapok	*knelt*
Sloth	*mist*
hesitated	*boa constructor*
buzz	*forest*
desert	*growl*

Possible connections:
- *Forest – desert:* Both describe a region of land.
- *Generations – hesitated:* Both have four syllables.
- *Sloth – boa constructor:* Both are animals.
- *Buzz – growl:* Both are sounds that animals make.

Images and Visualization

Many children today view visual images in a very passive mode. For example, as most children watch TV, they sit and passively observe the images.

It can be difficult for some students to develop active mental imagery and visualization. All are capable of constructing mental imagery, but years of passive exposure to television may have stunted their automatic ability to generate images. Constructing a mental image must be an active process, and there are many ways to teach and encourage it. Explicit instruction is required to help students recover their ability to generate visual images. Students who can generate visual images have a powerful word-learning and reading comprehension tool.

The strategies in this section follow the same three direct teaching steps: L–P–E. Use familiar and concrete terms such as *dog, car, cowboy hat,* or *large ice-cream cone* to begin your instruction. Here are the basic L–P–E steps:

L–P–E
L – Listen
P – Paint Structure
E – Explain

- **L — Listen:** Present the word, phrase, poem, or story.

- **P — Paint:** Have students close their eyes and attempt to paint a picture in their mind that relates to the word.
  - Some students respond to the cue, "Paint a picture on the blackboard in your mind."
  - Other students are assisted by imagining that they are drawing using colored spaghetti or Silly String® to create the image.

- **E — Explain:** Urge students to draw and/or explain their visualization.
  - Ensure your students that there is no "right" or "wrong" answer. However, encourage them to explain why they selected that image: have them back up their decisions.
  - This critical component is essential in enhancing the breadth and depth of your students' vocabulary development.

When teaching the strategies, consistently incorporate these three key components:
- **Modeling:** clearly demonstrate and explain each step.
- **Staging:** present the steps in small chunks.
- **Systematic:** use systematic and logical explanations, and encourage students to be systematic in their use of memory strategies.

Show Me: A Gallon Has Four Quarts
Images and Visualization

This activity is valuable for both elementary and middle school students. Begin by explaining the general purpose: "In our math lessons, we encounter many measurement terms that can sometimes become confusing. Today we're going to review one of those terms, *gallon*, in a silly way to help us remember there are four quarts in a gallon." You can adapt this type of activity to other measurement terms that can be related to something concrete.

1. Have two students come to the front of the room. One student stands or sits with his arms and legs extended. This student becomes "The Gallon Person."

2. Explain that each of this student's arms and legs represents 1 quart.

3. The second student touches each limb of "The Gallon Person" counting, "1 quart, 2 quarts, 3 quarts, 4 quarts," for each limb he touches.

4. Then the whole class repeats, "1 quart, 2 quarts, 3 quarts, 4 — a gallon has 4 quarts."

5. The students then work in pairs, taking turns being "The Gallon Person" and the counting person.

1 quart   2 quarts

The "Gallon" Person

3 quarts   4 quarts

When students are finished, review the terms with an exchange such as the following:

Teacher: A gallon contains 4 what?

Students: Quarts

Teacher: That's right. A gallon contains 4 quarts.

Teacher: So we can say that there are 4 quarts in a what?

Students: A gallon!

Teacher: That's right. There are 4 quarts in a gallon.

Teacher: Which container would be bigger — a quart container or a gallon container?

Students: A gallon.

Teacher: Which would you prefer to have for your party: a gallon or a quart of ice cream?

Students: A gallon.

Teacher: Which would be easier to carry: a full gallon container or a full quart container?

Students: A quart.

To review and consolidate the terms, have students draw a picture of "The Gallon Person" and label each "quart" (limb). Follow up with experiential activities using actual quart and gallon containers.

Word Imagery

Images and Visualization

Select some keywords from your content reading material. The example combines muscle memory with imagery and uses these words from the Native American Legend of "The Sleeping Bear Dunes":

might   *brilliant*   *slumbering*

Students may be somewhat familiar with the words, but they may not be aware of their meanings as used in this story. This activity serves to associate new information with what the child already knows. Here is a sample dialog for creating a visualization for *slumbering*:

1. Is anyone familiar with the word *slumbering*? (*Elicit responses.*)

2. That's right, to slumber is to "doze" or to "sleep." It's not like being sound asleep, but just a little bit asleep.

3. Who can show me what it might look like to slumber? *(Have students mime the action.)*

4. Those are a lot of good ways to slumber. Let's choose one and do it together.

5. Let's show slumbering by leaning back in our chairs, with our arms relaxed and our head hanging down. While we do that, let's make a snoring sound.

6. Okay, everybody show me slumbering. Great! Sit up straight, turn to your neighbor, give each other a high five, and say, "Great slumbering."

Create a similar dialog for *brilliant*. Students might be familiar with several meanings of the word. Explain that the meaning you will focus on today is "something that is very bright and shiny." You could have students raise their arms in the air and make a large circle while waving their fingers to indicate brilliance.

Students are probably familiar with the word *might*; however, they might not immediately think of it as as referring to "very strong, as in *mighty*." Begin by asking students, "Have you ever heard the word *mighty*?" Perhaps they will think of Mighty Mouse, The Mighty Morphin Power Rangers, or other TV characters. Have them create a movement for *might* by clenching their fists in a position to indicate strength.

Review each word by saying it and then having students perform the corresponding movement while they also develop a mental image of that word. Encourage students to explain their mental images. Emphasize that there are no right or wrong answers, but that each student also needs to be able to explain *why* he or she developed a particular image. Include affirmations such as high fives, thumbs up, or high tens.

LINCS
Images and Visualization

This strategy helps students develop a routine for analyzing words. Having a routine is important: good learners automatically develop routines to perform before they start to read a passage. The LINCS strategy is a routine students can use to explore new vocabulary. They may use words provided by the instructor or they select words from their reading (Conn Thomas, Learning Strategies Curriculum). Initially, the routine is especially important as students develop the skills and habit of manipulating components of a target word. A useful initial sequence is to have students first guess and confirm the definition for the target word and then perform the remaining steps to solidify the meaning. As your students become more skilled in using the strategy, they may manipulate the sequence of the steps: perhaps they may wish to begin with a story or picture. Explain that the key word, LINCS, reminds them of all the steps, although the order may vary.

There are five steps in the LINCS strategy, and it is useful for students to have a visual frame for each step, as shown and explained on the next page. It is important that you initially provide directed instruction to teach the strategy so that students can easily perform the steps in a group situation. When students become comfortable with the steps, have them work in pairs.

The LINCS mnemonic
L List the word
I Identify a reminding word
N Note a LINCing story
C Create a LINCing picture
S Self test: write a definition

A value of the LINCS strategy is that it helps students enhance the depth of their vocabulary knowledge. Rather than simply learn information by rote, they manipulate the meaning of the words themselves. In doing so, they are linking it to their prior knowledge. When students discuss why they selected a particular image or idea as a LINCing story or LINCing picture, they display higher order thinking as well as share background knowledge.

The 5 steps of the LINCS strategy:

1. List the word
   - Students write the target word.

2. Self-test
   - Students try to guess an operational definition for the target word.
   - When confirmed, they write a brief definition that includes the critical variables.
   - Underline the key words in the definition.

3. Identify a reminding word
   - This step is critical because it encourages students to create their own hook to help them remember the target word.
   - An effective reminding word includes sounds that are like part or all of the target word, is a real word, and helps the students remember the meaning of the target word.
   - It is critical that the linking word is personal to the student, as this makes it much more powerful as a recall hook.

4. Note a LINCing story
   - Students write a brief story (one or two sentences or thoughts) that uses the reminding word and that creates a visual image to explain the word. (The story may or may not include the key words underlined in the definition.)

5. Create a LINCing picture
   - Students draw a related picture. This step is critical because it helps them pull in visual imagery.

Completed LINCs Frame

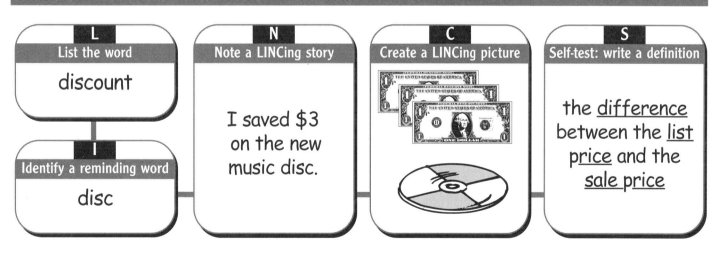

L — List the word	N — Note a LINCing story	C — Create a LINCing picture	S — Self-test: write a definition
discount	I saved $3 on the new music disc.		the <u>difference</u> between the <u>list price</u> and the <u>sale price</u>
I — Identify a reminding word			
disc			

Mnemonics

Mnemonics are a valuable way to provide key word associations for new vocabulary words. A mnemonic is a technique that assists memory. The following pages present several ways to incorporate mnemonics in vocabulary development. Use these as suggestions for developing your own mnemonics for vocabulary specific to your students' curriculum needs.

Measurement Terms

➤ *Hypotenuse*

The *hypotenuse* on a right triangle is the side that is across from the right angle.

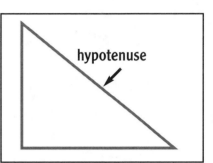

hypotenuse

You might integrate this activity with a strategy that helps students focus on the structure of the word while learning its definition:

1. Say *hypotenuse* and have students repeat it softly or loudly.
2. Have students repeat the word while clapping once for each syllable: *hy-pot-en-use*.
3. Ask, "What is the sound of the *y* in the first syllable?" Then ask if anyone can explain why it has that sound (*it comes from the Greek*).

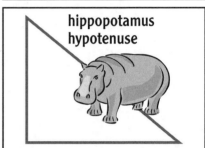

hippopotamus hypotenuse

To associate the visual mnemonic with the new word, show students the picture on the right and explain that this silly picture is to help associate hippopotamus and hypotenuse. Use a related hand gesture while explaining "big side" of the triangle. Then have them repeat this phrase several times:

- "The hypotenuse on a right triangle is as big as a hippopotamus. It's the biggest side."

Encourage your students to draw their own right triangle with a hippopotamus sitting on the hypotenuse. Have them repeat the mnemonics sentence multiple times with their peers.

➤ *Kilogram*

Ask students to tell you their favorite flavors of jam. Have the students examine and pick up one or more jars weighing 2-1/4 pounds (the weight of a kilogram). The jars may be actual jars of jam or other jars filled with something colorful, such as modeling clay, to simulate jam.

Explain to your students that they will learn a sentence to help them remember the weight of a kilogram. You might explain the parts that make up the word *kilogram*: *kilo-* is a Greek prefix similar to the Latin *mille-*. Both mean "1000." Therefore, a kilogram is 1000 grams.

Have students repeat the following mnemonic phrase to focus on the weight of a kilogram.

- "Two and a quarter pounds of jam, weigh about a kilogram."

Brain Terms

➤ *Hippocampus*

The hippocampus is a small but critical structure in the brain. It holds memory of the immediate past and sends memory to the cortex for higher-order processing. The hippocampus is involved in the recognition of novelty; therefore, it is important to provide novelty within learning situations so that the hippocampus can grab the information and hold it long enough to send it to the thinking part of the cortex.

46   *The Source for Reading Comprehension Strategies*

The word *hippocampus* is made up of Greek parts: *hippos* is a Greek term meaning "horse" and *kampos* means "sea monster." Hippocampuses is the scientific name for seahorse, which is convenient, because the brain structure looks somewhat like a seahorse.

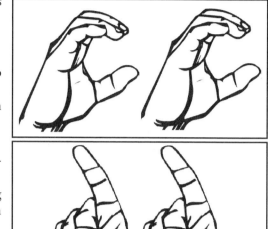

There are two parts to this mnemonic:

1. Say, "The hippocampus needs to grab onto information."
   - Show your hands "chomping," as in the picture on the top right.
   - Say, "hippocampus chomp, chomp."
2. Say, "When the hippocampus grabs information, it helps our retention increase."
   - Point your fingers upward while raising your hands to the sky as the picture on the bottom right.
   - Say, "retention tip top."
3. Repeat and practice.

➤ Corpus Callosum

The corpus callosum is a thick bundle of fibers in the middle of the brain that serves to keep the left hemisphere in contact with the right hemisphere. The word *corpus* is Latin for "body."

Here is a mnemonic rhyme to help students remember the name *corpus callosum* and its function (it is important to perform the gestures while saying the rhyme). Use rhythm and emphasis while chanting the words:

Left brain (*hold up left fist*),
Right brain (*hold up right fist*),
I use both of them (*bring both fists to about 4 inches apart*),
Because I have you,
My corpus callosum (*bring fists together with nails touching*).

Analogies

Mnemonics

An analogy is a way to compare similar elements between things that are otherwise not alike. Analogies are useful tools for helping students associate new information with what they already know. These associations help students hook a new word to a familiar image or knowledge base. Use the following examples as suggestions for developing analogies related to vocabulary words specific to your students' curriculum needs. Remember to add gestures for the key words as an added visual cue for your students.

➤ Hippocampus and a Keyboard

Have each student compare his or her brain to a computer. Say, "The cortex is like your hard drive where memories are stored. The hippocampus is like your keyboard; it is how memories are placed into your cortex."

Have students complete sentences such as these to repeat and review the information:

- In a computer, information is stored in the _____. (*hard drive*)
- We enter information into our computer by using a mouse or a _____. (*keyboard*)
- The part in our brain that is like a hard drive is called the _____. (*cortex*)
- Like a keyboard on a computer, information gets into our brain through our _____. (*hippocampus*)

➤ Kidneys and a Coffee Filter

Show your students a paper coffee filter (the type used in many automatic coffee machines). Explain how the filter works:

- The filter is filled with a mixture of coffee and water.
- Only the liquid passes through the bottom of the filter.
- The filter prevents solid particles — the coffee grounds — from getting into the coffee.

You might present similar examples, such as a colander filled with with small rocks and sand or a tea bag and a mug of hot water. Provide materials that illustrate the concept of filtering to your students and allow them ample time to experiment with the objects.

Provide experience before labels.

When the students are familiar with how filters work, explain that there is an organ in each of our bodies that works like a filter: our kidneys. Making an analogy between filtering and kidneys gives students a hook to help them remember a basic understanding of how kidneys work. When this hook is solid, students are ready for more detailed information presented in a lesson on kidney function.

Mapping Strategies

Learning a new vocabulary word as an isolated unit hampers students' attempts to perceive the patterns, similarities, and differences that contribute the word's meaning. In contrast, when students actively engage in interacting with the word — and with their peers — they develop a deeper understanding of the word and begin to appreciate the network of meaning that surrounds it. Visual organizers and other mapping strategies are valuable tools to use in conjunction with active engagement and interaction.

Basic Meanings   *Mapping Strategies*

A simple Basic Meanings word map begins with the target word usually placed at the top of the map (as seen in the first example on the next page) although it can be placed in the center (as shown in the second example). Students brainstorm what they know about the word and connect those suggestions to the target word. Associations might be characteristics, descriptions of use, or attributes. It is beneficial for students to interactively create these maps, followed by discussion. Basic Meaning Maps for *cooking* and *longitude* are on the next page.

This map was created by brainstorming different cooking methods.

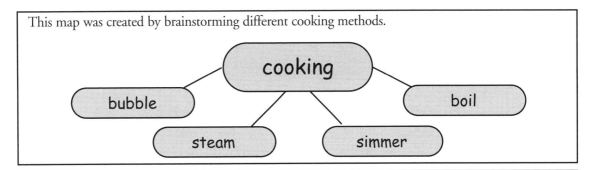

This format identifies the critical attributes of the word. Here is how to create this type of map:
- Students begin by brainstorming characteristics or attributes that describe the word.
- They write their ideas at the end of each line on the map.
- After they have recorded as many ideas as possible, have students identify the characteristics that *best* describe the meaning of the target word. Have them identify those words with a color or symbol, such as an asterisk.
- Work with students to define the word.
- Have students think of examples of when and how they could use the new word.

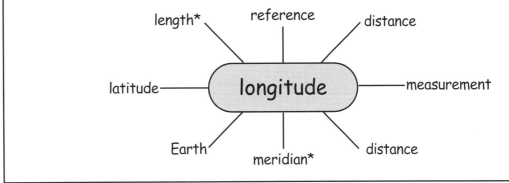

Multiple Meanings

Mapping Strategies

A Multiple Meanings Map is similar to the Basic Meaning Map: it begins with a target word in a box at the top. The various meanings of that target word are listed and associated with their meaning, as shown in the example on the next page.

A word can be stored in the brain in several ways, depending upon the student's exposure to and experience with the word, and a Multiple Meanings Map can help a student explore the many meanings of a single word. For example, *work* might mean "work a math problem" or "a task." *Dash* can refer to "a written symbol," "moving quickly," or "a small amount." The root word *dash* can be expanded to *dashing, dasher,* or *dashboard.* There are many ways to create Multiple Meaning Maps. Here are two suggestions using *run:*

Option 1:
1. Set up the frame, or template, for the word *run.*
2. Ask students for ways (phrases or sentences) to use *run* (prompt and cue as needed).
3. As a student states an idea, summarize the meaning and place it in a box. For example, if a student says, "I can run really fast," write "a fast way of moving" on the map. If another student suggests, "I scored three runs in baseball last night," write "a baseball score."

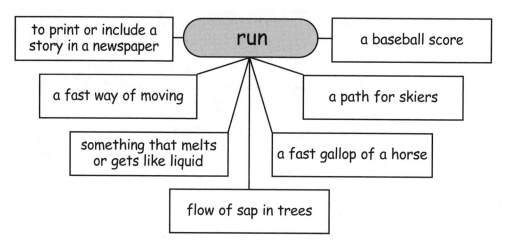

Option 2:

1. Set up the frame, or template, for the word *run*.

2. Say a sentence using *run* (or a form of the word), such as, "He caught the dog by running after him."

3. Ask students what *run* means in the sentence. If a student says, "It's a fast way of moving," write that meaning in a box on the map.

4. Repeat with additional sentences.
   - Include some sentences that use a meaning already stated, as in, "I can run really fast."
   - Include some sentences with different meanings, as in, "My ice cream was runny." A student might identify that meaning as "something that melts or gets like liquid."

"New verbal information is learned in accordance with prior knowledge. Effectively teaching elaborates various connections among better-known and lesser-known words, deepens and enriches existing knowledge, and seeks to build a network of ideas around key concepts . . ." (Moats, 2000, p. 112).

Word Trees

Mapping Strategies

Word Trees are extensions of Basic Meaning and Multiple Meanings Maps. Word Trees help emphasize that verbal knowledge is organized in networks of associations that have definable structures. A significant value of a Word Tree is that it helps students associate new words and concepts in relationship to one another and not as isolated units.

Use these steps to create a Word Tree:

1. Place the target word in the root area on the bottom.

2. Write the word's definition on the trunk.

4. Write a specific component related to the target word on each branch. The components will vary depending upon your students' age and your curricular goals. Here are some examples of components you might use:
   - Synonyms
   - Antonyms
   - Category (the function of the word rather than the grammatical label)
   - Alternate meanings
   - Examples (phrases using the word)
   - Linguistic structures (number of syllables, prefix, root, suffix)
   - Related body gestures

(For younger students, create a simpler Word Tree with fewer branches.)

Word Tree Template

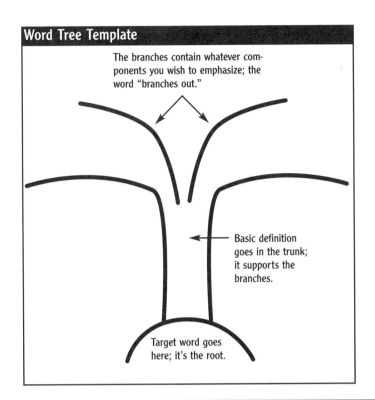

The branches contain whatever components you wish to emphasize; the word "branches out."

Basic definition goes in the trunk; it supports the branches.

Target word goes here; it's the root.

Completed Word Tree

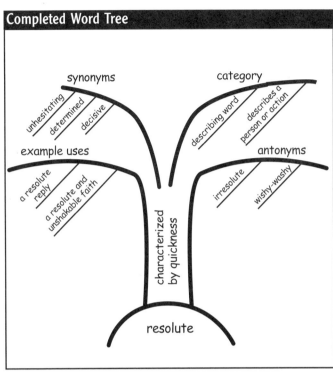

synonyms

unhesitating · determined · decisive

category

describing word · describes a person or action

example uses

a resolute reply · a resolute and unshakable faith

antonyms

irresolute · wishy-washy

characterized by quickness

resolute

Conceptual Strategies

When dealing with the conceptual strategies, it is most crucial to tap into your students' own knowledge as much as possible. Activating prior knowledge allows your students to make connections and develop deep associations for a word. We all remember information best when we can place it on a hook that already exists, which is the value of associations. Another major benefit of using the students' own experiences is that it provides connectedness for them.

Mel Levine notes that students with incomplete concept formation exhibit certain characteristics (Levine, 2001, pp. 114-115):

- A lack of awareness of the critical features of the concept
- Heavy reliance on rote memory
- A pattern of doing things without understanding why they are doing them
- Difficulty mastering abstract as opposed to concrete concepts

He also notes the various depths of conceptual understanding

None: unable to identify or cite examples

Tenuous: names one or two critical features about how the concept differs from others

Rote: mimics a teacher's explanation but can't use the concept or think of examples

Imitative: applies the concept but doesn't really understand it and can't generalize its use

Explanatory: explains the concept in his or her own words, cites examples, and compares and contrasts it with other concepts

Innovative: applies the concept in ways never directly taught

Connotation Organizer

Many students mistakenly believe that synonyms are words that have "exactly the same" meaning. That is not true because there are almost always slight differences in meaning among synonyms. Having a poor understanding of this concept often results in misusing vocabulary words in context. For example, although *gather*, *harvest*, and *congregate* are synonyms, it would be awkward to say, "Let's *congregate* the papers in a pile," or "Let's *harvest* the group." Consequently, it is important for students to learn how to use a given word correctly in the desired context.

> This system of presenting words in context, determining distinguishing features, and then reinforcing them in new contexts is a more effective and naturalistic way of instructing students in connotations than traditional methods which tend to present words in isolation (Baldwin, Ford, & Readence, 1981).

Words have a general or literal meaning, which is often called the *denotation*. For example, *clothing* and *raiment* have the same literal meaning: "items to wear." The connotations of those words, however, differ: there are different associations related to the use of each word.

- *clothing*: what people wear, garments in general
- *raiment*: clothing worn by princes and princesses on formal occasions

Developing a visual organizer assists students in identifying and grasping word connotations. When they create a visual representation of the similarities and differences among synonyms, they focus on the features of each word. You might do this activity with just basic information in a short period or you may extend and expand the activity to provide students ample time to explore the concepts more in depth.

The following steps explain how to create a Connotation Organizer for *gathered:*

1. Say, "We're going to discuss the word *gathered*. It has many synonyms, and it's important to know the similarities and differences between these various words."
2. Write a sentence frame on the board:
   The friends _____ in front of the movie theater.
3. Place the word *gathered* in the blank.
4. Encourage students to write their own sentences, using as many synonyms for *gathered* as they can name or find:
   - Interaction (small groups) is beneficial because it encourages analysis and discussion.
   - Encourage students to use a thesaurus in book form or electronically (a Franklin Language Master or a computer's word processor).
5. As a whole group, discuss differences among the meanings of various sentences. Decide whether each sentence appropriately uses the synonym of *gathered*.
   - You and your students might determine that some sentences are inappropriate or humorous, such as "The friends *harvested* in front of the movie theater."
6. Develop a Connotation Organizer, such as the completed one on the next page, using the synonyms the students have located.
   - Identify appropriate characteristics and determine whether each word relates to that characteristic. To make that determination, refer to the students' sentences, selecting those determined to be appropriate.
   - Have students use reference tools for confirmation.
7. To further extend the activity and help students apply the derived information, have them work in small groups to develop an appropriate and inappropriate contextual sentence for each synonym.

- Have them record their reasons (the distinctive features) and then have the group share.
- Appropriate sentence: "After the election, Congress *assembled* at the state capital."
  - Reason: *Assembled* is more formal than a word such as *congregated*.
- Inappropriate sentence: "Congress *accumulated* at the state capital."
  - Reason: *Accumulated* does not refer to people coming together.

word	done with people	done to things	formal	deliberate	work
gathered	+	+	?	+	?
collected	+	+	?	+	?
harvested	–	+	?	+	+
accumulated	–	+	–	–	–
assembled	+	+	+	+	?
congregated	+	–	–	+	?

8. To help further consolidate the information, ask the students questions that help them explore the use of the specific synonyms.
   - If you wanted to describe how people gathered for a wedding, which would be the best word? (*assembled*)
   - If you gathered signatures for a petition, what would be the best word to describe what you did? (*collected*)
9. Guide students to connect the relevant information to the context within their curriculum.

Feature Analysis

Conceptual Strategies

The Connotation Organizer activity described above can be adapted to any activity where students can benefit by analyzing similarities of and differences between features of particular words or concepts. The Feature Analysis organizer below compares and contrasts some characteristics among five U.S. presidents.

	Franklin D. Roosevelt	John F. Kennedy	Richard Nixon	Ronald Reagan	Bill Clinton
Democrat	+	+	–	–	+
Wartime President	+	–	+	–	–
Congress of the same party	–/+	+	–	–/+	–/+
Reelected	+	+	+	+	+
Served in Congress	–	+	+	–	–
Won majority of popular vote	+	–	–/+	+	–

A Feature Analysis is a powerful visual vocabulary chart. When used with literature, you may compare and contrast such things as different fictional characters, books by the same author, or genres of literature. Feature analysis is limited to sets of words from the same category that frequently occur in content areas. The process of comparing and contrasting is a critical prerequisite towards developing inferential analysis skills.

Venn Diagrams   *Conceptual Strategies*

A Venn Diagram is a visual organizer that helps students analyze and concretely represent similarities and differences between two or three concepts or words. The diagrams are another way to develop the comparing/contrasting skills, which are prerequisites to inferential thinking.

Create a Venn diagram organizer by overlapping two ovals. Place the distinctive features of one concept or word in one oval and write the distinctive features of a second concept in the other oval. Place characteristics common to the two concepts or words in the overlapping portion of the ovals. Students derive the most value from a Venn Diagram through the process of creating the organizer, especially if the process also involves interaction and discussion. Model the process at first and, through scaffolding, help your students develop independent skills.

You can use this strategy to compare any number of concepts. When preparing to read content material, select two related words that are important to the material. Prior to having the students read the chapter, create a Venn Diagram with the words to compare and contrast the two target words. Similarly, you might select two critical concepts to emphasize prior to the students' reading. Here are two examples of Venn Diagrams:

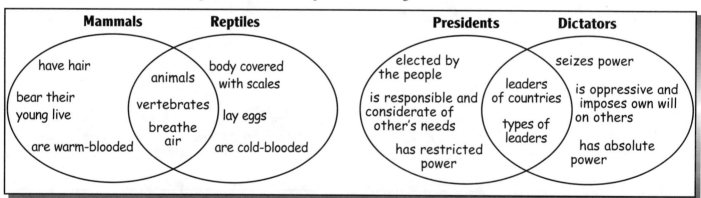

Here are some other concepts you can explore with Venn Diagrams:

- Debris and trash
- A rebellion and a protest
- Plants and animals
- Desert and rain forest
- A current rock band and Mozart

- The Civil War and the Revolutionary War
- Two characters in a story
- A pyramid and cone
- A volcano and a revolution
- A book and its related movie

➤ *Venn Diagrams — Extension*

Stories are a powerful teaching tool, and students often remember the stories they are told longer than other portions of a lesson. Stories are a great way to introduce or reinforce concepts. For example, before beginning to create a Venn Diagram with your students, you might present an introductory story such as the one on the next page.

One of the factors that initiated conflict between the American colonists and England was that **King George** (*have students mimic a hand motion to represent a crown on their head*) viewed the colonists' activities as rebellion against the crown. **King George** (*repeat the crown gesture*) considered his power to be absolute (*have students mimic a hand gesture, such as a raised fist, for absolute*). In contrast, the colonists viewed their activities as protest (*use gesture as of holding up protest signs*) against unjust laws. This difference in values and views led to conflict, which resulted in the Revolution. Repeat the story (with hand gestures) a second time. Then have students create a Venn Diagram to compare *protest* and *rebellion*.

> Manipulating and analyzing related words allows students to develop concepts, since the words crisscross the same conceptual landscape. As a result, students deepen their understanding and support their reading of more complex text.

A Venn Diagram does not need to be limited to only two ovals. You may create a more complex one using three ovals to compare compare and contrast three concepts (see page A-37 of the Appendix on the CD). You could create a Venn Diagram to compare the following:

- The three branches of the U.S. government
- George Washington, Thomas Jefferson, and Abraham Lincoln
- The contribution of auditory, visual, and kinesthetic processes to spelling or reading

Clusters
Conceptual Strategies

It is important to help students view the many facets of a word's definition rather than relying on a single block of meaning. For example, students may only associate the word *delighted* with a reaction to receiving a gift, which would be a narrow, stereotypic context. In contrast, students need an appreciation of the many facets of a word's meaning, which requires using the word in various activities.

Dealing with content material frequently involves technical terms. The nature of content material tends to link the meanings among the specific terms presented. Emphasizing these clusters helps students identify the inherent associations among the meanings of contextually related words. Exploring clusters of words is an important key to learning them, especially because our brains learn through patterns and connections. When working with words that share meaning, it is important to make the distinctions between them clear. One efficient technique to make such distinctions between words is to use related gestures and encourage interactive discussions.

An example cluster from a science chapter on airplanes might introduce terms like *flap, grade, soar,* and *lift*. Students might represent the Cluster as a visual Word Map or another organizer, or they may draw individual creative drawings that link the meanings of the various concepts. Using visuals makes the comparisons and interactions more concrete.

Another option, which may be used separately or combined with a visual representation, is to initiate discussion by asking your students questions about the similar terms. If the terms are linked, as in a logical cluster, the question (in response) will be logical, as in these examples:

- Can the *fuselage* cause *drag*?
- How do the *flaps* affect *lift*?
- How is *bellicose* different from *angry*?

Silly Questions

A related cluster procedure to reveal various meanings of a word and to enhance students' depth of understanding, is to create activities in which students are required to differentiate among examples of the word or between similar words. One approach is to provide descriptions and have students label each as an example or non-example of a description of the target word:

- *Banter*
  - A husband and wife argue about what to have for dinner. *(non-example)*
  - A husband and wife kid each other about something during dinner. *(example)*
- *Glum*
  - The class decides to have a party indoors when they learn that their picnic has been rained out. *(non-example)*
  - The class learns that the picnic has been rained out, and they have to do work instead. *(example)*

When words are somewhat related but not obviously connected, it is useful to contrive the relationship. Creating Silly Questions can combine typically unrelated terms in the same question and is a technique that encourages students to think about unlikely connections. When the answer to the silly question is "yes," a passable relationship is demonstrated through the resulting scenario. Here are some examples:

- Can someone who is *bellicose* be *loquacious*?
  - *Bellicose* means "willing to start quarrels or wars"
  - *Loquacious* means "excessively talkative"
- Can an *accountant* be a *philanthropist*?
  - An *accountant* keeps and analyzes financial records.
  - A *philanthropist* provides a charitable act or gift.
- Can an *virtuoso* be a *rival*?
  - A *virtuoso* is someone who is dazzlingly skilled in a field.
  - A *rival* is a contestant you hope to defeat.

Alternative Definitions

When students learn a single definition of a word, their understanding of that word is very narrow and restricted. To develop depth of understanding, students need rich instruction with variations. The Alternative Definitions activity provides students with opportunities to interact with different definitions of the word and then to respond under time constraints.

1. Present each target word several times during the week. Alter the definition each time somewhat so that students process the description of the word in a meaningful way. Students will then gradually learn the depth of the concepts represented by the words.

2. Here are some target words and alternative definitions that illustrate how definitions for the same word can be subtly different:
   - *ambitious*
     - really wanting to succeed in becoming rich or important
     - wanting to get ahead by becoming powerful
     - wanting great success in life

- *stern*
  - very strict about how you look and what you do
  - very demanding about how you and others behave
  - acting hard and serious
3. At the end of the week, do an activity like the one described below to help students develop rapid responses to the meanings of words so that when they meet the words in context, they will be accustomed to accessing the words' meanings quickly:
   - *Beat the Clock:* give students one-and-a-half minutes to complete 12-14 true/false items. Here are some example items:
     - An *ambitious* person is often lazy. (*false*)
     - *Shrill* sounds can hurt your ears. (*true*)
     - My mom is *stern* because she won't let me wear lipstick. (*true*)
     - *Gregarious* people would rather be alone. (*false*)

Complex Concepts

target word	examples of the word
definition of the target word	non-examples of the word

You can easily adapt many of the above techniques to use with concrete words. However, students also need strategies for associating meanings among more sophisticated concepts such as *ecosystem*, *democracy*, *liberty*, and *circulatory system*. A technique developed by Spiro called "criss-crossing the landscape" is very useful with abstract concepts (Spiro et al., 1994).

Students begin the "criss-crossing" activity by discussing the general category for the target word. For example, the word *liberty* is within a general category of *freedom*. Students generally understand the concept of freedom as being able to think or act without constraints. However, liberty is more complex.

Help students explore the concept of *liberty* by analyzing examples that apply to the target word, as well as those that don't apply. Use a 4-Square visual approach (such as those on the left), to concretely emphasize examples and non-examples. Since *liberty* relates to both personal as well as political situations, examples and non-examples for both are critical. Analyzing concepts in this way helps students understand a word's boundaries, and leads students to develop a full and rich understanding of a complex concept.

Discussing critical concepts with students and creating a matching visual organizer for them prior to reading are especially important in content areas. Doing so sets the stage that it is important for students to understand the unit or the theme.

target word	examples
liberty	Personal: • going to the mall • hanging out with friends • ability to choose Political: • ability to vote • freedom of speech • freedom of religion

definition	non-examples
political independence, freedom of choice, personal freedom	Personal • parents' rules • curfews • not talking in class Political • not being able to kill or steal • dictatorships • not being allowed to criticize

Cognates

English language learners present a special challenge related to vocabulary learning. Depending upon their language level, they may lack rapid access to partially known words. Strategies such as Cognates are very useful to students who are learning English. These children require repeated exposure to vocabulary, which is important for all students but especially critical for English language learners. Using thematically related texts offers multiple exposures to given words, as do books about a common theme.

Examples for the Cognates strategy refer to the Spanish language. Spanish-speaking children are the fastest-growing segment of America's school population. According to a 2000-2001 report, Spanish is the first language for 79% of the English language learners in American schools (Kindler, 2002). Furthermore, because an estimated 53.6% of English words have Romance language origins (Hammer, 1979), many words in our vocabulary have cognates in Spanish.

Begin this activity by explaining cognates to your students. You might say, "Cognates are words that look or sound alike in two languages, such as Spanish and English. They mean almost the same thing, although not exactly. Recognizing cognates will help you understand many new words in English."

The Cognate Strategy: IMR
  I – Identify the word
  M – Meaning of the word
  R – Read the sentence

Tell your students there is a special strategy that they can use when they encounter an unknown English word. The Cognate Strategy has three steps represented by **IMR**: **I** stands for "Identify the word that might be a cognate." **M** stands for "Meaning," because the students identify the meaning of the word in Spanish. **R** refers to "Read the sentence using the Spanish word." If the sentence make sense with the substitution, the word is a cognate. Here is an example sequence for teaching the strategy:

1. Provide your students with a sentence containing a cognate. Ask, "Do you notice any word that reminds you of a Spanish word?" (*Identify*)
   * *José was wearing two different shoes.*
   * Students suggest *different* might be a cognate.

2. Ask, "What does *different* mean in Spanish?" (*Meaning*)
   * Students suggest *different* is *diferente* in Spanish.
   * *Diferente* means "not the same."

3. Read the whole sentence together, using the Spanish word instead of the English word. (*Read*)
   * *José was wearing two* diferente *shoes.*

4. Ask students, "Does the new sentence make sense?"
   * This makes sense, so the word is a cognate. Your students now know that *different* in English means about the same as *diferente* in Spanish.

5. Provide the students with multiple opportunities to practice the Cognates Strategy: give them several sentences containing an underlined cognate and have them write the Spanish cognate for your underlined word.

6. As your students advance, provide them with a list of sentences containing a cognate, but have them identify which word might be the cognate.

You can vary this activity by having students do the same steps but with sentences presented auditorily instead of visually. As with many of the activities designed to help students develop associative vocabulary skills, small-group activities and discussions are extremely beneficial. Similarly, having them draw the meaning of words makes it more concrete for them.

Spanish/English Cognates

Cognates are words that have similar pronunciations and spellings in both languages, and frequently have the same meaning. There are thousands of cognates shared by Spanish and English. Many of these are words with Latin or Greek origins and words that have prefixes and suffixes derived from those ancient languages. Here are examples of 14 different groups of cognates that have English equivalents with only a few spelling changes. The Spanish examples are included so that readers can infer the rule or rules that govern the spelling changes to convert the Spanish form to English. Be aware of internal spelling changes required because of English spelling patterns and generalizations, such as double consonants (Mora [2005], used with permission).

Group 1	Group 4	Group 8	Group 12
Atlántico	artista	ambicioso	aristocracia
democrático	florista	famoso	democracia
patriótico	moralista	gracioso	eficacia
romántico	pianista	laborioso	farmacia
sarcástico	turista	religioso	urgencia

Group 2	Group 5	Group 9	Group 13
cliente	argumento	aniversario	abundancia
equivalente	monumento	disciplinario	conciencia
indiferente	sacramento	itinerario	distancia
patente	suplemento	literario	obediencia
suficiente	testamento	salario	permanencia

Group 3	Group 6	Group 10	Group 14
atención	abundante	comunidad	admirable
circulación	constante	necesidad	animal
edición	elegante	prosperidad	central
indicación	importante	publicidad	director
proposición	significante	universidad	noble

Group 7	Group 11
clásico	diagrama
cómico	idioma
histérico	problema
metódico	programa
técnico	sistema

Conclusion

Keep the following aspects in mind to incorporate within almost any strategy:

- Movement
- Repetition (including Think-Pair-Share)
- Visual representations
- Novelty
- Interaction
- Metacognition

And, most importantly, strive to build your students' established level of word knowledge and encourage your students to have fun with words!

Reflections

Since effective reading needs to be an active process, it is useful to reflect on a few of the key points within this chapter.

1. Select one vocabulary association strategy and develop a plan to use that strategy within one component of your current curriculum. Here is a recommendation of a number of words to include in a single session at various age levels:

   - Elementary grades students: 2-5 words
   - Middle school students: 5-7 words
   - High school students: 8-10 words

   Strategy: _____

   Words: _____

   Plan: _____

   _____

   _____

   _____

2. Develop two variations on your strategy to provide your students with further practice to understand the words with more depth.

   Variation 1: _____

   _____

   _____

   _____

   _____

   Variation 2: _____

   _____

   _____

   _____

   _____

    The Source for Reading Comprehension Strategies

CHAPTER 4

Our brain is a complex, unique, and wondrous organ, and it functions according to specific rules. One rule is that our brain strives to make meaning. We use a coding system to process words and derive meaning: "words must be analyzed by access codes into units, consisting of their bases or stems with prefixes and suffixes stripped" (Corson, 1985, p. 19). Because the meaning of a word is the sum of its parts, it is important for students to learn about structural analysis techniques: they greatly affect meaning, vocabulary development, and overall reading comprehension.

"For common readers, without Latin and Greek, the more serious reading becomes remote or irritating because the language of the page is not the language of the vernacular" (Corson, 1985, p. 39).

Vocabulary from science, social studies, mathematics, and other content areas are generally of Latin and Greek origin (disregarding foreign phrases). Students — especially adolescents — need to become quite familiar with the important Latin and Greek roots because those words are not encountered in everyday learning and interaction.

Curricular text contains far too many words to enable us to teach each word that is unfamiliar to one or more students in our classes. To attempt to do so is purely impractical because even if we select 20 new words each week, it is an insignificant number compared to the amount of words students need to learn to meet grade level expectations. To solve this dilemma, it is valuable to present students with a more efficient strategic approach to vocabulary development that will enable them to analyze unknown words independently. By developing efficient techniques for self-analyzing unknown words, students enhance their decoding accuracy and open the door for greater comprehension and fluency.

Exploring structural components of words can help students discover an excitement about our language. As they understand some of the historical forces that influenced the development of English, they realize English is a stable and learnable language rather than a language of exceptions. As Ramsden stated, "the English spelling system is tidy, behaves itself, and has a high degree of order" (Ramsden, 2001, p. 6). As stated by Nagy, it is critical that our students learn to "love language" and that they know how to "play with the parts of words" (Nagy, 2005). Berninger and Richards explain the benefits of teaching vocabulary strategies emphasizing consciousness:

> "The brain would be in chaotic overload if all knowledge of language were in consciousness all the time. From years of research it is well established that most knowledge of language is implicit and only becomes available in consciousness when it becomes the object of attention and reflection, leading to awareness. Such awareness plays an important role in creating the connections that allow written word forms to be created, stored, and retrieved in memory for purposes of reading" (Berninger & Richards, 2002, p. 220).

Evidence Base

The strategies described in this chapter incorporate specific components identified by the NRP as having a solid evidence base and match the mandates of both NCLB and Reading First. Studies supporting these techniques are referenced in the NRP Appendix A, Chapter 3 of *Vocabulary Instruction Methods: A Summary Of Vocabulary Instruction Methods* (National Reading Panel, 1999, pp. 3-33 to 3-35). Here are the evidence-based strategies represented in this chapter:

- Association method
- Concept method
- Interactive vocabulary techniques
- Roots/affix analysis
- Wide reading & background exposure
- Basic mnemonic techniques
- Decoding strategies
- Pre-instruction of vocabulary words
- Semantic mapping

Overview

Students benefit substantially by internalizing the importance of being able to analyze the structure of words. To increase their success, automaticity, and independence with these strategies, ensure that they understand word structure concepts including the schwa sound, syllabification, root, prefix, suffix, and accenting. These prerequisites are essential for analytical tasks. Review structural concepts periodically with your students as you progress through the activities in this chapter.

Remember that the activities described here are intended to be examples and models. Be creative in adapting the ideas to meet your curriculum as well as the age and linguistic level of your students. You might develop "cue cards" to remind students of the steps for any of the activities. Example cue cards are included in a few of the activities as models to use with any activity.

As with all activities, begin by modeling with the entire group. Have students progress to working in small groups or pairs before attempting an activity independently.

➤ Some Useful Definitions

Etymology: the history of words in the development of the structures and meaning of words (Henry, 2003, p. 109)

Morpheme: the smallest unit of meaning in a word (p. 182)

Bound Morpheme: a prefix, suffix, or root that cannot stand alone, such as *re-*, *struct*, and *-ure* in *restructure* (p. 285)

Affix: a bound morpheme attached to the beginning or end of a base or root that creates a new word with a meaning or function that is different from the base or root (p. 285)

Base Word: a word, such as *spell*, to which prefixes and suffixes may be added to form related words, such as *misspelled* and *misspelling* (p. 285)

Root Word: the main part of the word to which affixes are added to derive new words (for example, *struct* is the root of *destructive*); Roots are often, but not always, bound morphemes (p. 288).

Morphology and Comprehension

Morphological awareness makes a significant and unique contribution to vocabulary, reading comprehension, spelling, and decoding. It contributes to reading in two related but distinct ways, and each of these follow different developmental timetables.

- Morphology contributes to vocabulary and language comprehension.
  - Insight into the fact that words can be analyzed into meaningful parts is developed initially.

- Morphology contributes to spelling and word recognition
  - Insight into the way that morphological relationships are represented in the writing system is developed later.

Both of the assets listed above are critical for efficient reading comprehension because morphology is one way that written language differs from conversational language. Written language has richer vocabulary and more complex syntax than spoken communication. For example, the phrase "a certain unmistakable kingliness" is typical of written, rather than spoken, language. Low-frequency words, which often appear in written language, are more likely to be morphologically complex (Nagy & Anderson, 1984) than words in a spoken vocabulary. In the denser syntax of written language, suffixes play a greater role in signaling the syntactic functions of words. For example, the difference between the meanings of the phrases "residents manage collaboration" and "residential managers collaborate" is signaled by the suffixes of the individual words. By teaching morphology integrated with reading comprehension strategies, our students learn to appreciate and understand written language.

Children learn some aspects of morphology (base inflections and some derivational suffixes) before they enter school. There is a sharp increase in knowledge of prefixed and suffixed words between third and fifth grade (Anglin, 1993). The relationship between morphological awareness and vocabulary is especially strong in fourth and fifth grade (Nagy, Berninger, & Abbot, 2005). Children continue to grow in their knowledge of prefixes, suffixes, and Latin and Greek roots throughout high school and college.

When dealing with children with dyslexia, morphology can be considered — depending on the nature of the task — both a strength and a weakness (Casalis, Cole, & Sopo, 2004). It is a strength on tasks that rely heavily on meaning. For example, given a base word such as *act*, these children often are able to state many related words: *actor, active, action, react*. Also, they are frequently able to complete sentences by providing the corresponding derivative of the word:

- *politeness* — the boy was very _____. (*polite*)

Morphology appears to be a weakness for children with below average reading skills in tasks that depend on phonological abilities. For example, such students have problems segmenting affixed words into their parts as in, *sleepless — sleep, less*.

Because the meaning of a word is the sum of its parts, the origin of those parts becomes important. Anglo-Saxon, Latin, and Greek influences on word parts are most common. Generally, basic phonics instruction focuses on the Anglo-Saxon layer of language. When we move beyond this layer to the contributions of the Latin and Greek languages, we enable students to read text beyond the primary grades.

> "I strongly encourage teachers to move beyond phonics at the Anglo-Saxon layer of language, to the Latin affixes and roots and Greek combining forms that are used in upper elementary and secondary texts" (Henry, 2003, p. 140).

Examining structural components of words requires both conceptual analysis and metacognition. Students must think about the concepts as well as the linguistic components. When students use these techniques to explore vocabulary prior to reading, they increase their familiarity with the content words. This approach boosts their accuracy and efficiency for decoding and comprehension, and subsequently enhances their confidence and self-esteem, which will make reading more enjoyable for them and motivate them to read more often.

Some important morphological strategy questions to consider, and to have our students consider, are the following (Nagy, 2005):

- Can you analyze a new word into meaningful parts that gives clues about what the meaning of the whole word might be?
- Does the meaning for the new word that you infer on the basis of its parts make sense in the context?
- Can you think of other words that could be built from a familiar word by adding prefixes or suffixes?

Mapping Strategies

Collectively, the term Semantic Maps can be applied to the following vocabulary strategies, since semantics refers to word knowledge. One of the main advantages of using Mapping Strategies is that they encourage students to develop a greater *depth* of knowledge. By working with the various elements and relationships relevant to the word, students explore the word with greater processing depth and develop a more extensive network of meaning.

You or your students may convert any mapping strategy in this section into a larger format to create a bulletin board. Also, your students will enhance their involvement by using software programs such as Kidspiration® and Inspiration® because they can easily add graphics and sound to their word maps.

Basic Meaning Map   *Mapping Strategies*

A Basic Meaning Map is a concrete tool that enables students to perceive relationships among the components of a word that relate to meaning. In this activity, begin with an example of the word and describe its characteristics. After you have listed characteristics, develop a sentence that describes the word. Learning is anchored when students visualize and illustrate their sentences and then verbally explain their drawing to others.

A Basic Meaning Map for the word *cat* would include the following components:
- *Example*:   common pet
- *Characteristic*:   has 4 legs and likes to jump
- *Describing Sentence*:   My cat has four legs and jumps on our table.

Introduce the idea of word structure by asking, "What would we say instead of *cat* if we wanted to describe three of them?" (*cats*). Then have several students use *cats* in a sentence. Point out that the difference between *cat* and *cats* is the ending -*s*.

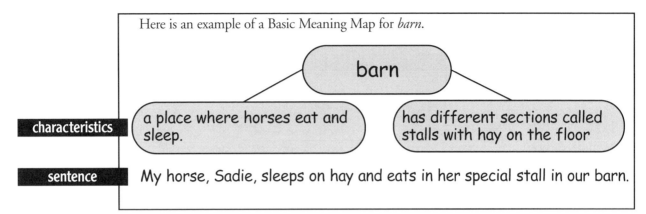

Here is an example of a Basic Meaning Map for *barn*.

barn

characteristics — a place where horses eat and sleep. / has different sections called stalls with hay on the floor

sentence — My horse, Sadie, sleeps on hay and eats in her special stall in our barn.

Word Association Map
Mapping Strategies

Have students create a word map for a given word to discover associations between the words. Page 49 contains an a Word Association Map for *cooking*. One example activity to use in developing the meanings and associations related to *cooking* is the picture book *Strega Nona* by Tomie de Paola. Go through the book with your students to identify words relating to cooking and then use the words to create a Word Association Map.

Multiple Meaning Organizer
Mapping Strategies

Multiple Meaning Organizers are similar to the Basic Meaning Maps but the focus is on the various connotations or meanings of a single word. Students will learn from one another's background knowledge if you initially create Multiple Meaning Organizers by having the whole class brainstorm ideas. Encourage students to determine (or guess) as many meanings as they can for the target word.

You can use a wide range of formats to create an organizer. The critical aspect is that the organizer presents a visual and concrete graphic for the different meanings of the target word. For example, you might use a "fence" format to link the various meanings of *web*, as shown on the right. Other formats include using lightning bolts or flags with meanings written on them to radiate from a central word. The verbal and visual information presented together helps students make connections among the meanings.

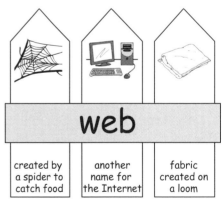

web

| created by a spider to catch food | another name for the Internet | fabric created on a loom |

Base Word Strategies

Word Family
Base Word Strategies

Use the analogy of a family to introduce your students to the concept of base words. Discuss that the people in a family are related but are not exactly the same. Then use that notion to expand students' concept of word families, and eventually, base words.

Relating word families to people families helps students recognize the relationship among words. For example, *build* is a base word that is part of a word family that includes *building*, *builds*, *rebuild*, and *buildings*.

Base Word Strategy

Explain to your students that the concept of a base word is critical because if they know the base word, they can easily find its relatives. Here is a cue card for presenting the Base Word Strategy:

Cue Card for Base Words

1. Look at the word and find a base word.

2. Determine the meaning of the base word.

3. Find similar words. If the same base word is inside a word, it's a relative of the family.

4. Determine the meaning of the related word(s).

Follow these steps to introduce the concept of Base Words:

1. Present and explain the cue card.

2. Give students a base word.

3. Discuss meaning of the base word.

4. Have students brainstorm as many words as they can think of that include the base word and include them in a graphic.

➤ Base Word Strategy for Younger Students

Begin presenting base words and affixes that your students commonly use in conversation. Guide students to discover and suggest affixes such as *-ed*, *-ing*, *-ly*, *-less*, *-er*, *-est*. Examples of simple word families include *like/likes/likely*, *stamp/stamping/stamped*, *play/playing*, and *big/ bigger/biggest*. Here are two examples of graphically presenting base words and word families:

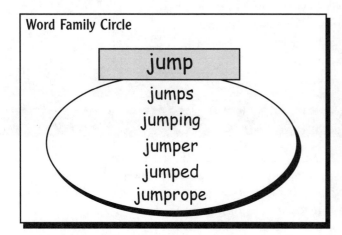

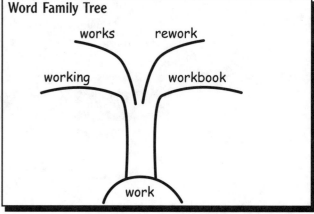

➤ Base Word Strategy for Older Students

Activities with older students are similar, but expanded and more complex. The following Word Web categorizes and lists options for *word* (Ramsden, 2001):

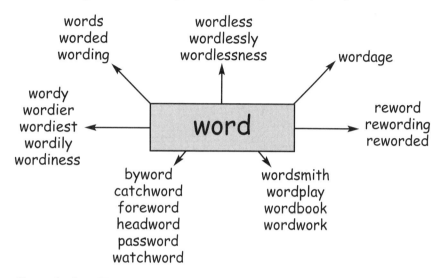

	words worded wording	wordless wordlessly wordlessness	wordage
wordy wordier wordiest wordily wordiness		**word**		reword rewording reworded
	byword catchword foreword headword password watchword	wordsmith wordplay wordbook wordwork	

The Knowledge Tree

Base Word Strategies

We organize our verbal knowledge in networks of associations based on definable structures. A Knowledge Tree, like a Word Tree, helps visually integrate information about new words and concepts: students explore words and concepts in relation to one another, not as isolated units. "New verbal information is learned in accordance with prior knowledge. Effective teaching elaborates various connections among better-known and lesser-known words, deepens and enriches existing knowledge, and seeks to build a network of ideas around key concepts that are well elaborated"

(Moats, 2000, p. 112). Helping students develop these associations provides a vehicle to increase the complexity of their understanding and their ability to comprehend and use more vocabulary words.

Adjust the components used in creating a Knowledge Map to your students' age and skills. Here are the basic steps:

1. Draw a tree outline (as shown on the right).
2. Write the base word on the root of the tree.
3. Discuss the base word.
4. Develop a brief definition and write it on the trunk of the tree.

category:
describing word, related to the uniqueness of a person or thing

synonyms:
strange, unusual, astonishing

word parts:
5 syllables, base word = ordinary,
prefix = ex- (out), extra
suffix = -ary (describing)

antonyms:
unexceptional, ordinary

something or someone notably unusual or exceptional

extraordinary

Trevor is an extraordinary piano player.

5. Add branches to the tree, with each representing a target component related to the word.

Your selected components for the branches will depend upon the age of your students and your curriculum goals. Use fewer components for younger students. Here are some components you can include:
- Synonyms
- Antonyms
- Category (speech part focusing on description and usage rather than a label)
- Linguistic structures (syllables, number of syllables, prefix, root, suffixes)
- Alternate meanings
- Examples of the word's usage
- Related body gestures
- Example sentence

Roots

A wide selection of activities exists for teaching and reinforcing the concept of root words, and this section contains several. As with any activity, incorporate and integrate brainstorming, mapping, personalization, associations, and interaction as appropriate. Many vocabulary authorities recommend an early start on the teaching of meaningful parts of words (Anglin, 1993; Biemiller, 2004; Moats, 2000; Templeton & Pikulski, 1999).

Base Word Strategies   *Roots Strategies*

This is a group activity enjoyed by students from about third grade through high school. You or your students select a specific root each week along with a visual organizer format. Throughout the week, students add words to the organizer.

Root Web: Suffixes
Use a Knowledge Tree (page 67) format for your Root Web and follow these steps:
1. Introduce a high frequency word that can stand alone. *form*
2. Define the word. *"shape or structure"*
3. Brainstorm words from the same word family. *forms, former, inform*
4. Record all of the words that your students generate in a list everyone can see.
5. Guide students to identify words on the list that have prefixes and underline those words.
6. Guide students to identify words on the list that have suffixes and circle those words.
7. Create a Root Web using only the words that have suffixes. Place those words on branches on one side of the Knowledge Tree.
8. Discuss each word in the Web and explain how the suffix combines with the root to create the word's meaning.

Root Web: Prefixes
1. Create a Suffix Root Web, as above.
2. Refer to the initial list and discuss the words that have prefixes.
3. Add the words with prefixes to the Root Web. Place them on branches on the other side of the Knowledge Tree.
4. Discuss these words to discover how the prefix combines with the root to create a word's meaning.

Root Web: Expansion
1. Select a common prefix or suffix, such as *-s* or *re-*.
2. Discuss words (in addition to those on the list) that can be created by adding the prefix or suffix.
3. Add these words to the Root Web.
4. Repeat this expansion activity with other common affixes.

Building Words Contests
Roots Strategies

The goal of this activity is for each group is to create a visual organizer by developing words related to a given root, such as *struct*. Have students work in teams for this activity and select a graphic organizer structure. Depending on your goals for the activity, you might include these components:
- Give a specific timeframe.
- Allow students to use a Franklin Language Master, dictionary, and/or thesaurus.
- Vary the size of the groups and/or the organizer format.
- Provide the root and a selected list of affixes, as in the example below:
  - Root: *struct*
  - Prefixes: *un-, re-, con-, de-, in-*
  - Suffixes: *-tion, -ing, -s, -ful, -ture, -ed*
- Provide the root and have students think of the variations.

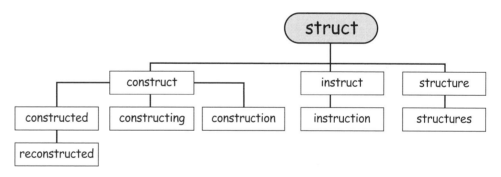

The winning group is the one with the most real words on its Web. At the conclusion of the contest, have each group select a given number of words from its organizer and develop sentences and pictures that illustrate the meaning of those words. Each group then explains its selections to the other groups.

Creating Real and Impossible Words
Roots Strategies

In this activity, students create words using word parts. Introduce the activity by emphasizing that the meaning of a word is the sum of its parts.

Present students with a list of prefixes, roots, and suffixes, as shown in the chart on the next page. Then have students use the word parts to create a variety of possible *and* impossible words by combining components from any row. Having students work in pairs or small groups will enable them to benefit from each other's background knowledge. Also, encourage them to check their answers using a dictionary or Franklin Language Master (Moats, 2000).

Prefixes	Roots	Suffixes	Real Words	Impossible Words
in-	spir(e)	-ed	invariable	dissectation
dis-	cred	-icate		
non-	sect	-(i)able		
pre-	var	-arian		
inter-	rupt	-(a)tion		

Real Word Possibilities:		Impossible Word Possibilities:	
interruptible	disrupted	noncredarian	presecticate
nonsectarian	prevaricate	disspiration	nonrupted
inspiration		intervarable	

CAUTION

Caution: When working with word parts (morphemes), guide your students to avoid finding "false" morphemes in words. For example, *sister* does not contain the comparative suffix *-er*, nor does *hundred* contain the past tense suffix *-ed*. Students should consult the dictionary for etymologies to clear up confusion.

Affixes

Affixes have already been included in the above activities because they are necessary when structurally analyzing words. Activities suggested in this section specifically focus on affixes.

Prefixes found most frequently with Anglo-Saxon base words are *in-*, *un-*, *mis-*, *dis-*, *fore-*, *re-*, *de-*, *pre-*, and *a-*. Of almost 3000 prefix words found in textbooks in grades three to nine, words beginning with *un-*, *re-*, *in-* and *dis-* occur in more than 58% of the prefixed words. (White, Sowell, and Yanagihara, 1989). Analyzing more than 2000 common suffix words revealed four common suffixes in 65% of the words: *-s*, *-es*, *-ed*, and *-ing*. Henry, in *Unlocking Literacy*, recommends a developmental approach and provides many example classroom activities and extensive lists (2003, Chapter 7 and Appendices).

Affix Challenge
Affixes Strategies

This activity challenges students to integrate a word, its affixes, and its meaning. Provide a list of words for students to use to make the activity more concrete and to provide a starting point.

Challenge 1
Challenge your students to use a word with and without a prefix in the same sentence.
- *Kind* parents sometimes seem *unkind* to their children when they insist on a curfew.
- I need to open this *vent* because the room is so stuffy, and I want to *prevent* becoming overheated.

Challenge 2
Students create a sentence using a word with and without a suffix.
- I think I am very *wise* about spending my allowance because I *wisely* plan my purchases.
- I am *working* hard on this project because I like this *work*.

Challenge 3

This is a combination challenge. The students create a single sentence using both a word without an affix (or with only one) and that same word using multiple affixes.

- I am *transforming* this complicated *form* so that it is easier to understand.
- I want to *inform* you about pizza day because you need the correct *information*.

Prefix or Suffix Chart

Have students work independently, in small groups, or as a whole class to complete the missing information in a prefix chart like the one below. Select words and prefixes for the chart from material the students will be reading.

Base Word	Meaning of Base Word	Prefix	Meaning of Prefix	Word with Prefix	Meaning of Word with Prefix
claim	to call for; to state as a fact	ex-	out	exclaim	to speak or cry out in strong emotion
		ac-	to, toward, in; use before roots beginning with c, k, or q	acclaim	to applaud or praise
change	to make or become different	ex-	out	exchange	to substitute one thing for another
		per-	through or completely	performs	
	to carry			export	
order		dis-			

For variation, create a Suffix Chart to focus on suffixes or an Affix Chart to include both prefixes and suffixes.

Ousting the Negatives

Many high frequency prefixes have a negative connotation, such as *un-, in-, im-, il-, dis-,* and *mis-*. Ousting the Negatives is a humorous activity that encourages students to practice manipulating these word parts.

1. Present students with a paragraph or longer passage that contains many high frequency words with negative prefixes. Depending on the level of your students, you might read the passage aloud or have students read it independently.

2. Working independently or in small groups, have students underline each word that contains a negative prefix.

3. Have students "Oust the Negatives" by crossing out the negative prefixes.

4. Reread the passage and discuss the difference in message.

An example story is on the next page. Guide students to discuss how they initially felt about Fido compared to their feelings about Fido after the revised story.

Original Story

My story is about my cousin's dog Fido. This dog has a very **unpleasant** smell and an **inability** to listen. He is an **insane** dog and **unusually** funny. He is **unaware** of rules and very **disobedient**. He likes to do things that are **unsafe** and creates **disorder** throughout the household.

Revised Story After "Ousting the Negatives":

My story is about my cousin's dog Fido. This dog has a very **pleasant** smell and an **ability** to listen. He is a **sane** dog and **usually** funny. He is **aware** of rules and very **obedient**. He likes to do things that are **safe** and creates **order** throughout the household.

Latin

Latin roots are reliable elements of word knowledge. Henry, among others, recommends that we teach individual Latin roots directly to students. As they begin to learn Latin roots, it is often beneficial to incorporate study of etymology in the curriculum. Word origin knowledge will enable students to realize the relationship among the different levels of language. For example, some Latin affixes may also be found in Greek or Anglo-Saxon: *ex-* can be found in both Greek and Latin. Corson reports, "Marked educational improvements have been reported for children who have followed programs focusing on the etymology and word relationship of English" (Corson 1985, p. 28).

An example of a word with a Latin root is *inspire:*
- Etymology: Latin
- Root: spir
- Prefix: in-

The following 12 Latin roots, along with the Greek combining forms *graph* and *ology*, provide clues to the meaning of more than 100,000 words (Brown 1947):

- *scrib, script* (to write)
- *spec, spect, spic* (to see, watch, or observe)
- *mit, miss* (to send)
- *fer* (to bear or yield)
- *duc, duce, duct* (to lead)
- *fac, fact, fect, fic* (to make or do)
- *tend, tens, tent* (to stretch or strain)
- *ten, tain, tin, tinu* (to hold)
- *sist, sta, stat, stit* (to stand)
- *pon, pose, pound* (to put, place, or set)
- *plic, ply* (to fold)
- *cap, ceit, ceive, cep, cept, cip* (to take catch, see, hold or receive)

Since spellings of Latin roots are very phonetic, the order of presentation may not be as critical as finding connectedness with words used within our curriculum.

About Schwa

Schwa is the vowel sound in many lightly pronounced unaccented syllables in English words of more than one syllable. It is a short, neutral vowel sound and is written phonetically with a rotated e (ə). It is the most common sound in the English language and it depends on the adjacent consonants. Any vowel may be used to represent a schwa sound, as in the examples on the next page.

- *a* in *about, ago, adept*
- *e* in *synthesis, silent, camel*
- *i* in *victim, decimal*
- *o* in *harmony, pistol, reason*
- *u* in *medium, circus, album*

- *y* in *syringe*
- *ai* in *mountain, captain*
- *au* in *authority, author*
- *ou* in *limousine, glamour*
- *oi* in *tortoise, pension*

"The name (schwa) is derived from the Hebrew point system devised to indicate vowels in a writing system that normally did not use them. The phoneme and the associated grapheme (ə) were identified in the late 19th century. Schwa has been part of the International Phonetic Association (IPA) notation since 1897, when it was first published.

When English speakers try to speak Spanish, which has no schwa, they invariably introduce it. Fiesta (fee-e-stah) becomes "fee-es-tuh" and mesa (mā-sa) becomes "mei-suh."

In 1971, Dewey claimed there were 42 different ways of spelling schwa in an unabridged dictionary" (Shwa [sic], 2005).

The Schwa Sound *Latin Strategies*

While Latin roots are quite phonetic, the affixes generally contain the schwa sound. Therefore, we need to teach students explicitly to attend to both phonological clues and grammatical usage when decoding and spelling multisyllabic words. Here is an example:

- *-ous* and *-ess* both say /əs/:
  Governess: *-ess* is used for feminine nouns
  Mountainous: *-ous* is used for adjectives

Invite students to develop lists of other words that end in an affix that sounds like /əs/. Separate the lists into words that end in the suffix *-ess* and those that end in the suffix *-ous*.

Morpheme Web *Latin Strategies*

You may easily adapt the semantic mapping activities described above for Base Words, Knowledge Trees, and Root Webs to activities focusing on Latin roots. In the following activities, a Morpheme Web provides students with a matrix for a given root. They use the information to develop words using that root. For example, the Morpheme Web on the next page lists possible words for the root *struct*, including *reconstructing, destruct, obstruction, infrastructure*.

After the Web is constructed, guide students to increase their depth of understanding by discussing the meanings of some of the words generated, focusing on similarities and differences. Select students to create a sentence using one or more of the words. As a challenge activity, encourage students to use several words in a short paragraph that makes sense.

An appropriate activity for elementary students may use a simplified matrix and a root word, such as *have* or *fright* (Ramsden, 2001). Activities appropriate for middle or high school students might use *struct* (as shown in the example on the next page) or *preci* (Ramsden, 2001).

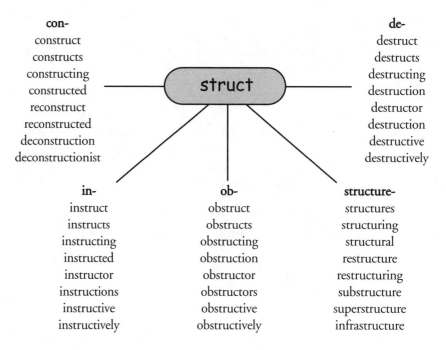

con-		de-
construct		destruct
constructs		destructs
constructing		destructing
constructed		destruction
reconstruct		destructor
reconstructed		destruction
deconstruction		destructive
deconstructionist		destructively

in-	ob-	structure-
instruct	obstruct	structures
instructs	obstructs	structuring
instructing	obstructing	structural
instructed	obstruction	restructure
instructor	obstructor	restructuring
instructions	obstructors	substructure
instructive	obstructive	superstructure
instructively	obstructively	infrastructure

Morpheme Search

Latin Strategies

Have students look for words of Latin origin in newspapers or in their texts. You might structure and simplify the activity by providing a cue card with specific Latin roots. The students may circle the words (if using a newspaper) or create a list of words found. Have students provide a reference (page number, paragraph number, line number, etc.) that explains where they found each word.

An important follow-up activity is to discuss the relationships and meanings of the words students found. This discussion phase is critical in establishing greater depth of processing regarding the words. Select a limited number of words and have students use them in a written activity, such as one or two of the following:

- Write sentences using the words.
- Write a story incorporating as many words as possible.
- Create a Morpheme Web with one or more of the words.
- Create a Root Web with one or more of the words.
- Illustrate one or more of the words or a group of words.

Finding Latin Roots and Affixes

Latin Strategies

Following are variations of activities that require students to search for a specific Latin root or affix and determine its meaning in words.

1. Students read a list of words and underline the root.
2. Students create a chart using a given list of words, forming columns for prefixes, roots, and suffixes.
3. Discuss a Latin root such as *dic/dict* (to say or tell). Provide students with a list of words that use this root and have them match each word to its corresponding meaning as shown on the next page.

   The Source for Reading Comprehension Strategies

Words containing root *dic* or *dict*		Word meanings	
1	malediction	an absolute ruler	(5)
2	benediction	to express the opposite	(3)
3	contradict	to point out	(6)
4	prediction	a blessing	(2)
5	dictator	a reference book of words	(7)
6	indicate	a curse	(1)
7	dictionary	something foretold	(4)

4. Provide students with a passage, such as the one below. Have them underline the prefixes and circle the suffixes.

> The hyperactive kid jumped over the puddle. He appeared to make it, but slipped and crashed to the sidewalk. He started to cry since he had misbehaved. He complained to his friend that the ground was too slippery. His friend laughed and helped him up. They continued running, jumping and playing around the parking lot. Then they saw a bunch of people getting out of their cars. They were musicians. They saw violinists and trombonists. Their stuff looked expensive. The two kids were interested in the musicians but they disappeared into the building.

Greek

In English, many of the words based in Greek relate to science and math. Greek words often combine or compound, such as in *biology, geology, geography, chemistry,* and *physics.* The technical term for combining those word parts is *combining forms.* Explain to the students that the words usually combine two parts of equal stress and importance, which is similar to the way Anglo-Saxon compound words are formed (*cowboy, lighthouse,* etc.). Using the terms *root, prefix, and suffix* is appropriate when discussing Greek forms as long as the terms are used consistently.

Henry (2003, p. 114) recommends teaching some of the common Greek forms along with the root words beginning in fifth grade because the science and math texts at that level begin to depend on Greek-based words as key content words. She recommends providing at least four to six Greek combining forms in a given lesson, which will allow the students to generate a larger number of words from each combining form.

Greek words can be recognized by their use of combined elements that are analogous to English compounds: each part has equal value in determining the meaning of the word but (each Greek combining form) must exist in combination with others before it can make a word in English" (Moats, 2000, pp. 89-90).

Prerequisites

Teach the students the sound symbol correspondences that are exclusive to Greek, such as:

- ph for /f/ — *photograph*
- ch for /k/ — *chemotherapy*
- y for /ĭ/ — *symphonic*
- y for /ī/ — *hydrogen*
- ps for /s/ — *psychology*

- rh for /r/ — *rhinoceros*
- pn for /n/ — *pneumonia*
- pt for /t/ — *pterodactyl*
- mn for /n/ — *mnemonic*
- words beginning in x — *xylophone*

Initial Combining Forms

These 12 combining forms are useful for the initial study of Greek forms (Henry, 2003, p. 115):

- *phon, phono* (sound)
- *photo* (light)
- *gram, graph* (written or drawn)
- *auto* (self)
- *tele* (distant)
- *logy* (study; from logos, logue [speech or word])

- *micro* (small or minute)
- *meter, metr* (measure)
- *therm, thermo* (heat or hot)
- *bio* (life)
- *scope* (to watch or see)
- *hydr, hydra, hydro* (water)

Generating Greek-Based Words, Level 1

1. Give students two Greek combining forms and discuss the meaning of each.
2. Have students generate as many Greek-based words as they can for each form.
3. Write the words on the board as students say them.
4. With the class, practice reading and air writing the words.
5. Discuss the meaning of each word.

An example using the combining forms *bio* and *logy*:

bio (life)	logy (study of)
biology	biology
biosphere	mythology
biochemistry	phonology
biodegradable	geology
biography	zoology
autobiography	pathology

Generating Greek-Based Words, Level 2

1. Give students a list of four Greek combining forms. Discuss the meaning of each and have them generate as many Greek-based words as they can that use that form.
2. Write the words on the board as the students say them. With the class, practice reading and air writing the words.
3. Have students look for patterns and create a visual organizer, similar to one of the maps described in previous activities. The map on the next page is based on some possible words generated from the following combining forms: *phon/phono, photo, gram/graph,* and *tele*.

	phon/phono	photo	gram/graph	tele
phon/phono			gramophone	telephone
photo				telephoto
gram/graph	phonogram	photograph, photographer		telegram, telegraph
tele	telephone	telephoto		
ology	phonology			
copy		photocopy		
bio			biography	
biblio			bibliography	
geo			geography	
scope				telescope
vision				television

4. Encourage students to create other words using the same combining forms. Have them guess if the word is a real word or not. If students identify a real word, have them guess its meaning based on what they know about one of the combining forms.
   - Use a dictionary or Franklin Language Master to confirm accuracy of their guesses.
   - Here are some words students might generate from the forms in the chart:

photogram	*phonocopy*	*photology*	*gramology*
geophoto	*photoscope*	*bibliophone*	*phonoscope*
bibliogram	*telecopy*		

   - The real words are *photogram*, *phonoscope*, and *telecopy*.

5. Have students search one of their textbooks for words that contain Greek combining forms.

Mapping
Greek Strategies

You can easily adapt the semantic mapping activities described previously for Base Words, Knowledge Trees, and Root Webs to activities focusing on Greek combining forms.

Contrasting and Describing Meaning
Greek Strategies

Encourage your students to try to determine the meaning of the target words and check their answers using a dictionary or Franklin Language Master. To scaffold the activity, provide students with a visual cue card of some Greek combining forms and their meanings.

Statement for student to analyze	Word meanings
Describe a person with *megapods* and *megadonts*.	*Megapods*: large feet *Megadonts*: large teeth
Compare an *introvert* and an *extrovert*.	*Introvert*: behavior turns inward *Extrovert*: behavior turns outward, is outgoing
Compare a *tyrannosaurus* and a *brachiosaurus*.	*Tyranno*: terrible *Saurus*: lizard *Brachio*: arm *Tyrannosaurus* is "terrible lizard" *Brachiosaurus* is "arm lizard"; its arms are longer than its legs

A related activity is to have students use Greek combining forms to describe the following dinosaurs: *triceratops, microceratops, megaceros, anchiceratops, anchisaurus,* and *asiaceratops.*

Combining forms	Concrete meaning of dinosaur names
tri — three	*triceratops* — 3 horns on face
cera — horn	*microceratops* — small, horned face
tops — face	*megaceros* — gigantic, large horn
micro — small	*anchiceratops* — horn near face
mega — gigantic, large	*anchisaurus* — near lizard
anchi — near	*asiaceratops* — Asia, horned face
saurus — lizard	
asia — Asia	

Defining and Identifying
Greek Strategies

1. Present and discuss the meanings of words such as *telescope, autograph, automatic, and biped.*
2. Create a chart to define each word. After the definitions are in place, determine the word parts and the meaning of each part.

Word	Definition	Word Parts
telescope	instrument with lenses or mirrors used to view distant objects	*tele* — distant *scope* —to watch or see
autograph	a person's handwritten signature	*auto* — self *graph* — write, writing
autobiography	a biography written about one's own life	*auto* — self *bio* — life *graph* — write, writing
bibliography	a written list of books	*biblio* — book *graph* — write, writing

Latin and Greek Forms
Greek Strategies

A familiarity with Anglo-Saxon, Latin, and Greek word origins is useful for understanding variations in English spelling. Here are some interesting spelling guidelines for using suffixes (Henry, 2003, p. 108; Moats, 2000, pp. 65-78):

- Use *-or* with Latin roots for nouns (*inventor, conductor, elevator*), but use *-ar* for adjectives (*popular, singular, circular*).
- Use *-or* with Latin roots (*spectator*), but use *-er* for Anglo-Saxon roots (*heater, swimmer, baker*).
- Although *-ous* and *-ess* sound alike because both are unstressed syllables containing a schwa sound, use *-ous* for adjectives (*dangerous, tremendous, fabulous*) and *-ess* for feminine nouns (*princess, hostess, governess*). The similar sounding *-ice* is a noun suffix (*office, malice, practice, apprentice*).

- Use *-est* for comparative adjectives (*greenest, loveliest, smallest*), but use *-ist* for people nouns (*dentist, pianist, socialist*).
- Although not always the case, *-able* is usually added to Anglo-Saxon base words (*likable, reasonable, eatable*) and *-ible* is usually added to Latin roots (*credible, edible, impossible*).

Mental Imagery

Powerful Words
Mental Imagery

Explain to your students how using powerful words within a sentence influences the way you develop a corresponding picture in your mind. Give examples of sentences that use nonpowerful descriptive words. Then provide a similar sentence that uses powerful descriptive words. Ask your students to create a visual image in their mind for each, using the cue, "What picture do the words paint?"

1. The ship was on the sea. The sea was *rough.*
   - The ship tossed *violently* on the *brutal* seas.
2. The bear looked *mean* with *ugly* fur.
   - The bear's fur was *spiky*, and his face was *scary* because of his *humongous* teeth and *wide* eyes.

Discuss how both groups of words (*rough/brutal, ugly/spiky, mean/humongous*) are describing words (adjectives or adverbs), but that one conveys a more vivid mental image than the other. To extend the concept of using powerful words, have students identify powerful words in literature in their curriculum and encourage them to use powerful words in their own writing. Guide students to reflect on how affixes contribute to the imagery power of a word.

Poetry
Mental Imagery

Read poems to your students and encourage them to be mentally active by using imagery as they listen. Developing imagery cannot be a passive process, even though excessive TV viewing encourages passivity with visual images. Introduce concrete, short poems to younger students and challenge them to visualize what they hear. With older students, increase the complexity and abstraction of the poems. Through discussions and group interactions, encourage students to draw upon their background knowledge as they form images in their minds. They will also expand their experiences by sharing their images and experiences with others.

Here is a suggested sequence for using poetry to encourage Mental Imagery:

1. Have the students close their eyes while you read a verse or whole poem. Instruct them to "let the writer paint a picture in your mind while you listen."
2. After the reading, have students open their eyes and read the first line or verse by themselves. (This helps chunk the activity into smaller components to enable the students to focus on their imagery.)
3. Encourage students to picture the image in their mind that is suggested by the verse. Then have them draw a corresponding picture that illustrates their mental image.
4. Repeat steps 2 and 3 until the poem is finished.

Reflections

1. Select an expository text appropriate to your grade level and curriculum. Create the following using vocabulary within the text:
   - A Multiple Meaning Map for at least one of the key words
   - A Knowledge Tree for at least two different key words
   - A Morpheme Web using a root from at least one of the key words

2. Consider how you might incorporate information about word structure into your content curriculum. For example, what words in your current science lesson could you use to create one of the visual organizers in this chapter?

   _____

   _____

   _____

3. Create an activity relevant to your students' age and goals to utilize information about Greek combining forms. You might do a Web (page 67), questions to compare and contrast meaning of word pairs (page 77), or create an activity using dinosaur names or word parts (page 78).

   _____

   _____

   _____

   _____

4. How do you think your students would benefit from learning about Latin roots and affixes? Which area or areas of your curriculum would be most applicable?

   _____

   _____

   _____

5. Which of the 12 Latin roots listed on page 72 best match your current curriculum? Develop two activities to focus on these roots.

   Activity 1: _____

   _____

   _____

   Activity 2: _____

   _____

   _____

CHAPTER

CONTEXTUAL STRATEGIES

Students need multiple experiences with and exposure to new words to enhance their vocabularies. Incorporating novelty in your instruction encourages your students to focus and attend more completely. Integrating new words in novel and varied activities also provides word redundancy that helps establish a network of meaning for students. The entire process encourages students to use, enhance, share, and extend their background knowledge.

> **Word redundancy establishes a network of meaning for new words.**

Students need to generate rich connections between new vocabulary and information that is already familiar to them. Seeking connectedness is one of the brains' major rules for learning. Generating rich connections involves more than learning a simple association: students need to process the word deeply and create links between the word in different contexts while activating their own prior knowledge of other words.

The contextual strategies in this chapter suggest techniques for previewing the words, concepts, and content of text before students actually read the material. Some of the activities represent ways to use the upcoming text as a starting point on which to elaborate words or concepts while also building critical comprehension skills. Such strategies are useful as we seek to deal with the conundrum of striving to meet standards while also adapting to individual students' needs. Other strategies in this chapter are basic prereading recommendations.

Select an activity to match the needs of your group and the goals within the upcoming text. Vary your activities to provide novelty and increase your students' focus while also calling attention to the importance of networks of meaning.

Evidence Base

The strategies in this chapter incorporate components identified by the NRP as having a solid evidence base and match the mandates of NCLB and Reading First. Studies supporting these techniques are referenced in Appendix A, Chapter 3 of *Vocabulary Instruction Methods: A Summary Of Vocabulary Instruction Methods* (National Reading Panel, 1999, pp. 3-33 to 3-35). Here are the evidence-based strategies represented in this chapter:

- Association method
- Concept method
- Elaborate and rich instruction
- Pre-instruction of vocabulary words
- Semantic mapping

- Basic mnemonic techniques
- Decoding strategies
- Interactive vocabulary techniques
- Roots/affix analysis
- Wide reading & background exposure

Listening Activities

Listening activities provide a critical foundation for developing reading comprehension efficiency. It is critical that your students learn to listen actively. Providing a purpose for listening avoids passivity and encourages students to take responsibility for what they hear. Examples of some "purposes" include tasks students participate in after reading:

- Discuss information
- Retell the story
- React critically
- Answer questions

Listening activities are critical for building students' world knowledge while simultaneously enhancing their vocabulary and comprehension. These types of activities are an excellent starting place for students who have inefficient decoding or fluency because in doing so, you eliminate poor decoding or fluency as a roadblock to comprehension. Thus, the student is better able to focus on what the material means. These activities are also efficient initial skill builders for students who lack world knowledge skills. By presenting information in small chunks, you help those students with language processing problems for whom it is easier to comprehend small passages. Furthermore, retelling a story after listening helps build students' working memory. In general, it is more efficient to start with small passages, but you may judge this based on your students' skill levels.

Word Up Activities

Listening Strategies

Word Up Activities benefit students most when used in conjunction with a listening activity. These activities are valuable to emphasize specific key words in narrative or expository text, with each student taking responsibility for a specific word. Instead of presenting material in a traditional lecture format where students are more inclined to be passive listeners, Word Up Activities provide students with ownership of at least one small part of the lesson. This ownership encourages more active listening overall. Furthermore, students often become interested in other students' words, which expands the depth of the activity.

➤ Word Up: Prereading a Story

This strategy works well with all ages, but it is especially effective with young and at-risk students. Select a few vocabulary words that are critical to a story's meaning. Write each word on one or more large, colored index cards. Limit the number of new words at first; however, you might want each student to have a card so some words will be on more than one card. For example, if you have 20 students and you select seven key words, most words will be repeated on three different cards.

Prepare:
1. Hold up a word and read it. Have students repeat the word and follow these directions:
   - Have students clap the syllables for the word (this increases the number of repetitions and reinforces linguistic concepts).
   - Elicit brief discussion about the word's meaning. Summarize the desired meaning based on your content. Keep this step short — no more than 10 seconds.
2. Repeat the above step with all of the selected target words.
3. Distribute the word cards, one to a student. Randomly distribute cards with the same word throughout the room.

Read the story:

1. As you read the story aloud, each student listens for his word.

2. Every time a student hears you read his word (or a derivative), he holds up his word card. For example, if a student has the word *talk*, he raises his card if you say *talk*, *talks*, *talking* or *talked*.

After Reading Review 1:

1. One student holds up her card and reads it.

2. All students with that same word then hold up their cards and read them.

3. Discuss the word and use it to create sentences. Students will often suggest sentences from the story.

4. Repeat with all the words.

After Reading Review 2:

Each student keeps her card, which gives ownership of that part of the instruction. Then the student uses multiple colors to illustrate her word on the back of the card

When the students later read the story themselves, their word understanding will be substantially higher. Their "own" word will be automatic to them and they will be familiar with the other words previewed in the initial activity. This activity is valuable for students because it previews the story while also exposing them to new words in isolation and in context.

- In isolation:
  - Initial reading and discussion of the word
  - Holding up the card
- In context:
  - Listening for their own word

➤ *Word Up: Content Material*

The Word Up Activity is performed as described above when using content material (from a textbook, for example). When you select your words, choose those that are critical for understanding the concept. During the preparation, you might wish to spend additional time and elaboration in helping students understand the concept.

Rather than read the text to your students, you state a verbal overview of the material they will be reading independently. As you provide your overview, each student holds up her card when it corresponds to the word you say.

The review activities are the same as described above. It is particularly useful for each student to illustrate her word's meaning when dealing with content material.

Combining Strategies for Listening
Listening Strategies

The following example Combining Strategy uses a listening activity as a base while simultaneously developing a variety of vocabulary and comprehension skills. The activities build breadth and depth of vocabulary skills while incorporating many cognitive strategies. Students create a stronger foundation for reading comprehension by learning and practicing critical skills within a listening task. As a result, the skills they build will be readily available when reading and comprehending on their own. Learning the skills while listening often allows students to attend more fully on the cognitive strategy because listening eliminates the demands of decoding and fluency.

Adapt this activity to your own needs. Some days you may wish to implement just a few of the activity steps. Other days you may wish to use more or add steps of your own.

The activity is described in detail on the following pages. Here are the basic steps:
1. Identify and explore vocabulary related to the story (Naming, Categorizing, Ranking, Relating Words, Describing).
2. Work with the story (Listening, Retelling, Identifying Components, Visualizing Components, Summarizing).

The story explored in the following example is about cars and Henry Ford's implementation of the assembly line, "The End of Cheap Oil: Wheel Life Begins" (found on page 87).

➤ Vocabulary: Naming

Introduce the activity by telling students you will later be reading them a story about cars.

Have your students name any item they think of when they hear the word *car*. The activity should proceed quickly (encourage students to call out items without having to raise their hands). Ignore duplicate items and keep the brainstorming moving to encourage students to rapidly name items.

Continue brainstorming until your students can think of no more associations with *car*. The general purpose is to encourage students to substantially widen their network of associations with the word.

Here are some things students might name:

gas	travel	radio	front seat
convertible	fast	vacation	McDonald's®

➤ Vocabulary: Categorizing

In this step, your students will become more precise in naming items by providing a categorical structure for the items they name. Sequence the categories from general to specific to encourage students to become progressively more precise. Depending upon your group's skill level, you might create a list of the students' responses. If you suspect students might name some items that do not fit within the target category, then having a written list will aid discussion and adaptations afterwards.

On the next page are some ideas for categories related to cars, with a few examples of specific items in each category. Ask your students to name items within each category.

- Name some makes of cars:

  | *Honda* | *Toyota* | *Mercedes* | *BMW* | *VW Beetle* |

- A station wagon is one type of car. Name some other types:

  | *sedan* | *convertible* | *SUV* | *van* | *minivan* |

- Name parts of a car that are essential for the car to work:

  | *steering wheel* | *brake* | *gas pedal* | *engine* | *spark plug* |

- Name parts of cars that are useful and we like to have, but that are not critical or essential in order for the car to work.

  | *radio* | *air-conditioning* | *TV* | *leather seats* | *power windows* |

To avoid discouraging students from participation, it is important to be positive in your comments, even when the student is "wrong." For example, if the student names *radio* as an item that is the essential for the car to work, you might make comments such as the following after the list is complete:

- "This is a really good list. We thought of a lot of parts that are essential for a car. *Essential* means 'the car really needs them in order to run.' Let's look at some of our words."

  - "*Brakes* — that's a really good word. Why is this part essential for a car?" (Guide students to discuss that a brake is necessary in order for the car to stop in time and not crash.)

  - "*Radio* — that's another really good word. Why is this part essential for a car to run?"
    - ✔ Some students might say that a radio is nice because otherwise you get bored riding.
    - ✔ Lead students to discover the difference between the concepts of *essential* and *useful*. You might say, "Right, a radio is really nice to have in our car. Some people think it's real important. However, a car can run without a radio. So let's circle it and we'll find another category later where it fits even better."

➤ Vocabulary: Ranking

> Ranking offers students more depth of understanding and leads them towards understanding multiple meanings and inferential thinking.

Ranking words is extremely valuable for students because it helps develop the concept of *connotation* (an idea that is implied or suggested). Ranking encourages students to explore the meaning of the word as well as other ideas that relate to the word. This activity offers students more depth of understanding and leads students towards understanding multiple meanings and inferential thinking.

Begin by selecting some items from the list of makes of cars generated earlier. Limit your selection to cars that will have obvious differences in rank for the students. Have the students rank the car makes from "least luxurious" (or "least fancy") to "most luxurious" (or "most fancy"). Here is a possible ranking:

1. VW Beetle, 2. Honda, 3. Mercedes

Discuss how the concept of the car's relative rank can provide information to students while they are reading. This leads them towards the concepts of multiple meanings and inferential thinking. Here are some questions you can ask to provide meaning to the ranking:

- What does it imply about a character who drives a VW Beetle? *He may be practical and frugal; he may not have a lot of money.*

- What does it imply about a character who drives a Mercedes? *He may be wealthy; he may be a movie star or someone famous.*
- What does it mean if an author mentions that a character has the "Mercedes of computers"? *The computer doesn't have anything to do with a car — it means the computer is fancy or very expensive, just as a Mercedes is fancy.*

➤ *Vocabulary: Related Words*

Encourage students to think about words that relate to cars, such as the word *make*. In the factory, they make cars. Then generate other meanings for the word *make*, perhaps creating a visual organizer similar to the Multiple Meaning Map for *run* on page 50. When dealing with related words and multiple meanings, the goal is to encourage students to name as many categories as possible.

➤ *Vocabulary: Describing*

In this step, students look at pictures related to the topic. You might restrict the activity by presenting pictures only of cars or expand it to include pictures of any vehicle. You might have students search for their own pictures or select from pictures you provide.

The students' task is to describe the picture in a very organized way. Provide students with a structure to use as they describe their pictures. A structure will help them organize their thoughts when they are not sure what to say about an object. Students who become efficient at verbally describing objects frequently generalize that skill into their written expression.

Here is an example hierarchy:
1. Name the object.
2. Tell the category the object belongs in.
3. Tell the function or uses of the category.
4. Discuss the attributes of the object.
5. Compare the object to something similar.

A visual structure consisting of a visual organizer with boxes (a frame), such as the one below, is one way to have students describe an object.

Name	Category	Function of Category	Attributes	Comparison
racing car	vehicle	transportation	convertible, low to the ground, very fast, no back seat, four wheels	A racing car is faster than a sports car but not as fast as an airplane.

Summary description: This is a racing car. It is a vehicle used for transportation. It is a convertible that is low to the ground with no back seat. It has four wheels and a steering wheel. It is very fast and the driver needs to wear a helmet and seat belts. A racing car is faster than a sports car but not as fast as an airplane.

➤ *The Story: Listening*

In this step, you will read the story about cars and Henry Ford — "The End of Cheap Oil: Wheel Life Begins." In the story below, some words appear in boldface. These words are key to understanding the story. As you read, use pictures, basic graphics, or gestures to illustrate the meanings of the key words, possibly to integrate with the Word Up activity (see page 82).

The End of Cheap Oil: Wheel Life Begins

We see cars everywhere we go. Can you imagine a world without any cars? Cars have been around for only about 100 years.

New York around 1910 had its share of the **wealthy**, especially in Manhattan. This city also had **paved** roads, something other places did not have. Around 1913, there were hardly any cars on our **city streets**. Cars were very **expensive**. Most families could not **afford** to buy one. Therefore, cars were a rich man's toy but they were some in Manhattan.

It took a long time to make a car back then. There were many parts and it took many hours to put the car together. That's why they were so expensive.

A man named **Henry Ford** thought that cars needed to be faster to make. In 1913, he developed a new idea for car factories called the **assembly line**. This made mass **production** of cars possible.

In an assembly line, many workers stood along the table. Each person only needed to put one part on the car. Then the car moved down the **line** and the next worker put on the next part. Each person had to learn how to do only one thing. Henry Ford had many people working on the assembly line so that they could make cars much faster. All the cars were similar. They had the same parts and the same colors.

The assembly line made the cars much less expensive and many more people could buy a car. Henry Ford gave people a new way to travel. By 1920, there were 9.2 million vehicles in the United States. Half of those were **Ford Model T's**. As **supply** of the cars grew, the prices decreased. Our streets became more crowded.

➤ *The Story: Retelling*

Students need a model in order to retell stories efficiently. As you model how to retell a story, arrange the key word pictures/graphics developed earlier in the activity in sequence and use them as cues for the events. Using the specific keywords in your retelling will increase the likelihood that students will use those same words when they retell the story.

Next, have students practice using the pictures as cues while they retelling the sequence of events in the story. You might have individuals take turns retelling to the class or have students work in small groups. Simplify the task by selecting fewer keywords or providing cue phrases for each step in the sequence.

➤ *The 5 W's*

The story on the previous page is a narrative, a format that answers five basic questions: Who?, What?, When?, Where?, and Why?. When students can answer those five questions about the text they have read, they obtain a valuable tool for understanding narratives.

Set up the activity by defining a narrative and explaining its structure. Then tell students they will be answering the five important questions related to the structure.

1. Have each student cut five squares out of different-colored paper and write one of these question words on each square: Who?, What?, When?, Where?, and Why?

2. Have students line up the five squares vertically along the left side of their workspace, in the order listed in Step 1.

3. Tell the students, "While you're listening to the story, these are the five questions you need to keep in your head. Afterwards, you will think about each question and answer it."

4. Reread the Henry Ford story to your students and then ask questions similar to those listed at the bottom of this page.

As students answer the first question, have them physically move the square to the opposite side of their work area. This movement creates physical involvement as well as a reminder for each component: it is a concrete encouragement to think systematically about the components within the passage. Students proceed similarly with each question.

A major advantage of using the cards is to encourage students to read the whole passage before answering the questions. This approach prevents merely reading the questions and searching for answers; it encourages students to think about possibilities related to their choices.

Initially, use modeling, direct teaching, and scaffolding to help the students learn to answer the 5 W's. As students progress, have them work in small groups or pairs. The eventual goal is for them to perform independently. Here are some tips for presenting the questions:

- *Who?*
  - Name the characters.
  - Identify the main characters.
    - ✔ Look for repeating words and the title for cues.

- *What?*
  - Identify the most important thing that happened in the passage.
    - ✔ Review the events in the story and ask students, "What was most important?"
  - Narrative stories sometimes have two important events:
    - ✔ One is the initiating event: it has to be the here or there is not a story.
    - ✔ The other is the event that causes the character to act or decide something. The character needs to change and something happens that allows the story to end the way it does. This is the most important event.

- *When?*
  - Identify when the action took place.
  - Identify the day or approximate time.

- *Where?*
  - Identify the location or place where the important action occurred.

- *Why?*
  - Identify why the most important event took place.
  - Note: Students often have the most difficulty with this question.

A recommendation:
You will probably need to model the 5 W's with several different stories with younger students, second-language learners, or students with language processing issues before having them work in pairs.

Further exploration for older students:
To encourage more use of higher order thinking skills, encourage students to explore the meaning of the title for the story. You might have them complete a 5 W's frame like the one on page A-21 of the Appendix on the CD.

➤ The Story: Visualizing Components

In this step, students visualize each of the 5 W's.

Working in a whole group
After the group decides upon an answer to a given Wh- question, encourage students to create a picture in their mind of that response. Then have each student draw a picture to represent the response.

Working in pairs
Have students brainstorm answers to a given question. Then have students each take a moment and visualize their own mental image to represent that answer. Next, have each student draw a picture of the mental image. When completed, each pair compares and discusses their individual pictures. Emphasize that there are no right or wrong answers for visualizations.

➤ The Story: Summarizing

It is often difficult for students to learn to summarize a story succinctly. Use the 5 W's cards as a concrete tool to teach the skill. To begin, the students rearrange the cards into three sections, in this order:

    1. Who?

    2. When? Where?

    3. What? Why?

Explain to your students that they can use the cards as a framework for developing a succinct summary in three sentence groups. Model how to develop a summary through questioning:

- The story is about **Who**?   *Henry Ford*
- The story takes place **When** and **Where**?   *Early 1900s, in New York*
- **What** happens   and **Why**?   *Henry Ford developed the assembly line so it was easier and faster to make cars. More people could afford to own cars and the streets became more crowded.*

Example Summary:
Henry Ford was an inventor. Around 1910, New York had many wealthy people and even a few cars. Ford developed the assembly line so workers could make cars faster and then more people could afford to own them. The streets became more crowded.

Text Talk

Text Talk is a vocabulary technique that incorporates several steps (Beck, McKeown, & Kucan, 2003). It provides a valuable bridge linking a target word used within a specific context to examples of that same word in a variety of different contexts. Students respond verbally, and the quick-paced activity can be done in two to three minutes. The components are as follows:

- Conceptualizing a word from the story
- Repeating the word
- Defining the word
- Using the word in other contexts
- Stimulating students' examples
- Saying the word repeatedly

The following example of Text Talk introduces the word *absurd* from the story *Burnt Toast on Davenport Street* (Egan, 1997).

Sample Dialog	Component
In the story we are going to read, a fly tells Arthur he could have three wishes if Arthur didn't kill him. Arthur said he thought that was *absurd*. That means Arthur thought it was silly to believe a fly could grant wishes.	*Conceptualizing a word from the story*
When something is absurd, it is ridiculous and hard to believe.	*Defining the word*
If I told you that your teacher was going to stand on her head to teach you, that would be absurd. If someone told you that dogs could fly, that would be absurd.	*Using the word in other contexts.*
I'll say something, and if you think it is absurd, say, "That's absurd!" If you think it is not absurd, say, "That makes sense." • I have a singing cow for a pet. *absurd* • I saw a tall building that was made of green cheese. *absurd* • Last night I watched a movie on TV. *makes sense* • This morning I saw some birds flying around the sky. *makes sense*	*Using the word in other contexts.*
Excellent job! If I said, "Let's fly to the moon this afternoon," that would be absurd. Who can think of another absurd idea?	*Stimulating students' examples*
When a student answers, ask another student if he agrees with the answer. If so, the student says, "That's absurd!"	*Saying the word repeatedly*

Function Words

You might use the Schoolhouse Rock song "Conjunction Junction (What's Your Function?)" to "prime" or introduce the concept of function words. Discuss how each word has a function and when we can recognize the function of words, we can understand more about what we are hearing or reading.

  The Source for Reading Comprehension Strategies

Nonsense Sentences

Explain to your students that you are going to read them a sentence composed of mostly nonsense words. Read a sentence like the one below and then ask your students questions about it:

Before the nisty dipple rattled, Pesby pobbed dillfully around the josk to glink the gorder.

Ask your students to complete questions like the ones below, with each followed by a question such as, "How did you know?" Encourage students to explain their answers. It is important that you teach the function of words rather than the labels (for example, the student should say, "It is a name," rather than "noun"). Requiring explanations is critical because students learn best by having experience with a concept prior to developing a label for it. This type of activity provides experience in identifying the function of words within a sentence.

Question	Response	Follow-up
Who is the story about?	Pesby	*How do you know?* "The word has a capital letter," *or* "It's before a word that ends in *-ed*" suggesting someone did it.
What did Pesby do?	He pobbed *or* He pobbed dillfully around the josk.	*What led you to that idea?* "The word is after Pesby, and it ends in -ed, so it must be an action."
When did Pesby pobb?	Before the nisty dipple rattled.	*What cues led you to that?* "The word *before* suggests a time."
Where did Pesby pobb?	around the josk	*How did you find out?* "The word *around* suggests a location."
Why did Pesby pobb?	to glink the gorder	*Why do you think that?* "The word *to* suggests a phrase that explains something."

The next step is to help students elaborate upon the activity. Have them substitute the nonsense words with real words that conceptually fit within the sentence. This critical skill is a component within many high stakes examinations, such as the California High School Exit Exam.

Here are some examples of elaboration questions:
- What word might you use instead of *dillfully* in "he pobbed dillfully"? *carefully, slowly, quickly, skillfully*
  - Why did you choose that word?
- What word might you use instead of *glink* in "to glink the gorder"? *fix, paint, rearrange, lift*
  - Why did you choose that word?

As your students become more skilled, you might expand this activity to short paragraphs. You could have students work in groups to create their own nonsense stories. They can then ask questions like the ones above of other groups.

Function Words: Real Word Sentences

Function Words Strategies

A single sentence can stimulate a great deal of conversation and thinking about comprehension. Working with one sentence also provides an excellent preview or prereading activity for an upcoming story that students will read.

Here is an example sentence based on the legend, "The Sleeping Bear Dunes"*:

> The Bears leaped wildly into the big lake to get away from the flames as they burned through the many tall pine trees.

Here are some questions to ask about the sentence:

Who is the story about?	the bears
How do you know the story is about bears?	It says in the beginning that they leaped.
What is the Bears' problem?	There is a big fire burning.
How do you know there's a fire?	The bears ran to get away from the flames.
What is the setting of the story?	a forest
How do you know the story takes place in the forest? (does not directly say "forest")	There were many tall pine trees.
How do you think the Bears are feeling right now?	They are probably scared.
Why do you think the Bears are probably scared?	They leaped wildly, and the story says they needed to get away from the flames, which would be scary.

Combination Activity

Function Words Strategies

Research informs us that a combination of strategies is more effective than any single strategy in isolation. The reasoning makes sense: using a combination of strategies provides more opportunity for students to increase the depth, as well as breadth, of their vocabulary knowledge.

The following example will incorporate several strategies as the students listen to an Indian legend, "The Sleeping Bear Dunes*."

The activity incorporates a variety of strategies, including previewing, visualizing, related movements, "owning," and using derivatives.

Follow these steps to proceed with the activity:
1. Preview the meaning of the underlined words in the story on the next page using the Show-Me and Word Imagery Strategies (as described on pages 42-43).
   - Have students visualize the meaning of each of the underlined words.

---

* The Sleeping Bear Dunes are on the northwestern shore of Michigan's Lower Peninsula. Some sources say this is an Ojibway Indian Legend and others refer to it as a Porquoi Legend.

2. Divide the class into three groups. Each group will be responsible for one of the underlined words (*slumber, brilliant, might*). Tell each group, "Your word is _____. When you hear that word you will do the action for it (demonstrate an action for each word)."

  • Have each group practice its movement in response to the cue word several times.

3. Read the legend, "The Sleeping Bear Dunes" (printed below) to the class.

  • Every time you say a target word or one of its derivatives (slumbering, slumber), the group responsible for that word performs the related action.

The Sleeping Bear Dunes

Long ago, in the land that is today Wisconsin, Mother Bear and her two cubs were <u>slumbering</u> peacefully. Suddenly, a <u>brilliant</u> light appeared and woke up Mother Bear from her slumber. The brilliant light came closer. With a start, she realized that it was a raging forest fire. She awoke her cubs quickly. They ran into Lake Michigan. The cubs swam and swam with all their <u>might</u>. However, the distance and the water proved too much for them. They fell farther and farther behind and ultimately slipped beneath the waves. When Mother Bear reached the Michigan shore, she climbed to the top of a bluff and peered back across the water, searching vainly for her cubs. All she saw was the brilliant light.

The Great Spirit Manitou saw her and took pity on her plight. He raised North and South Manitou Islands to mark the place where her cubs vanished and he then created a solitary dune to represent the dedication of the faithful mother bear who tried with all her might to save her cubs.

Visual Cue Activities

The visual cue activities are a group of strategies used with a text before beginning to read. They serve to prepare students to understand the concepts and organization of the context more thoroughly. Some of these strategies rely on graphic organizers and others upon the use of signal words. The Detective Activities encourage students to actively seek specific visual cues.

A picture is worth *more* than 1000 words.

Value of Graphic Organizers

Graphic organizers are a powerful tool for enhancing reading comprehension. Students who use visuals in learning situations discover something fascinating: they strengthen their initial learning by engaging their visual system. This is because visuals stimulate neural pathways: a huge number of associations are launched into their consciousness. As a result, these connections provide a rich context for the learning.

Our brain communicates to itself through associative images. Symbolic language and metaphoric associations characterize this communication. "Most of our normal conceptual system is metaphorically structured; that is, most concepts are partially understood in terms of other concepts" (Lakoff & Johnson, 1980). When we use visual organizers with our students, we stimulate associations and metaphors that help solidify concepts in our brains.

Visual Organizers: Venn Diagrams *Visual Cue Strategies*

The Venn diagram is one type of visual organizer, as previously described in Chapter 3 (page 54) and on page A-37 of the Appendix on the CD. A Venn diagram helps students identify attributes of concepts for the purpose of comparison and contrast. Here are the steps for creating a Venn diagram:

1. Have students look through the passage or chapter and identify the key concepts. Here are some examples:
   - *Science*: mammals and reptiles
   - *Social Science*: presidents and dictators

2. Have students create a Venn diagram format to compare and contrast the key concepts.

3. As students read the text, encourage them to search for and record characteristics related to each concept in the diagram. Have them record characteristics that apply only to one concept in one circle and characteristics that apply to the other concept in the second circle. Characteristics that apply to both concepts are recorded in the center circle.

4. After students complete the passage and their diagram, encourage substantial discussion about the similar and different features of individual students' Venn diagrams.

Elaborate upon the activity by incorporating other components previously discussed. The following illustrates example pictures, key words, and related gestures to compare and contrast *democracy* and *autocracy*. When doing the gesture, exaggerate the word's pronunciation to emphasize the association.

- Democracy
  - *Key word: Crazy* — The end of the word *demo<u>cracy</u>* sounds almost like *crazy.*
  - *Picture:* a group of people (stick figures) with smiles
  - *Gesture:* say "de–mok–kracy" and on the last syllable make a circle with one finger and point toward your head and smile to indicate "crazy"

- Autocracy
  - *Key word: Auto* — That's the prefix and it means "self" or "oneself."
  - *Picture:* a group of people (stick figures) with sad faces and one larger person separate from the group
  - *Gesture:* Say "auto–cracy." While saying "auto" point to yourself, and then fold your arms in an authoritarian stance. Use emphasis and rhythm while saying the word.

Visual Organizers: Feature Analysis and Attribute Maps *Visual Cue Strategies*

Feature Analysis and Attribute Maps were also discussed in Chapter 3 on page 53. Have students prepare their organizers prior to beginning to read. As they read, have them complete the various components within the organizer. After reading, encourage students to discuss their results. Many of these visual organizers are especially useful with expository text in content areas.

Initially, present your students with a specific organizer format and have them complete it as they skim or read the text. Eventually, encourage your students to decide for themselves which format would be most appropriate with particular types of chapters.

Signal Words

Signal words are specific words within the text that provide a signal to the student. Familiarity with common signal words provides students with specific context clues to use while they read. It is valuable for students to begin learning about signal words in early elementary grades; however, as they mature, they will need further learning to increase the complexity of their understanding of these important signals. Content textbooks, such as social science and science, often contain large numbers of signal words that contribute to or interfere with comprehension.

Signal words provide important clues for students as they read. One strategy to use when teaching a group of signal words is to use a stop sign — either a picture, such as the one on the left — or a three-dimensional stop sign. The visual cue reminds students to stop and think about what the word is signaling.

There are various categories of signal words. In teaching a category of signal words, whenever possible, have your students create a visual organizer or picture to reinforce the concept. Some categories of signal words with a few examples are listed below.

Category of signal	Examples	These words/cues:
Defining words	*refers to, means*	define or tell about something
Adding words	*furthermore, also*	indicate something is added
Sequencing words	*first, next*	indicate that events are in a sequence or order
Example words	*for example, including*	point to an example of a previous statement
Comparing words	*just like, similar to*	compare things similar or alike
Opposing words	*but, however*	contrast things that are different
Cause and effect words	*because, consequently*	indicate relationship and that one thing causes another

 Teach only one category of signal words at a time to avoid overloading your students. Provide multiple experiences for students to locate the signal words in short passages. Remember the guideline: "Too much, too fast — it won't last."

When students are familiar with a category of signal words and they can easily locate relevant signals within text, provide them with a section from the text they will be reading and have them locate the appropriate signal words. Follow the activity with either group discussion or Pair-Share, focusing on how the signals aid the students' understanding.

Detective Activities

A fun way for students to search for specific words, signals, or target words within a category is to have them become "detectives." Searching for specific words provides novelty as well as additional exposure to the words.

Give each student a paper magnifying glass similar to one associated with a being a detective. Cut a circle in the lens area of the magnifying glass. Have each student "be a detective" while she passes her magnifying glass over text and searches for specific words you have identified in the following activities.

➤ I Spy

This game helps students elaborate upon words and hold them in working memory for a longer period. Students play I Spy while looking for signal words from any of the categories in the chart on the previous page. You might say, "I spy *example* signal words." Students then use their "magnifying glasses" to search the text for words that signal an example.

A variation is to encourage students to search for a specific word in various contexts. This approach actively engages them with the word as they experience repeated exposures to it. Redundancy increases the probability that they will retain the word and its meaning in long-term memory. For example, if the target word is *bumpy*, you say, "I spy something bumpy."

Have students identify instances of *bumpy*, such as these:
- The bark on a tree outside the window is *bumpy*.
- An Almond Joy bar is *bumpy*.
- A sentence in a story: "they took a *bumpy* ride."
- A sentence in a story that refers to using sandpaper: "It felt very *bumpy*."

Extend the activity by having students do one or more of these variations:
- Draw a picture of one or more *bumpy* items.
- Create a visual organizer illustrating several meanings of the word *bumpy*.
- Search a story for words that are similar to *bumpy*.

You might also have student use I Spy to scan a passage before reading it to find or to "spy" derivations of a given word. For example, if the key word is *responsible,* have students identify words such as *responsibility, responsive, responsibilities.*

➤ Base or Root Word Search: Younger Students

In a variation of I Spy, students scan a passage to find a given base word. The concept of a base word is critical because if you know the base word, it is then easy to find its relatives. Younger students may particularly benefit by using a cue card to help them remember the steps. (Refer to the sample cue card for Base Words on page 66.) Follow these steps:

1. Present and explain the cue card to your students.
2. Identify a base word, such as *send*.
3. Discuss the meaning of the base word.

4. Present each student with a copy of a one-paragraph story that contains the base word and several related words (derivations).

5. Read the story to the students (an example is shown below).

Example Story

I like to <u>send</u> Christmas presents to my cousins. My favorite cousin, José, always <u>sends</u> me something very special. I don't remember what I <u>sent</u> to José last year, but this year I am <u>sending</u> him a special robot. It is fun to be the <u>sender</u> of gifts. I'll admit that I do like having them <u>sent</u> to me even better!

---

6. As you read the story, have students use their magnifying glasses to find each related word in the story. Have them underline each word they find.

7. Have students create a graphic of the base word and related words from the story, as shown on the right.

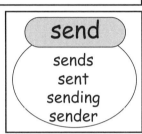

➤ Base or Root Word Search: Older Students

You might vary the I Spy activity for older students by having them search for words that containing a specific root, such as the Latin root *rupt*. Have students list the words they find and determine the meaning of each. Encourage them to use clues from the word's structure, as well as from the context of the passage, to determine word meanings. For example, they might notice *abrupt, abruption, bankrupt, bankruptcy, corrupt, corruptible, disrupt, destruction, disruptive, erupt, eruption, incorrupt, incorruptible, interrupt, interruption,* and *rupture*. Discuss how each of the words relates to the meaning of *rupt* as "to break or burst."

An option is to create a frame, such as the one below. The frame could have four columns: root, prefix + root, root + suffix, prefix + root + suffix. If desired, leave room in each section for students to draw a small picture that represents the meaning of some of the words.

root	prefix + root	root + suffix	prefix + root + suffix
rupt	corrupt	rupture	interruption

➤ Base or Root Word Search: All Ages

This variation of I Spy can be adapted to any age level. Have your students search a reading passage to find words that contain a particular prefix or suffix. You might say, "Find at least four words that end in _____," to present the criteria of the activity.

Vary the complexity of the target affix according to the skill level of your students. Here are three possible levels of difficulty:

1. words that have the suffix *-ing* (meaning "action or process")
   dancing   drying   skipping   swimming

2. words with the prefix *post-* (meaning "after, behind, or following")
   postclassical   postmark   postpone

3. words ending in *-tude* (meaning "condition, state, or quality of")

| altitude | aptitude | gratitude | magnitude | solitude |

Extend the activity by having the students determine meaning of the target prefix or suffix and then writing a sentence using one or more of the words. An option is for the sentence each writes to differ from the sentence in their book but maintain the same conceptual meaning.

Post-It® Notes Preview

Have students work in groups to research and analyze words within their text. As they read, have them identify difficult words with a Post-It® Note. Provide each group with a list of relevant, familiar word analysis strategies and encourage students to select an appropriate strategy for two of their words. Have students explain why they chose each strategy. Then have students analyze those two words. Afterwards, have students determine if the strategy they selected was efficient and have them explain why. If they determine it was not an efficient strategy, have them select another strategy and repeat the process. If they determine the strategy was efficient, have them select another two words to analyze. Provide them with a frame, such as the one below, for each word.

Strategy Selected	Why did you select this strategy?
Word	**Definition**
Was your strategy efficient?	Why? or Why not?
If not, repeat with a different strategy.	*If yes, continue with new words.*

As a variation, have all the students contribute their words to a total class list. Select a specific number of words and work with the whole group to complete the frame. This technique provides you with multiple opportunities to model appropriate self-talk.

The overall purpose of the Post-it® Notes activity is for students to think about whether or not they are comfortable with a specific word's meaning and use. Being aware of their comfort level with particular words encourages them to monitor themselves while working with text. Explain to your students that their job as they read is "to be a good word detective." Being a good word detective also allows them to simultaneously use strategies to increase their knowledge of given words prior to actually reading the passage. At the same time, they focus on metacognitive strategies of decision-making and judging the effectiveness of that decision.

Predicting

One of the major values in encouraging students to predict information is that it provides great opportunity for them to make connections between new and familiar information. As they activate existing background knowledge, they also build additional background and vocabulary knowledge. The importance of having students use prior knowledge in reading comprehension has been extensively documented (Hirsch, 2003; Nagy, 1985; Nagy et al., 1986).

Background knowledge is extremely important at the word and the text levels because the words represent concepts that students must understand in order to comprehend what they are reading. Evidence strongly indicates that we can maximize student learning by building and activating background knowledge because doing so helps students make important connections between new and familiar information. To exemplify the importance of background knowledge, consider these lines from the chorus of The traditional Australian folk song, "Click go the Shears":

"Click goes his shears, boy. Click, click, click.

Wide is his blow and his hands move quick."

One listener might hear those lines and visualize shears clipping the hedges along a row of bushes in someone's yard. Another may visualize a shearer in Australia shearing a sheep. Each of these listeners will interpret the chorus — and the song — very differently. Consequently, discussions and use of graphics are critical to bring a group of listeners to a common understanding. In this situation, the song is about the sheep shearers and the "blow" is the swipe made by the shears.

Besides activating background knowledge, another value of prediction activities is that prediction requires inferential thinking and necessitates active engagement by students. Such activities provide skills that form the foundation for inferential reading comprehension.

Readers often make predictions and draw conclusions about text without adequately using what they have read to support their thinking. They infer meaning without regard to clues in the text. Consequently, they miss important meaning in the material. It will be easier for students — even older students — to support their thinking with excerpts from text after they have experience trying the strategy with a simple picture book first.

Predicting Detectives

Predicting Strategies

When initially teaching prediction, use only small chunks of material. Stop and ask students to predict and explain the thinking behind a prediction. After reading additional text, have students seek to confirm the prediction. Have them explain why their predictions were accurate or why they weren't. Use a chart such as this one to help students organize their predictions.

Prediction	Thinking behind the prediction (Why I made this prediction)	Prediction Confirmed	Why the prediction was or wasn't accurate
The bears will sleep through the whole winter.	I know that bears hibernate, and the story says that winter is coming.	No	The bears went out to find food a few times during the winter.

Predicting with Pictures

Having students use a picture from the text or a book cover to predict vocabulary words likely to be in the upcoming text is a great way to present essential vocabulary and provide background knowledge at the same time that you preview and build excitement about an upcoming topic.

➤ Predicting with Pictures: Younger Students

In this example, students are about to read a section of a social studies text about the 1980 eruption of the Mount St. Helens volcano. Follow these steps to present the activity:

1. Show students a picture of Mount St. Helens after the eruption.
2. Create a two-column chart labeled "Predicting With Pictures Word Chart":
   • Label one column, "Words I predict I'll find."
   • Label the second column, "The reason for my prediction."
3. Ask your students questions, such as these:
   • What do you think the story will be about?
   • Which words do you think the author will use to tell the story?
4. After each response, write the word in the first column. Then ask the student to explain his reason for the prediction and write the reason in the second column.
5. When students run out of ideas, provide prompts to encourage them to think of additional words. Here are some example prompts:
   • What you think caused the volcano to explode?
   • What do you think happened when the volcano exploded?
   • What do you think the people did?
   • What do you think happened to the peoples' houses and gardens?
6. Provide the students with a printed version of the text.
7. Read the selection to the students. As you read, have your students follow along and raise their hands each time you read a word that is on the prediction chart.
8. Create a second two-column chart or add two more columns to the existing chart:
   • Label one column "More important words."
   • Label the second column "Why these words are important."
9. Ask students if there were any other important words in the story and record these words and reasons on the second chart.

Example words the students may think of in the above prediction include *mountain, rock, underground, melted rock, lava, landslide, eruption, explosion,* and *earthquake.* You might prompt students to think of additional important words, such as *destroy, destruction, underground, Earth's surface, shaking, ash, escape, wipe out, damage, devastate,* and *damage.*

➤ Predicting with Pictures: Older Students

Predicting with pictures is useful to help your students prepare to comprehend challenging texts. In the following example, the topic is Pearl Harbor:

1. Present a picture of the U.S.S. Arizona Memorial at Pearl Harbor.
2. Have students create a "Predicting with Pictures Word Chart" (as described in the previous activity)
3. Guide students to predict words and prompt them as necessary with key questions.

4. Have students write the words and reasons in the chart.

5. Read a section of the material to the students as they follow along in their books.

6. Tell students that they will be responsible for listening for words that were predicted.

7. After reading, go through the chart and discuss if each word was used, as in the example dialog below.

8. Make a check mark by each word in the chart that is used in the story.

Example words the students may predict include *attack, harbor, death, fleet, invade, war, explosion,* and *memorial*. A sample dialog:

Pearl Harbor

Americans remember December 7, 1941, as "a day that will live in infamy." It is the day the Japanese bombed Pearl Harbor. The attack caused heavy casualties and destroyed much of the Pacific Fleet. The attack sank or seriously damaged 18 warships. It also brought the United States into World War II.

Dialog

Teacher: We have the word *harbor* on our chart. It's used in the second sentence of the story, just like we predicted. We predicted it is a place with water for ships. The story says, "The Japanese bombed Pearl Harbor . . . and sank or damaged 18 warships." We predicted that. Check off the word *harbor*. Do you see any other words we predicted?

Student: We said *death*, and the story says *casualties*. Aren't they like the same thing?

Teacher: What do you think? (Encourage discussion.)

Teacher: Let's add the word *casualties* to our chart.

Continue the conversation, encouraging students to identify words in the text, discuss them, and then check them off or add them to the chart. Point out the relationship of any new words to the picture.

As a conclusion, have each student select a word from the chart that is new to him and that he likes. Allowing students to select a word they prefer creates some ownership and provides a critical cognitive anchor for students: they each have at least one word that they have chosen. Each student then draws a picture to represent the word's meaning and creates a key word and gesture to help remember the word.

Predicting with Title   *Predicting Strategies*

Activities for predicting based on the title of a text are very similar to activities for predicting based on a picture, except that the prediction is based on the title rather than a picture.

Here are some suggestions for possible questions to ask students about a title:

Younger Students
- What do you think this book will be about? Tell me (or write) one sentence that tells what you think this whole book will be about.

- Is this book fact (a true book about real things) or fiction (a made-up story?) How do you know?
- Look at the title and the picture on the cover. Write two or three sentences that tell what you think the book will be about and what will happen in it. Also, tell whether the book will be fact (a true story) or fiction (a made-up story).

Older Students
- What you think this article will tell you about _____ (topic)?
- Tell me (or list) three things you think you might learn by reading this article.
- Is this article fact or fiction? How do you know?

Here are some general strategies and questions to use in guided questioning/commenting about a passage's title. Use the sample dialogs as models:

- Think through your predictions about the story.
    - "The title of the book is _____, so I think it will be about _____."
    - "When I look at the picture on the cover, it makes me think of _____."

- Make direct links to prior knowledge.
    - "In the first paragraph, the main character _____. That makes me think of another story I read where _____."

- Pretend you don't understand something.
    - "I don't know what the author means when she or he says _____. Maybe the author is talking about _____."

- Show how to check predictions and comprehension.
    - "I was right about _____ but wrong about _____. I'd better read that again."

- Pause to summarize and make new predictions.
    - "Okay. What has happened so far is _____. I think what will happen next is _____."

Predicting in Early Grades

Select a storybook with an illustrated cover. Display the cover to your students and ask a variety of questions to encourage them to predict the story. If the story relates to other familiar stories, ask your students to predict how this story may differ from the others. You might ask closed questions (requiring a one-word or yes/no response), or open questions (encouraging expansion of what students see and how that relates to their response). Allow students to point to items in the picture, such as colors, objects, or characters. Here are three options for continuing the activity:

Option 1
- Discuss each picture in the book and have students make predictions as described above.
- Read the book aloud.
- Discuss the decisions and predictions the students made in their initial exploration of the title and pictures.

Option 2
- Record key elements of the students' predictions.
- Read the book aloud.
- Discuss the decisions and predictions and how they relate to the actual story.

Option 3
- Record students' predictions based on the title of the story on a large sheet of paper.
- Have students read the first few paragraphs (or first page) to determine the accuracy of their predictions.
- Return to the predictions and discuss the accuracy of each.
- Have students make predictions on the next section, considering the previous passage and any upcoming illustrations.
- After reading the next few paragraphs, return to the predictions and discuss the accuracy of each.
- Continue the procedure through the story.
- As you discuss and compare the predictions, cross out inaccurate ones and place a colored star by those that are accurate.

Predicting in Upper Elementary Grades   *Predicting Strategies*

Help students realize that they can use the title and other visual clues to infer important concepts and vocabulary, especially because stories at this level have few pictures. The following strategy emphasizes the importance of those components in understanding storylines, characters, context, mood, and general meaning.

This procedure is the same as that used for younger students, except that it is more important to use a visual organizer to organize the information. Students brainstorm predictions based on the title and/or other cues in the story, and then read the story. After reading, they review and discuss their list of predictions. While reviewing their predictions, have them visually indicate the relevance of each to the actual story (by circling, crossing off, or highlighting). Guide students to categorize their initial predictions based on their level of importance to selected key elements, such as story line, characters, context, mood, and general meaning.

As an alternative, you might assign a pair or small group of students to each of the key elements, such as "predictions relevant to the story line" or "to characters." Students take turns using Think-Aloud (see Chapter 7, page 130) to determine the relevancy level (none, slight, high), while others in the group record the steps used in determining the level.

A more advanced alternative is to present a list of literacy learning strategies you wish the students to focus on (predicting/guessing, using what I know, asking questions, etc.). Briefly explain each strategy and have students complete a chart by finding examples for each using the following tasks. Here are some example tasks, along with related stories:

- *Song:* "You're in Trouble" (by Bill Harley, www.billharley.com)
  Task: "Look at the title. What do you think the song will be about? Read the first few lines. Now expand your prediction."

- *Story: Charlotte's Web* by E.B. White
  Task: "Imagine that you have to write a song or a poem about Wilbur, Charlotte's friend. What steps would you take to prepare for this assignment?"

- *Story: The Wind in the Willows* by Kenneth Grahame
  Task: "Look at the title. Are there any words you don't understand? How can you guess what they mean? What do you think will happen in the story?"

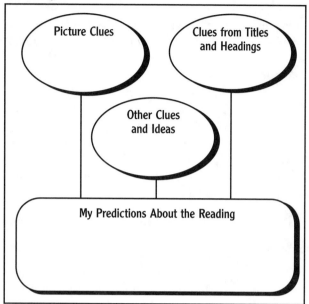

Predicting Story Using Organizer
Predicting Strategies

One predicting strategy is to present students with a basic organizer like the one on the left and on page A-20 of the Appendix on the CD. Another option is to create a chart with five columns based on the 5 W's. (Place one word in each column — Who?, What?, When?, Where?, and Why?) Tell your students they are going to read a new story and tell them the title. You might also briefly discuss the cover illustration. Then provide students a list of seven to ten key words and phrases from the story, as in the example below. Make sure your students are able to read the words and that they know their approximate meanings. There is no need to discuss the words in depth at this point.

Here are some example words/phrases you might supply your students before reading the story, "Mrs. Redwing's Speckled Egg" in *Old Mother West Wind* (Burgess, 2003):

Old Mother West Wind	*golden light*	*Merry Little Breezes*
Mrs. Redwing	*bulrushes*	*great distress*
nest	*singing for joy*	*whisked hat off*

Guide students to use their thinking and prediction skills to decide where the words might fit into the story. Use the 5 W's organizer to help them focus their thinking. Have them place each word in any of the five columns, but do not allow them to repeat a word in more than one column.

After students enter each word into a column, have them use the words to create a short story that predicts what will happen in the story they will read. Have students share their prediction stories with the class.

After reading the story, discuss the predictions again to determine which ones accurately foretold what would happen in the story. Ensure students that there are no right or wrong predictions — predictions are guesses based on partial facts. When students have all the facts (the actual story), they then have more information.

Remind your students that good readers use the words and pictures in a story, along with things from their own lives, to think about what is probably true in story. Using those pieces of information is called making inferences, and explain to students that inferences help us understand the story better.

Predicting and Sorting
Predicting Strategies

This activity can be used with a complete chapter in a content area text. The students predict words, just as they did in the Predicting With Pictures activity on page 100. Students will create a chart with a labeled column for each section title or major heading from the chapter. Follow these steps:

1. Have students read the title of the chapter and make an extensive list of words they predict will be in the passage.

2. Have students record major headings in the chapter in a separate column on the chart:

3. Have students sort the predicted words into the appropriate columns on the chart.

104

4. Have students read one section of the chapter and check off words on their chart as they hear or read them in the chapter section. They may check off additional words, if appropriate.
   • Initially, read the section to students as they follow along.

5. Students repeat step 4 for each column on the chart.

Predict-O-Gram

The Predict-O-Gram prepares students for reading a content chapter and is a beneficial activity for upper elementary, middle school, and high school students. Prepare students by briefly (in about one sentence) summarizing the content of the chapter they will be reading.

Present your students with two items: a Predict-O-Gram (an example is shown on the next page) and a list of relevant phrases from the text. Have students write a section title or major heading from the chapter in each column of the Predict-O-Gram and follow these steps:

1. Use their best guess to place each phrase from the list in the appropriate category on the Predict-O-Gram.

2. Scan the text and locate the passage that contains the phrase to confirm or correct each prediction.
   • Indicate correct predictions with a check mark. If they did not predict correctly, they use an arrow to show the correct category.
   • Write the the page and paragraph number of where each phrase appeared.

3. Discuss the items in each category as a group.

Example 1: Daily Life in Feudal Europe
Present students with a two-column chart labeled "Reading for Information — Look for Keys". Place a picture of a key in each column: label one "Nobles" and the other "Peasants." Provide a list of phrases and ideas, such as those listed below. Have the students predict and place each item in one of the columns. Then, as they read, have them look for the phrases and ideas and verify the correct placement of each.
   • Slept behind a curtain in main dining hall
   • Borrowed oxen for farming
   • Took over the manor when their husbands were gone
   • Tilled the land
   • Little power by women in the castle
   • Women managed the making of clothes and medical care
   • Women produced food and clothing for their household

Example 2: Evidence Supporting Ancient Life
Present your students with a Predict-O-Gram, such as the one on the next page, and the following list of phrases:
   • Evidence of activities of ancient animals
   • Turning into stone
   • Preserves delicate parts of leaves
   • Shell buried in sediment
   • Copy of the shape of the organism
   • Gases escape from the organisms

Petrified Fossils	Molds and Casts	Carbon Films	Trace Fossils
Page/Paragraph #:	Page/Paragraph #:	Page/Paragraph #:	Page/Paragraph #:
Page/Paragraph #:	Page/Paragraph #:	Page/Paragraph #:	Page/Paragraph #:

When creating a Predict-O-Gram, leave enough room for students to draw arrows to change categories. Also, provide space for them to write the page and paragraph numbers that confirm their predictions.

It is valuable to encourage your students to predict patterns and other information prior to actually reading the text because then students begin to think about the content prior to actually beginning to read. Predicting is a component of inferential analysis and encourages your students to analyze cues and make determinations based on these cues.

Previewing for Text Structure

Reading is much more than moving one's eyes over the line of print. Previewing a text prior to beginning to read is beneficial to help students set the stage for what will come. Previewing strategies are valuable because they enhance active reading. When students survey the material first, they develop a general understanding and expectation of the concepts and events.

The following prereading strategies provide mnemonics that encourage students to use metacognitive awareness in analyzing the content and/or structure of the material. To use a strategy, students need to understand its function so that they know when it may be useful. Here are the general steps for presenting a strategy:
1. Present and explain the first step in the strategy.
2. Practice it in various situations so that you can automatically use it.
3. Repeat steps 1 and 2 with each step in the strategy.
4. Explain to students how the mnemonic provides a cue for remembering the steps for the strategy.

Generally, students use text structure to aid their comprehension. Even young children do so with narrative text. As students get older, they typically improve their ability to use text structure. Some students, especially those with learning disabilities, are slower to understand and use text structure. Because they may not automatically pick out important story information, make inferences, and identify story themes, using appropriate previewing strategies encourages them to focus on such components, which will significantly enhance reading comprehension.

Page A-15 of the Appendix on the CD presents a chart of some previewing strategies, indicating the appropriateness of each for narrative or expository text.

The Source for Reading Comprehension Strategies

KWL: Know, Want to Know, and Learn
Previewing Strategies

This strategy works well with many types of text and is an excellent way to encourage students to activate their background knowledge. You may use KWL as a large-group brainstorming activity or students can create KWL charts in small groups or individually. Initiate the activity by creating a KWL chart, as shown on the right, with your students. The KWL chart provides students with a frame to organize their ideas. (A larger KWL chart plus an expanded version are on pages A-15-18 of the Appendix on the CD.)

K	W	L
What I **K**now	What I **W**ant to Know	What I have Learned

The KWL strategy involves three basic steps, corresponding to the three columns on the KWL organizer.

1. **K** for *Know* — What I already know
2. **W** for *Want* — What I want to know
3. **L** for *Learned* — What I have learned (from my reading)

Follow the activity with a whole group discussion, and emphasize that reading content material serves several purposes. Many students realize that content reading involves finding out what the author thinks is important about the topic. Content reading should also engage your students and encourage them to identify questions they want to know and search for answers.

Basic Organizer
Previewing Strategies

Some students, especially younger ones, benefit from using a basic frame that reminds them about the clues they need to find while reviewing the passage. A Prereading Organizer can be found on page A-20 of the Appendix on the CD and provides spaces for students to record the clues they find while previewing, as well as a spot for them to write their predictions.

TELLS and TP
Previewing Strategies

The mnemonics TELLS and TP provide organized ways for students to preview the structure of either fiction or nonfiction stories. There are five steps in the TELLS mnemonic (**T**itle, **E**xamine, **L**ook, **L**ook up, and **S**etting) and two basic steps in TP (**T**extbook structure and **P**aragraph structure). Both of these mnemonics are described in more detail on page A-15 of the Appendix on the CD.

Select the previewing strategy that best meets the needs of your students' skill level and age, the type of material presented, and your goals for the activity. TELLS works well with both narrative or expository text and TP works best with expository materials. The important aspect of using these strategies is that your students will use a systematic procedure for going through text prior to beginning to read.

Frames with 5 W's

Previewing Strategies

In the 5 W's Listening activity earlier in this chapter, students had 5 cards that each contained a "W" word: Who?, What?, When?, Where?, and Why? Use a similar procedure as explained in that activity to preview the text by having students create a frame for the information. You can find an example format on page A-21 of the Appendix on the CD.

Your students will need some moveable markers such as paper squares, chips, or Post-It® flags. Post-It® flags work best — especially with text of more than one page — because they stick to the paper and do not fall off the desk. Students will need five different colors and several of each. Assign one color to each of the "W" words and have students color in the related word on the visual organizer, or frame. You might come up with these combinations:
- Who? — red
- What? — yellow
- When? — blue
- Where? — green
- Why? — purple

Instruct your students to keep the 5 W's in mind as they read. When they encounter a phrase that might answer one of the "W" questions, have them place the corresponding color marker (Post It®) by that phrase. For example, if they read a character's name, they put a red marker there to indicate "Who?"

After reading, have students review their markers and use the related information to fill in their frame with the appropriate answers. They might find they have more markers than are necessary to answer each question. For example, students might have six or seven red markers indicating characters. They need to decide which is the "main" character to answer the "Who?" question.

Frames for Expository Text

Previewing Strategies

Authors write expository text to inform, explain, describe, present information, sequence events, compare/contrast, problem solve, or persuade. Expository text is subject-oriented and contains facts and information with little dialog. Because different structures exist for expository text, the format of the frame may vary, depending on the structure of the text. Provide students with a frame to organize their approach as they decide which format to use. Some suggestions are on pages A-12–13 of the Appendix on the CD. Page A-23 of the Appendix presents an example format of a frame to use with expository text that has a describing or defining structure.

Visualization

Both thinking and language comprehension have a foundation in imagery. This similarity is because the brain "sees" in order to store and process information. Visualization is directly related to language comprehension, language expression, and critical thinking because imagery is a primary sensory connection in the brain (Bell, 1991, p. 8). The following sample suggestions illustrate questions to encourage visualization with younger and older students. It is important to emphasize that there is no right or wrong answer when a student is describing an image in his own head. The important aspect is to be able to explain the cues that led to that image.

> The strategy of visualization helps to record and store information in your brain as pictures!

Explain visualization to your students by adapting the following example to meet their maturity level:

"When authors write, they use words to describe information. You can change the information from words into a picture. A picture is easier for your brain to understand and remember. You can see the picture in your mind, and/or draw the picture on paper. When using visualization strategies, you might wish to draw and label your picture on paper. You can also use the picture as notes to help you remember the information later."

There are four basic steps for students to follow when visualizing:
1. Read or listen to the text.
2. Picture the information in your brain.
3. Plan how to draw it on paper.
4. Draw and label your picture on paper.

Present students with a basic sentence and ask them to imagine an elaborate image of the components and actions in the sentence. Stimulate their images with questions such as those below. Follow each question with "Why did you choose that?" or "How do you know?"

Example for younger student
1. The cute puppy bounded across the yard.

   Questions
   - What does the image of your puppy look like?
   - What color is your puppy?
   - Does your puppy have big legs or little legs?
   - What are his ears like?
   - What does the yard look like?
   - Is it daytime or nighttime?
   - Is it winter or summer?

Examples for older students
1. The panda eats shoots and leaves.

   Questions:
   - What picture does this sentence create in your mind?
   - How big is the panda? What color is it?
   - What is the panda doing?
   - Where is the panda?
   - Are there other animals in your image?
   - Is it daytime or nighttime?
   - Is it winter or summer?

2. The panda eats, shoots, and leaves.
   - Ask similar questions as the above example, but add, "What is the difference between sentence 1 and sentence 2?"

Imagery with Poems
Visualization Strategies

This activity can be adapted for students at varying age levels. The value in using poetry to encourage visualization comes from poetry's frequent use of descriptive and interesting words. Also, "The purpose of using poetry as a means to vocabulary development is to teach children to savor perfectly chosen words" (Lubliner, 2005, p. 108). Having students interpret and write poetry can be a valuable stepping stone to more descriptive writing.

Introduce the poem with a brief overview. Then proceed with the steps below. If your students are struggling to "paint a picture in their mind" refer to the suggestions on pages 43-44 in Chapter 3.

1. Say, "Students, please close your eyes while I read this poem. Let the author paint a picture on the chalkboard in your mind."

2. Read the poem aloud.

3. Provide students with a written copy of the poem.

4. Discuss any words that may be unfamiliar.

5. Reread the poem again and encourage students to create visual images.

6. Ask questions to stimulate more elaborate visualizing such as, "Can you see the _____ in your mind?" or "What color is the _____ in your image?"

7. Encourage students to discuss their various images, relating them directly to the words in the poem that stimulated a particular image.

8. Encourage students to elaborate upon their images by using color and movement.

Select a poem that matches your students' age and interest levels. Here are some poems you might use:

- "People" by Lois Lenski
  "Tall people, short people; Thin people, fat . . ." (Lenski, 1927)

- "In Indianapolis" by Jack Prelutsky
  "In Indianapolis, what did we see? An elephant perched on a sycamore tree . . ." (Prelutsky, 2002, p. 20)

- "September" by Helen Hunt Jackson
  "The goldenrod is yellow; The corn is turning brown . . ." (Jackson, 1959)

Pamela Nelson (2005) suggests using the metaphor of a suitcase to introduce poetry to students. She places the poem and a related object in a "suitcase." Here are some ideas:

- *a suitcase full of science:*
  - *Object:* a model stegosaurus
  - *Poem:* "Stegosaurus" by Jack Prelutsky (1988, p. 11)

  - *Object:* a paper or plastic snowflake
  - *Poems:* "First Snowfall" or "A Blank White Page" by Francis X. Alarcón (2001, p. 27)

- *a suitcase full of language arts:*
  - *Object:* a model ear
  - *Poem:* "I Hear, I Hear" by Pat Mora (1996, p. 17)

- *a suitcase full of social studies:*
  - *Object:* a Navajo weaving doll
  - *Poem:* "Storm Pattern" by Shonto Begay (1995, p. 37)

  - *Object:* a package of almond cookies
  - *Poem:* "Grandmother's Almond Cookies" by Janet Wong (1996, p. 27)

  - *Object:* a reproduction of a U.S. Civil War cap
  - *Poem:* "Civil War" by Carol Shields (2002, pp. 34-35)

Imagery with Figurative Language
Visualization Strategies

Students always benefit from exposure to and practice in manipulating figurative language. Figurative language refers to words or sentences that have multiple meanings. A large number of English words have more than one meaning, especially those derived from the Anglo-Saxon layer of language. The meaning of figurative language phrases depends upon both the individual word meanings and the structural combination of words (the word order and their grammatical role). Homographs and homonyms are forms of figurative language that cause substantial confusion for students and interfere with comprehension.

* *Homograph:* One of two or more words that have the same spelling but that sound different and differ in meaning, such as *polish* (to rub to make shiny or a substance used while doing so) and *Polish* (the nationality).

* *Homonym* (also called homophone): One of two or more words that have the same sound and often the same spelling but that differ in meaning, such as *die* (stop living), *die* (a device for cutting/stamping objects), and *dye* (color) (Henry, 2003, p. 287).

Use a selection from a humorous story or a story that contains figurative language to perform this imagery activity. One of many available examples is the Amelia Bedelia series. In the first book, *Amelia Bedelia* (Parish, 1963), Amelia has a new job as a house cleaner. Explain to your students that one of Amelia's instructions was to "dust the furniture." Then read the following passage and encourage your students to "let the author paint a picture on the chalkboard of their minds":

> "Dust the furniture?" said Amelia.
> "Did you ever hear tell of such a silly thing?"
> Amelia took one last look at the bathroom. She saw a big box with the words *Dusting Powder* on it.
> "Well, look at that. A special powder to dust with!" exclaimed Amelia. So Amelia Bedelia dusted the furniture with the dusting powder.
> "That should be dusty enough. My, how nice it smells."

Continue the activity by asking questions such as, "Can you see the _____ in your mind?" or "What color was the _____?" Expand your students' understanding of figurative language by discussing how concretely Amelia interprets "dusting the furniture." Guide students to discuss what meaning was presented and compare it to the concrete meaning of the phrase intended by the original request.

Imagery Using Structure Words
Visualization Strategies

Nanci Bell, in *Visualizing & Verbalizing for Language Comprehension and Thinking* (Bell, 1991), created a highly sequenced program designed to enhance visualization while strengthening the connection between visualizing and verbalizing. The program, called V & V, uses structure words printed on cue cards (examples are on the following page). Students visualize a picture and then describe the picture generated in their mind. As they verbalize their mental picture, they refer to the cards, using the specific structure words as reminders. The structure words help students more thoroughly describe physical, as well as emotional, aspects of the image or text. Using structure words to describe mental images encourages students to verbalize in a more structured and sequential manner. V & V expands the technique for use with text.

The initial set of structure words provides information that is more global. These words are listed in their importance to overall comprehension:

What?	Size	Color
Number	Shape	Where?

When students become proficient using the above words, present them with additional structure words to help them delineate finer distinctions. These words are listed in order of their impact on the clarity of the visualization:

Movement	Mood	Background
Perspective	When?	Sound

In providing feedback to the students regarding their verbalization, Bell recommends using phrases such as, "Your words make me picture . . . ." Feedback is critical because it enables students to better relate verbal messages with the images in their heads.

Metaphors and Clichés   *Visualization Strategies*

Some expressions, because of frequent usage, develop a meaning that goes beyond their concrete meaning. These expressions frequently cause confusion in text for many students, especially second language and learning disabled learners. Encouraging students to visualize the meaning of metaphors and clichés greatly enhances their understanding of these language forms and enables them to obtain deeper understanding of what they read. It also guides them away from only a concrete interpretation.

A metaphor is a figure of speech that connects two objects or ideas that are different from each other but have some similarity, often in a significant way. It is a way of explaining something abstract in terms of the concrete. Lederer states, "small wonder that we take our most common metaphors from things that surround us in our daily lives and that we find a rich vein of descriptive phrases in the most familiar of all things in our lives — our own bodies" (Lederer, 1990, p. 5). "Rule of thumb" and "tongue in cheek" are good examples of metaphors that rely on comparisons with parts of the body.

Another common category of metaphors uses clothing, as in "putting on your thinking cap" and "keep your shirt on." Lederer describes metaphors in relationship to categorical patterns. Other categories include household items ("dead as a doornail"), colors ("white elephant"), the earth ("cream of the crop"), the weather ("on cloud nine"), and animals ("pigheaded"). Metaphors add depth to descriptions and are often useful in helping students sort out attributes of concepts.

A cliché is a worn-out sentence or phrase that has become completely predictable (Lederer, 1990, p. 79). For example, if you hear the first half of a cliché, it is often automatic to think of the second half. Give these clichés a try:

1. Cut _____
2. Beck _____
3. A babe in the _____
4. A backhanded _____

5. Sleeps like a _____
6. Better late than _____
7. Between a rock and a _____
8. Can't see the forest _____

Answers:
1. and dried, 2. and call, 3. woods, 4. compliment, 5. baby, 6. never, 7. a hard place, 8. for the trees

Some clichés, especially when found in narrative text, use a simile format: "(adjective) as/like a (noun)." Here are some examples:

1. Happy as a _____
2. Bald as an _____
3. Busy as a _____
4. Snug as a _____
5. American as _____
6. Slow as _____
7. Blew up like a _____
8. Came out smelling like a _____

Answers:
1. clam, 2. eagle, 3. bee, 4. bug in a rug, 5. apple pie, 6. molasses, 7. balloon, 8. rose

Use metaphors and clichés with any of the visualization and drawing activities described previously to encourage students to compare the concrete and abstract meaning of the phrases.

Phrase Detective

Visualization Strategies

An excellent way to increase students' awareness of the meaning and function of figurative language phrases is any of the "Be A Detective" activities presented earlier in this chapter (pages 96-98). Have students search a section of text for phrases that make connections between an abstract and concrete meaning and fill in an organizer like the one below. Using a concrete frame encourages students to recall all of the components and provides a mechanism for them to use in making the important connections.

Location of Expression	Expression	Meaning in Context	Concrete Meaning
page 62, paragraph 3	"He was a real pig at dinner."	He ate more food than anyone else.	He wasn't human; he was a pig.

Have students select their favorite expression from the organizer and draw two pictures of its meaning — one picture for the meaning of the phrase in context and another for its concrete meaning.

Reflections

1. List three previewing activities you might use with your students prior to reading the text. Explain how each activity you would use relates to how your students learn. Use a frame to record your ideas that contains these three columns:
   a. previewing activity
   b. reason to use activity
   c. how activity relates to how my students learn

2. Select one of the Listening Activities and adapt it to a portion of your current curriculum. Expand upon the activity to help your students elaborate the concepts and deepen their understanding.

   _____

   _____

   _____

   _____

   _____

3. Create an activity to encourage students to become more aware of figurative language in their reading or the environment.

   _____

   _____

   _____

   _____

   _____

4. Develop a system that you will use consistently with the I Spy activities. Some options include establishing a frame, creating a visual organizer with specific components (i.e., word, word parts, relating picture, definition, sentence), and/or sequencing the steps in a specific way.

   _____

   _____

   _____

   _____

   _____

   _____

    The Source for Reading Comprehension Strategies

CHAPTER 6

TEXT STRUCTURE

Students have a better chance of comprehending and remembering what they have read when they understand how the material is structured. For example, the text might present a main idea and then details, or it might present a cause and its effects. Each text form has a corresponding basic structure that relates to varying purposes and to the types of questions students need to ask themselves as they read.

Most narrative or fiction materials follow similar organizational patterns. The structure of expository text, on the other hand, can vary substantially. Because of narrative text's consistency in form, it is best to use it to begin instruction of text structure. However, it is critical that students advance to a level where they also recognize common text structures found in expository texts as well.

Comparing Narrative and Expository Text

The chart below compares some of the characteristics of narrative and expository text. Keep these features in mind as you explain text structure to your students.

	Narrative Text	**Expository Text**
Purpose	Tells a story	Delivers information
How students are invited to the text	Through characters to which students can relate	Through explaining information but has no characters or situations that typically draw students into the situation
Pattern	Has a relatively predictable storyline; often begins with setting, character, or event	Uses a variety of text patterns; may change patterns within a selection; options include sequencing, compare/contrast, question/answer, cause/effect, and problem/solution
Relationship to other material	Story stands alone as a complete text	Text often relies on other resources to support understanding of the selection
Illustrations	Uses illustrations to support understanding of the story	Uses graphic aids, illustrations, or graphs to deliver information
Vocabulary usage	Includes common usage vocabulary; much is often familiar; generally includes few new words	Includes technical vocabulary related to the content; some words have a common usage; meaning as well as technical meaning, which creates confusion; often includes unfamiliar words
Context	Provides more context to support understanding of new vocabulary words	Typically provides one exposure to new vocabulary word, with varying degrees of support

Chapter 6

Evidence Base

The strategies in this chapter listed below incorporate components identified by the NRP as having a solid evidence base and match the mandates of NCLB and Reading First. Studies supporting these techniques are referenced in Appendix A, Chapter 3 of *Vocabulary Instruction Methods: A Summary Of Vocabulary Instruction Methods* (National Reading Panel, 1999, pp. 3-33 to 3-35).

- Cooperative learning
- Multiple strategies
- Text structure
- Graphic organizers
- Prior knowledge

Narrative Text

Students generally understand narrative text better than expository forms: the content is often familiar and the structure is consistent. When students are familiar with these strategies, they will increase the efficiency of their comprehension:

- seeing relationships in stories
- answering comprehension questions
- retelling what they have read

Narrative text is based on life experiences and is person oriented. It often uses dialog and familiar language. Here are three of the most common purposes of narrative text:

- to entertain
- to tell a story
- to provide an aesthetic literary experience

There are a variety of genres or narrative text types:

- fantasy
- historical fiction
- science fiction
- folktales (tables, legends, myths, tall tales, realistic tales)
- contemporary fiction
- mysteries
- realistic fiction
- essays

Narrative stories follow a particular story grammar, or structure, and when students understand that structure, they improve both their comprehension skills and retelling abilities. They also acquire an organizational framework for future reading. Torgesen states, "using story grammar elements should be considered best practice for improving comprehension of students with learning disabilities. Teacher modeling and feedback are important components" (Torgesen, 2001).

Components of Narrative Text
Narrative Text

Most narratives contain a beginning, middle, and ending. Students need to understand these concepts before progressing further with the components of story grammar. These components vary slightly for a narrative story or a narrative essay.

➤ Narrative Stories

- *Beginning*
  This part of the story contains the setting, characters, and characters' problem(s).

- *Middle*
  The *plot* makes up the middle of the narrative. The plot includes a series of events designed to hold a reader's attention and build excitement. It consists of three main parts:

  1. *Initiating event*
     - This event starts the main character on his path to solve a problem.
  2. *Series of events*
     - During these events, the character attempts to solve the problem and excitement builds as the events progress.
     - Roadblocks or setbacks for the character may appear as he attempts to solve the problem.
  3. *Climax*
     - The high point of the story is where the problem is solved.

- *Ending*
  When the problem — as initiated in the plot — is solved, there is *resolution*. The resolution provides the ending to the narrative text.

Other Aspects of Narrative Stories
- *Theme:* A narrative story contains a basic theme, which is one of the most difficult components to teach because theme is more abstract than other components. A theme is often based on an abstract concept
- *The 5 W's :* The 5 W questions are usually answered by specific story parts: Who? (character), What? (problem/resolution), When? (setting), Where? (setting), and Why? (character action, problem, etc.). Further strategies for explaining and using the 5 W's are on page 160 in Chapter 8.

➤ Narrative Essays

Essays written in narrative style also contain a beginning, middle, and ending; however, the internal components are slightly different.
- *Beginning:* The beginning of an essay provides the introduction. An introductory sentence presents the thesis or purpose of the essay. This part may also include a general outline of the essay.
- *Middle:* The middle of an essay is the body. It includes transitional sentences, topic sentences, major and minor supporting details, and examples.
- *Ending:* The ending concludes the essay. This portion summarizes the points previously mentioned, and might offer suggestions, give predictions, or ask for action about the topic.

Identifying Text Structure
Strategies to help students identify a text's structure include TELLS and TP, as described on page 107 in Chapter 5.

Expository Text

Expository text is more difficult for many students to understand than narrative text because its structure is less consistent, denser, and contains vocabulary that is more technical. These aspects of expository text create challenges for students as they attempt to summarize and synthesize content. Help your students understand how a text's structure enables them to understand both how the material is organized, and how it aids in monitoring comprehension.

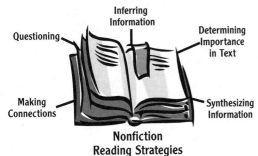

Nonfiction
Reading Strategies

Students further increase their comprehension and understanding of expository text by activating their prior knowledge. Some ways to activate prior knowledge include having students think of experiences they may have had that relate to the content, connecting the content to their own lives, and previewing critical vocabulary by relating new words to familiar words and/or ideas. Remind students to search for and then focus on the purposes of reading expository text by creating graphics such as the example on the left.

Students also benefit by being able to recognize and understand signal words that identify a text's organizational structure. Page 95 of Chapter 5 contains suggestions for helping students focus on signal words prior to reading the text. You might provide a cue card for students to remind them of the key features related to common text structures they will encounter in their curriculum. The example cue card below presents a few of the forms: descriptive, sequencing, compare/contrast, and cause/effect. Create your own cue card focusing on the structures relevant to your curriculum. Use small graphics to help students focus on the components. Page A-12 in the Appendix on the CD presents a table describing the seven main categories of expository text structure and an example graphic organizer to use with each.

Expository Text Structures – Cue Card			
Text structure	**Signal words**		**Signal to reader**
Description or list	such as for example for instance most important beside		The following tasks will present a list or set of characteristics.
Sequence or time order 1900 1950 2000 ① → ② → ③	first second third before next then	on (date) not long after after that at the same time finally	The text will describe a sequence of events or steps in a process.
Compare and contrast	like unlike but both also	in contrast on the other hand however too as well as	The text will present and/or discuss likenesses and differences.
Cause and effect Problem and solution	therefore so this led to as a result because if . . . then		The text will describe evidence of cause(s) and effect(s) or problems and solutions.

118   *The Source for Reading Comprehension Strategies*

Another type of cue card to help students with expository text includes a series of questions they ask themselves. You might title the card, "Be a Reading Detective." An example is on the right.

As an alternative, you may provide students with a frame to complete prior to reading the text. Organize your frame in any format that contains these four sections:

Be a Reading Detective

- What kind of reading is this?
- What signals tell me how the text is organized?
- Are there headings?
- Are there diagrams or illustrations?

- Scan the text. What do you think is the text's purpose?
- Circle (or put Post-it Flags®) by signal words you find in the text.
- What is the main structure of the text? (Hint: give 4 choices)
- What do you think the main idea is of this text? (Hint: list the topic and 3-5 words that elaborate on that topic. This is probably the main idea.)

Components of Expository Text
Expository Text

The elements and structures listed below are frequently found within expository text, especially in textbooks. As you explain these elements to your students, have them find examples of each in different textbooks.

Elements
- Introduction
- Bold Headings
- Definitions
- Visuals (graphs, pictures)
- Chapter Summary
- Chapter Questions

Structures
- Advance Organizer
  - Outlines chapter and indicates what will be included

- Introduction
  - Gives a summary about the topic of the chapter
  - Might link the previous chapter to the current one
  - Might include questions for students to keep in mind while reading, new vocabulary words, and/or objectives

- Bold Headings
  - Divide the chapter into meaningful sections.
  - Identify the major topic of the paragraphs that follow.
  - May identify definitions, facts, or visuals that support the content.
  - Typographical features — including boldface, italics, or colored type — highlight new words or information. Notes in the margin and captions are other typographical features that provide additional information.

- Summary
  - Provides key points of all of the sections
  - Helps identify the most important information
  - Pulls the chapter information together

- Chapter Questions
  - Helps identify what to focus on while reading
  - Includes questions about facts
  - Includes critical thinking questions
  - Includes discussion questions

When students are familiar with the concepts listed above, they can adapt strategies such as TP (found on page A-15 of the Appendix on the CD) to approach expository text:

- **T**=Textbook Structure: Preview for elements (introduction, headings, definitions, visuals, chapter summary, chapter questions) and review the structure of the sections within each chapter (advance organizer, introduction, headings, summary, chapter questions).

- **P**=Paragraph Structure: Preview the structure of the paragraphs in the first section of the chapter and look for topic sentences, key words, and conclusions.

Activities Related to Text Organization

Understanding Story Grammar with Narrative Text   *Text Organization Strategies*

A useful technique for explaining the grammar, or structure, of a story is to use a metaphor: the human spine. Compare the structure of the spine to the story grammar.

1. Explain to your students that our spine provides a structure for our body. Show them the spine in a picture of a skeleton or on a model. Elaborate the concept.

2. Compare the structure of the story to a spine by explaining, "Our story structure holds up the story. This is called the 'story grammar' and helps give the story a backbone. A backbone is another word for our spine."

3. Introduce the components, one at a time (character, setting, problem, initiating event, climax, and ending).
   a. Focus on fewer components with younger students (perhaps just character, setting, problem, and ending).
   b. Use a concrete representation or graphic as a hook or visual tag for each component.
   c. Provide substantial practice with each component before moving on.

You (or your students) might develop graphics by sketching related pictures or by using clip art for each story element.

Identifying Fiction or Nonfiction
Text Organization Strategies

1. Show students two reading selections: one fiction and one nonfiction.

2. Use group brainstorming to have students identify the characteristics of one selection and label it as *fiction* or *narrative*.

3. Have students brainstorm the characteristics of the other selection and label it appropriately.

As students become more skilled, show them three or more selections to identify so that they do not automatically label the second selection whatever the first selection was not.

Examining Nonfiction Materials
Text Organization Strategies

1. Provide students with a frame that contains questions about expository material.

2. Have at least four boxes within your frame with one question in each box. Here are some example questions:
   a. How does nonfiction text look different from fiction?
   b. How are graphic aids used?
   c. How is the vocabulary in nonfiction different from the vocabulary in fiction?
   d. What do we know about nonfiction?

3. Have students work in pairs or small groups to examining the text and complete the frame.
   a. Have some groups use nonfiction social studies examples.
   b. Have others use nonfiction science examples.

4. Initiate a whole group discussion regarding the components of nonfiction materials and have students share the discoveries they made.

Sharing Information About Nonfiction Materials
Text Organization Strategies

1. Have students share experiences they have had with nonfiction text.

2. Use question prompts such as these:
   a. What books have you read about real people, places, and events?
   b. Do you enjoy reading these types of books? Why or why not?
   c. When you look at an article or a biography, do you look at the illustrations and read the captions?
   d. What Websites do you visit?
   e. Have you ever had to read directions for a board game or ingredients in a cookbook?
   f. Have you seen a travel brochure? How was it organized? What did it include?

Examining Different Nonfiction Texts

1. Have students work in small groups.

2. Decide upon the text structures you wish to focus on and obtain articles illustrating each of those structures. Some common structures are sequential, compare/contrast, description, point of view, problem/solution, and cause/effect. Page A-12 of the Appendix on the CD describes seven categories of expository text.

3. Provide each group with two expository articles that use different structures.

4. Provide students with a frame like the one below. Students might also benefit from a cue card, such as the one shown on page 118.

5. The group examines each article, determines its structure, and completes the boxes in the frame.

6. Discuss each group's completed frames.

Frame for Examining Nonfiction Text				
Title of article	Organizational structure	Signal words	Questions to consider	Visual organizer to summarize information

Discussing Structure After Reading

1. After reading a nonfiction article, have students answer questions about the content of the text, as well as its structural components.

2. Here are some sample questions based on an article about the Leaning Tower of Pisa.

    a. Why was the Leaning Tower of Pisa so famous? (*content*)

    b. What was the problem with the tower? (*content*)

    c. How did the engineers solve the problem? (*content*)

    d. What text features did you find most helpful? (*structure*)

    e. What clues in the article helped you figure out the text structure? (*structure*)

    f. What was the text structure? (*structure*)

Reflections

1. Why do you think it is important to teach your students about text structure?

_____

_____

_____

_____

_____

2. What problems do you anticipate your students might encounter as they begin to identify and work with different types of text structure?

_____

_____

_____

_____

_____

3. Develop an activity related to your students' goals for teaching text structure. You may modify any of the activities discussed in this chapter to fit your needs.

_____

_____

_____

_____

_____

_____

_____

_____

_____

_____

CHAPTER 7

Asking appropriate questions and teaching students a variety of questioning strategies are critical components in helping them develop efficient reading comprehension skills. When students use strategies, they break through their passivity because they are involved in their own learning. Thus, they are better equipped to achieve the overall goal of competent and self-regulated reading.

> The overall goal for students is competent and self-regulated reading.

This chapter addresses asking questions that encourage greater depth of processing and includes four of the five top promising strategies suggested by the National Reading Panel: Monitoring Comprehension, Using Graphic and Semantic Organizers, Answering Questions, and Generating Questions. The fifth strategy, Summarizing, is addressed in the next chapter. (A summary of all five strategies appears on the next page.) These strategies efficiently help students conceptualize reading: they expand the depth of their understanding and use specific cognitive strategies and/or reason strategically when they encounter barriers to comprehension during reading.

Evidence Base

The strategies described in this chapter incorporate components identified by the NRP as having a solid evidence base and match the mandates of NCLB and Reading First. Studies supporting these techniques are referenced in Appendix A, Chapter 3 of *Vocabulary Instruction Methods: A Summary Of Vocabulary Instruction Methods.* (National Reading Panel, 1999, pp. 3-33 to 3-35). These strategy categories are included:

- Basic mnemonic techniques
- Cognitive strategies
- Elaborate and rich instruction
- Interactive vocabulary techniques
- Visual mapping
- Wide reading & background exposure

The chart on the next page reviews the top five promising strategies for improving text comprehension according to scientifically-based reading research, identifying why the focus on what we know about cognition has led to the development of practical strategies for improving students' comprehension. "The cumulative result of nearly three decades of research is that there is ample research supporting the efficacy of cognitive strategy training during reading as a means to enhance students' comprehension" (Baumann, 1992, p. 162). The commonality among the strategies in the chart is that they all encourage students to think actively as they read.

Strategy	Strategy is effective because students . . .
Monitoring Comprehension	• become aware of what they understand • identify what they do not understand • use appropriate strategies to resolve comprehension problems
Using Graphic and Semantic Organizers	• focus on the structure • develop a tool to examine and visually represent relationships • use the components as a frame for organizing concepts and/or writing cohesive summaries
Answering Questions	• obtain a purpose for reading • focus attention on what to learn • are encouraged to monitor their comprehension • review content and relate to prior knowledge • use text clues to draw inferences, think ahead, discern a theme, and speculate on what is to come • determine important ideas • support an answer by revisiting text
Generating Questions	• ask their own questions about the text • integrate information from different parts of the text • synthesize information • combine new information with existing knowledge
Summarizing	• identify or generate main idea • connect central ideas and synthesize information • illuminate repetitive or unnecessary information • focus on key concepts • remember what was read

Asking Questions to Encourage Processing Depth

Successful comprehension involves building coherence among details and global ideas. Past research has suggested comprehension is automatic if the student successfully decodes the text and recalls the information. More current research reveals that comprehension is not a unitary process, but rather that it consists of several interacting levels of processing (Kintsch, 1998; van Dijk & Kintsch, 1983; Kintsch & Kintsch, 2005; Kintsch, 2005; Caccamise & Snyder, 2005). The table on the following page summarizes the three main levels of processing (*Local, Macro,* and *Situation*) and relates each to types of questions needed to probe at that level. The questions form a continuum of increasing depth in engaging a student's understanding.

As we develop questions to ask our students, we should tap all three levels of text comprehension. When we reach all three levels, we gain a more complete picture of what the student knows and also encourage deeper learning. While it is important to insure that students understand the basics of a text at the local and macro levels, we also need to ask questions that target the cause, precondition, or goal of an event or process; the process of events that occurred; and the outcome. You can reach this deeper level — the Situation Level — by asking questions such as, "Why did something happen?" "How did it happen?" and "What was the result of an action, event or process?"

Levels of Processing

	What these processes do	Mental representation required	What is required by the student	Related types of questions	Common types of questions
Local Level	Tie sentence meanings together. Example: relating pronouns and synonyms to their referents and filling in connectors not specified in the text	Minimal, mostly associative connections	Processing at this level proceeds fairly automatically in an easy reading task with familiar content.	Questions require students to recognize and recall facts or details from text.	• Fill-in-the-blank • Multiple-choice • Concept definition • Short answer
Macro Level	Establish the overall level and meaning of the text content. Spell out the relationships of individual sentences and groups of sentences to the global topic.	Sufficient to support recall of the text or recognition of particular ideas	Processing at this level proceeds fairly automatically in an easy reading task with familiar content.	Questions ask students to summarize and recall the general content.	• Fill-in-the-blank • Multiple-choice • Concept definition • Short answer
Situation Level	Effectively integrate the ideas in the text with the information in the reader's personal knowledge base.	Deeper representation necessary for true learning. Allows new knowledge to be easily accessed from memory and used in novel situations.	Processing at this level requires conscious, effortful comprehension, and problem solving.	Questions probe problem-solving, relationship analysis, forming connections among ideas, explaining relationships between content and personal knowledge, and/or formulating thoughtful questions.	Open-ended questions requiring a longer response: involves expressing understanding in their own words

Our activities with students need to challenge them to process more actively, which results in memory representations of the content that are more elaborated and more integrated with their existing knowledge. Effortful comprehension results in a deeper understanding of concepts and situations. Students are then able to more readily access the information needed to solve novel inference problems (Kintsch, 2005, p. 53).

Applying Multilevel Questions

Questioning Strategies

As you develop questions to ask your students after they have read a text selection, be aware of the multiple levels of processing depth and generate your questions so that they engage each level of processing.

Here are some examples of questions at several levels based upon Aesop's Fable, "The Ant and The Dove."

- Local level questions:
  - Why did the Ant go to the river bank?
  - What happened to the Ant?

- Macro level questions:
  - How did the Dove help the Ant?
  - How did the Ant help the Dove?

- Situation model questions:
  - Why did the Ant sting the bird catcher?
  - Have you ever experienced a similar situation? How was your situation similar? How was it different?

General Considerations with Strategies

In guiding your students to select appropriate strategies, first review the similarities and differences between narrative and expository text. Strategy selection decisions depend on the type of text being read. In teaching any strategy, remember to demonstrate, model, and guide your students to understand and use the strategy automatically. Once students achieve automaticity with a strategy, demonstrate, model, and guide them to use it independently and spontaneously.

Expository Text

- General purposes:
  - Inform
  - Describe
  - Present information
- Persuade
- Uses little, if any, dialog
- Usually deals with less familiar content
- Basis of 2/3 of standardized test questions

Predictable structure

Predictable genres

Narrative Text

- General purposes:
  - Entertain
  - Tell a story
  - Provide aesthetic literary experience
- Based on life experiences; often uses dialog and familiar language
- Has a specific story structure or story grammar

Students need to focus on comprehension strategies at all levels throughout the learning continuum. Research reveals benefits when such instruction begins in the early grades. Research also indicates that comprehension monitoring strategies are most effective when used in conjunction with other strategies: the multiple strategy approach.

It is important to encourage student interaction while working with the Questioning Strategies. Interaction with others enables students to work together to learn and practice the strategies in the context of reading. When peers instruct others or interact over the use of reading strategies, they increase their understanding of the strategies and enhance their intellectual discussion. Results show reliable effects on instruction, indicating, "Cooperative learning produces reliable and replicable near transfer" (National Reading Panel, 1999, p. 4-45). Cooperation enhances your students' overall reading comprehension: you save teacher time, have more control over students' learning, and allow them to socially interact with their peers.

Monitoring Comprehension

Comprehension is the goal of reading, and good readers are both purposeful and active: they think actively as they read, use their experiences and knowledge of the world, and use their knowledge of vocabulary and language structure. Good readers incorporate reading strategies to make sense of the text. All of this requires that they monitor their comprehension while they are reading.

Students who effectively monitor what they are reading are aware when they understand the text and when they do not. They have strategies available and are capable of using them to deal with or fix any problems in their understanding. They employ these strategies efficiently as problems arise.

There are three primary goals when teaching comprehension monitoring strategies. Appropriate scaffolding best accomplishes these goals:

- Teach students to be aware of when they understand the text.
- Teach students to identify what they do not understand.
- Teach students to use appropriate strategies to resolve problems that may occur during reading.

Using Highlighters

Students frequently enjoy using colored highlighters or pencils to underline text when reading. When it is not feasible to write in a textbook, you might have students use Wikki Stiks® or Post-it® flags in lieu of highlighters. Direct teaching of this strategy is critical because many times students "over-highlight" the text. As they struggle to identify salient information, they often highlight practically everything. While that approach creates colorful text, it does not aid reading comprehension. Here are some general suggestions for using highlighters:

- Explain that the goal is to highlight as few words as possible.
- Use an overhead to model highlighting different passages.
- Begin by identifying a specific component to highlight, such as the main idea.
- Provide students with substantial practice in identifying each component before adding another.
- Have students focus on a specific component and work in pairs to identify and highlight it.
- Provide positive affirmations and incentives for correct highlighting.

➤ Highlighting Instructions

Some students have a problem reading instructions. Teach them to use highlighting within instructions to increase their understanding. When students appropriately highlight important components of instructions before beginning, they "chunk" the information into smaller pieces and identify a starting point. The task provides a visual approach for verbal information and helps students focus on the key parts of an assignment. Students correlate the instruction (the "you do it" aspect) with their response (the "I did it" aspect). Most importantly, they gain ownership of and empowerment over how they progress through the task.

Begin framing the strategy by providing a rationale for why students should learn the technique appropriately. You might begin by telling an anecdote based on these situations:

- A student missed something very exciting because he did not complete all the steps in the instructions for his assignment
- A first-person account about being confused about multi-step instructions and wishing you had a way to deal with them

Next, present the highlighting strategy as a solution to the problem you established in your anecdote. Display a set of instructions on an overhead or whiteboard that is appropriate to your students' skill level. Use substantial self-talk to instruct and model the following steps (initially, students may need considerable assistance):

1. Identify the first part of the instruction. Find and highlight the key word.
2. Identify the next chunk. Find and highlight the key word.
3. Continue in the same manner through the entire instruction, discriminating essential from nonessential information.
4. When finished, review the steps by writing a numbered list of the key words in sequence.

Prior to attempting math word problems, have students highlight the words that determine which operation they must use to solve the problem. They might identify words such as *difference*, *in all*, or *how many more*. You might have your students explicitly match the operation they will use with the key words (for example, *in all* means addition), especially with younger students.

➤ Highlighting Expository Text

Highlighting is a powerful tool to help students identify main ideas and supporting details within a paragraph or passage. It is essential to use a different color for each component.

> The goal in highlighting is to highlight as few words as possible.

Begin by teaching one component, such as main idea. Guide students to identify and highlight the main idea in several paragraphs. Then teach another component, such as supporting facts, and proceed similarly but with a different color. It is important that students remember the goal is to highlight as few words as possible.

Once students develop skill in identifying main idea and supporting facts, and they are able to highlight key words for each using two different colors, they will be pleasantly surprised at their increase in comprehension and retention. They will have a foundation for using the information further and can easily use the highlighted material to create a visual organizer, an outline, or study cards to use in preparing for a writing assignment or test.

"Meaning doesn't arrive because we have highlighted text, used sticky notes, or written the right words on the comprehension worksheet. Meaning arrives because we are purposefully engaged in thinking while we read" (Tovani, 2004, Chapter 1).

Post-It® Notes
Monitoring Comprehension

Students can use Post-it® Notes or Flags as an alternative to highlighters, especially when they are unable to write in their text. Post-It® Notes provide a surface for writing additional notes, such as the main idea or detail, which can later be transferred into a graphic organizer.

Think Aloud
Monitoring Comprehension

"Think-Alouds are just what their name suggests. The teacher models a silent reading strategy by thinking aloud as she processes a text, thus making explicit skills that normally cannot be observed. Originally a research technique for studying reading processes, Think-Alouds are used to model comprehension processes such as making predictions, creating images, linking information in text with prior knowledge, monitoring comprehension, and using a fix-up strategy when there is a problem with word recognition or comprehension." (Gunning, 1996, p. 295)

130   *The Source for Reading Comprehension Strategies*

As teachers and parents, we frequently use the Think-Aloud strategy with young students while reading to them. For example, we might pause to explain something by linking the text to something familiar: "This _____ reminds me of _____." Comments such as those provide a tool to model and verbalize your thinking as you connect with the text.

The Think-Aloud strategy provides a vehicle to make observable and model those effective strategies that are generally "silent." As you Think-Aloud, you verbalize internal cognitive behaviors and demonstrate strategies used by thoughtful readers, including how to generate questions. This modeling helps students learn how to ask themselves questions as they read silently.

You can use the Think-Aloud strategy as an instructional or assessment tool at any age level. When students Think-Aloud, they become more active readers and have control of monitoring their own thinking and comprehension. This strategy is effective with a wide range of techniques. Keene & Zimmerman (1997) recommend seven techniques that integrate well with Think-Aloud when your students are unfamiliar with the strategy:

- Predicting
- Clarifying
- Visualizing
- Using prior knowledge
- Building new connections
- Summarizing
- Synthesizing

Begin by selecting a book to fit the particular cue(s) you wish to emphasize, and initially, you may wish to focus on one or two strategies and model your thoughts using many different types of books.

The following example illustrates some Think-Aloud cues for Aesop's Fable, "The Ant and the Dove." Initially use only some of the clues and/or focus on a single strategy. Sometimes it helps to reread a phrase after making a comment to maintain continuity. This example incorporates several techniques, which are numbered to correspond with the list on the bottom of the next page. When moving to a new strategy, it is often useful to use the original story once again, which will provide familiarity and allow greater focus on the process.

Story Text	Think-Aloud Comments/Cues
An Ant went to the bank of the river to quench its thirst.	I can just picture this little bitty ant crawling through the grass and the mud to the side of the water[1]. It looks so hard. Poor guy. (Show concern[2].) It must be like walking through very tall weeds for us[4].
The ant, being carried away by the rush of the stream, was on the point of drowning.	Oh my! That poor ant. He must have slipped on the mud at the side of the river and fell in. I feel bad for him[2]. I can see him struggling in the rushing waters[1].
A Dove sitting on a tree overhanging the water plucked a leaf and let it fall into the stream close to her.	That makes me feel so good! I just hope the Ant sees the leaf[2]. I picture the Dove as a very pretty white bird[1].
The Ant climbed onto the leaf and floated in safety to the bank.	Hooray for the ant! I feel so happy for her! (Show "happy" expression[2].) I can picture a smile on her little face because she is saved[1]. I remember one time I was getting stuck and was helped. Wow! I felt so glad[4].

Continued on the next page.

Story Text	Think-Aloud Comments/Cues
Shortly afterwards, a bird catcher came and stood under the tree. He laid his lime-twigs for the Dove, which sat in the branches.	I think the bird catcher is a mean-looking man with a mean look on his face. (Model "mean" expression[1, 2].) I wonder what "lime-twigs are[10]." Let's see, it says he's a "bird catcher" and he laid them for the Dove. Hmmm, "lime-twigs" must be some kind of trap[5].
He laid his lime-twigs for the Dove, which sat in the branches.	Yes, I can just see him bending over and setting the trap for the bird with his twigs[1]. (Demonstrate action[9].)
The Ant, perceiving his design,	Huh? What was that? I'll go over that part again[5].
The Ant, perceiving his design,	Hmmm, "perceiving his design"? A design is like a drawing, but I don't think that's what it means[10]. I remember hearing that a design is like a plan. That must be it. I'll read on and see. Could it be that the ant is guessing his plan? The ant is watching the bird catcher[3, 8].
The Ant, perceiving his design, stung him in the foot.	Yes! I was right. The Ant did figure out the bird catcher's plan. (Show excitement[10].)
In pain, the bird catcher threw down the twigs, and the noise made the Dove take wing.	I feel so glad for the Dove[2]. The Ant saved him just like the Dove saved the Ant. I wonder what it means that the noise made "the Dove take wing"[3]? Why did the authors say it that way[8]? It must mean something about the Dove flying away. Oh, of course. He uses his wings and flies — that means he escapes. Now I get it[10].

As students become more confident with the technique, you may extend the types of and variety of strategies used. Other instances that lend themselves well to modeling the Think-Aloud strategy during reading activities include those in the following list. Eventually, when you ask your students to share what they are thinking about a story, they will be able to do so in a broader manner.

1. Making pictures in my mind
2. Exploring how I feel about what's happening
3. Asking myself questions regarding my thoughts or the text
4. Making connections to other stories, other authors, familiar experiences or people
5. Stopping and rereading for clarity
6. Looking at story structure
7. Considering story genre
8. Examining the author's word choice
9. Acting out a passage
10. Monitoring comprehension

CAUTION

Remember how critical it is to model the technique with different types of texts. Most students require many examples of using this technique in order to discriminate Think-Aloud from just asking questions that have a specific right or wrong answer.

Self-Monitoring

A strategy to encourage students to develop a habit of monitoring their own comprehension is to provide them with a checklist of questions to answer after reading a passage. The questions are not about the content of a passage but provide self-feedback on students' own use of strategies. Below are example checklists for elementary and middle/high school students. As always, adapt your questions to your students' needs.

Self-Feedback Form for Elementary Students

When you are reading for information, how often do you . . .					
Stop to think about what you undersand.	never	not very often	sometimes	most of the time	always
Continue to consider your questions about the topic.	never	not very often	sometimes	most of the time	always
Use context in all possible clues to get to the meaning of the unknown words.	never	not very often	sometimes	most of the time	always
Try to identify key ideas and concepts	never	not very often	sometimes	most of the time	always

Self-Feedback Form for Middle/High School Students

When you are reading for information, how often do you . . .			
Adjust your reading speed to match your purpose for reading?	never	sometimes	often
Try to identify the main idea?	never	sometimes	often
Take notes while you are reading?	never	sometimes	often
Predict what is coming next in the reading?	never	sometimes	often
Look for answers to your own questions about the topic?	never	sometimes	often
Use context clues to figure out the meaning of words you don't know?	never	sometimes	often
Get so absorbed in the reading that you lose track of everything else?	never	sometimes	often
Go back and reread what you don't understand?	never	sometimes	often
Visualize while you are reading?	never	sometimes	often
Connect new information with what you already know?	never	sometimes	often

Fix-It Strategies

One of the major reasons students need to monitor their comprehension is to identify when they encounter a problem, especially one that reduces their comprehension. Such monitoring enables them to adjust and fix their techniques, which increases their understanding.

A Fix-it Strategy is any strategy that a reader uses to "get unstuck" when the text becomes confusing. Students need to know that such strategies are flexible and will depend upon the text and situation. Teaching students to use Fix-It Strategies requires substantial direct instruction and plenty of practice with different types of text. Continually model and use guided practice as you scaffold the steps of each strategy.

Students must understand that they will need to determine, on a very conscious level, which strategy would be best to use in a given situation. The following lists detail the types of strategies students can use with different Fix-it needs. Select the items you feel are most appropriate for your students and create a cue card that students refer to as they read. Only include strategies your students thoroughly understand on your cue card and add to it as students learn additional strategies. An initial cue card, for example, would probably only include two to eight strategies, depending on a student's skill level:

General strategies:
- Notice patterns and text structure.
- Notice when you lose focus.
- Stop and go back.
- Reread to enhance your understanding.
- Identify what is confusing.
- Select an appropriate strategy for that confusion.
- Make a connection between the text and your life, your knowledge of the world, or another text.

General strategies for monitoring your understanding:
- Stop and think about what you have already read.
- Locate the difficulty:
  - Identify what the difficulty is.
  - Determine what part seems to be causing the difficulty.
- Restate the passage in your own words.
- Look back through the text.
- Look forward in the text.
- Ask yourself a question and try to answer it.

Strategies for clarifying or identifying confusing words or phrases:
- Identify unfamiliar words.
- Identify the part of a phrase that seems confusing.
- Use statements such as these:
  - I don't understand the part where _____
  - This _____ is not clear.
  - I can't figure out _____
  - This is a tricky word because _____

Strategies for clarifying ideas and concepts:

- Reread the part you don't understand.
- Think about what you do know related to the topic.
- Talk to a friend or your teacher.
- Read on and look for additional clues.

Knowing how to remedy an inefficiency in comprehension is a critical aspect of metacognitive knowledge and control. Beyond being aware of their understanding or lack of understanding, students must learn how to regulate and enhance their own reading processes.

Using Graphic Organizers

Graphic organizers provide visual structure for vocabulary, content, and organization of text. The visual connections students make with text are powerful tools to facilitate comprehension, especially in content areas. Using a concrete framework to analyze and visualize important concepts helps students focus on key elements and use metacognitive techniques. This focus enhances their comprehension and ability to organize the content, which helps them generate an organized summary and/or gain greater efficiency in studying the material.

There are many types of graphic organizers, and it is valuable to have a variety of them in your strategy toolbox. Proficient readers create mental pictures as they read stories because it helps them monitor their developing understanding of the text. However, it is more difficult to visualize content materials since they are primarily expository text. By illustrating relationships, graphic organizers help students transition or link their ability to visualize stories into visualizing relationships with expository text. Organizers are key to helping students "read to learn" from informational text, especially in the areas of social and natural science.

Selecting Graphic Organizers
Using Graphic Organizers

Because there are so many different types of graphic organizers, it is important for a student to know how to select or create an appropriate organizer for a particular task. The student needs to match the text structure and/or the desired learning outcome to the selected format. Therefore, when teaching strategies for a given organizer, explicitly demonstrate its importance and how it matches the text structure and information addressed. Students need to ask themselves these questions as they select a graphic organizer format:

- What is the text structure?
- What information do I want from this material?
- How can I best organize this information?
  - What relationships within the material are important?
  - How can I best represent these?
- What category of organizer will best meet my needs?
- Which specific format will best meet my needs?

Any time you develop an organizer with students, discuss the results they achieved. Explicitly guide your students to understand the "frame" or purpose: discuss how the organizer helps them to systematize their thinking while they read. Show students how using a graphic organizer with expository text is similar to the visualization that happens spontaneously when they read narrative text. Instead of automatically seeing the "mind pictures" that narrative text inspires, though, a graphic organizer is a deliberate way to visually organize the concepts, vocabulary, and information their textbooks contain.

The tables on pages A-12–13 of the Appendix on the CD display two groups of graphic organizer structures: those that relate to various types of text structure and those based on the information desired from the text. Use these tables to help your students decide on the best type of graphic organizer format that will meet their text needs.

Concept Mapping *Using Graphic Organizers*

Concept Maps are particularly useful with science and social studies materials and can exist in a variety of structures. This strategy encourages students to organize concepts and determine the relationships among them. Rather than merely memorizing facts, students work with concepts and ideas. Determining relationships between these concepts and ideas encourages students to use the vocabulary associated with them appropriately. You can review and analyze your students' Concept Maps to determine their understanding of the lesson or reading material.

Here are the three critical components for students to keep in mind as they construct Concept Maps:
- Identify and focus on the main idea — the organizing concept.
- Locate supporting details.
- Determine the relationship between the details and concepts.

Students will initially need substantial modeling and guidance to implement this strategy. Progressively guide them to work with peers before completing Concept Maps independently. This is especially critical with Step 2, selecting the concepts, and Step 5, arranging the concepts from general to specific.

Have your students perform the following steps to create their concept maps.
1. Decide upon the structure/format most relevant to the task.
2. Select several concepts from the chapter, ideally 8 to 12.
3. Write each concept on a separate Post-it® note or index card.
4. Determine the main idea by selecting the organizing concept. Place the card with this concept at the top (or center) of the Concept Map.
5. Arrange the other cards in a distinct hierarchy as related to the main idea or organizing concept. Arrange the concepts from general to specific.
6. Transfer the concepts to the Concept Map, maintaining their hierarchy by taping the cards onto the paper or rewriting the concepts.
7. Draw lines to connect each concept to the main idea and write linking words on each to explain the relationship.
8. Review the Concept Map and reflect upon the concepts and organization. When satisfied with the arrangement of the concepts and their links, construct a final map using color and drawing or pasting small pictures.

Answering Text Questions

As discussed at the beginning of the chapter, it is common to ask students questions to guide and monitor their learning. When students have specific questions to answer before they begin reading, they have a purpose for reading and are better able to focus their attention on what they are to learn. Knowing they need to answer questions encourages them to think actively as they read, monitor their comprehension, and consider the content in relationship to what they have already learned.

Model techniques that encourage your students to look back in the text to find answers to questions they cannot answer after the initial reading. As students learn to answer questions more efficiently, they comprehend at a deeper level.

QAR — Question-Answer Relationships
Answering Text Questions

The QAR strategy requires students to analyze questions about the text. They differentiate among various types of questions in a strategic way and recognize that different types of questions require different types of answers. For many students, the processing used for the QAR strategy will be a new experience. Model the strategy with Think-Aloud and demonstrate how to utilize the strategy effectively before providing your students with guided practice.

Begin by creating a frame with four sections, similar to the one on the next page. QAR focuses on the four primary relationships between questions and answers (Raphael, 1984).

Right There
- Relationships are text explicit.
- The answer is right in the text and usually easy to find.
- The answer is often within a single sentence.
- The words that make up the question and the answer are frequently the same.
- "Right There" questions usually ask Who?, What?, When?, Where?, and occasionally, Why?

  Example:
  Question: On what date did our forefathers sign the Declaration of Independence?
  Answer: Our forefathers signed the Declaration of Independence on July 4, 1776.

Think and Search
- Relationships are text explicit.
- The answer is in the text but you need to search within different sentences to find its parts and put them together.
- The questions require you to synthesize different bits of information from the text.
- Words for the question and the answer are usually not the same.

  Example:
  Question: What are the main organs of the digestive system?
  Answer: The digestive system is made up of the esophagus, the stomach, and the intestines.

Author and You

- Relationships are script implicit.
- The answer is not in the text, but you use the text to find the answer.
- You need to combine information from the author with what you already know.

Example

Question: Why do you think the Channel Tunnel that connects England and France is an amazing project?

Answer: I think the Channel Tunnel is amazing because it is 31 miles long and most of that is underwater. It's an incredible engineering feat to create such a Tunnel and make it sturdy and safe.

On My Own

- Relationships are script implicit.
- Answer is not in the text.
- You must use prior knowledge and experience.
- You can answer these questions without even reading the text.

Example

Question: Why is it a good idea to conserve water?

Answer: It's a good idea to conserve water because _____.

Struggling readers may not possess the background knowledge required to answer script implicit questions ("QARs in my Head"). Their knowledge base is often lower, usually due to their lack of exposure and practice with reading. In such situations, use techniques to enhance students' knowledge base (Pair-Share, hands-on experiences, etc.).

Here is a passage about Mount St. Helens and a completed QAR frame:

QARs in the Book	QARs in my Head
Right There: The answer is in the text. What type of mountain is Mount St. Helens? Describe what happened to Mount St. Helens in 1980.	**Author and You:** The answer is not in the text. What does *destroyed* mean? Approximately how many feet shorter was Mount St. Helens after the explosion?
Think and Search: Put it together. What happens when a volcano erupts? Why was Mount St. Helens shorter after the eruption?	**On my Own:** Your own thoughts How do you think people who lived in homes near Mount St. Helens felt? Do you think the eruption of a volcano is over quickly?

Mount St. Helens

Mount St. Helens was a 9,677-foot-tall mountain in 1980. This mountain is also a volcano: a place where melted rock squeezes out from the inside of the earth and goes through the earth's surface. Mount St. Helens erupted in 1980. First, it began to shake like an earthquake. Then it rumbled and spit out steam and hot lava, which is melted rock. Next, a landslide began. Mud, gravel, and rocks destroyed trees and homes and everything else in its path. Afterwards, Mount St. Helens was only 8,364 feet tall.

ReQuest

This self-questioning strategy involves interaction between students. Initially, you and your students take turns asking each other questions about a given chunk in the textbook. In doing so, you model appropriate development of questions along with efficient techniques for determining answers to questions. Additionally, you provide your students with feedback about their questions and their strategies for question answering. Students then use ReQuest with each other, while you observe and monitor.

As they progress, the value of the ReQuest strategy surfaces: students learn to construct effective questions as a skill they generalize and use in their independent reading (Helfeldt & Henk, 1990).

A Road Map

The Road Map Strategy uses study guides as a tool for questioning students while they read a chapter and is an especially useful strategy for approaching difficult chapters in textbooks.

> Study Guides provide support for students and help them become more sophisticated in their reading.

Construct study guides to chunk the material. When you intersperse questions throughout the text, you reduce the amount of text your students deal with at one time. Study guides also prompt your students to use metacognitive control by adjusting their reading rate, monitoring their comprehension, and focusing on significant information in the text.

This strategy uses the visual cues of road signs to indicate reading speed, thus helping students learn to adjust their reading rates when they encounter more detailed, technical, or difficult passages.

"While good readers subconsciously know when to skim over material that is not significant, less proficient readers tend to read all textual material at the same rate — either too laboriously or too quickly and carelessly. By the use of 'road signs' to depict reading speed, the Reading Road Map can help students learn to adjust their reading rates based on the different purposes for reading a particular passage" (Wood & Harmon, 2001, pp. 87-88).

The sample Reading Road Map on the next page is based on a section in a middle school History Book regarding explorers and the nature of 15th and 16th century exploration. It scaffolds the students' progress through reading the material. Follow the activity with whole group discussion. Here are the steps to follow:

1. Establish a focus question and explain it to your students. Then read the corresponding section from which you derived the question.
   - *Focus Question:* How did the meeting between Christopher Columbus and the Taino people change the world?
   - *Text:* "October 12, 1492. On this fall morning, three ships landed near a small island in the Western Hemisphere. The island was home to Taino people. A sea captain named Christopher Columbus, who was sailing under the flag of Spain, waded ashore. Neither the Taino nor Columbus knew their meeting would change the world" (McGraw-Hill, 2002, p. 132).

2. Provide previewing activities and/or mini-lessons about Columbus, using shared reading and vocabulary development to enhance students' background knowledge.

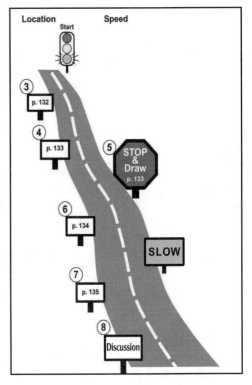

Location   Speed

3. Introduce the Reading Road Map. Have students work in "Traveling Partners" (pairs) to complete the tasks using their U.S. History textbook.

- The students read to each road sign page number on the map and answer the questions associated with it.
- When students encounter a road sign, they follow the instruction. For example, they would stop at sign #5 and slow down at sign #7.

Questions for the Christopher Columbus Road Map:

Start 1   Write down everything you know about Christopher Columbus.

Start 2   Read the Focus Question and predict what you think you will be learning.

Sign 3   *Read to page 132:*
Who was Leif Ericson? Why is it important to know about him when we talk about Christopher Columbus?

Sign 4   *Read to page 133.*
List 2 words that survive from the Taino language. What do we mean when we talk about a "dead language"?

Sign 5   Draw a map of the Taino Islands. What are they called today?

Sign 6   *Read to page 134.*
Explain who Christopher Columbus was.

Sign 7   *Read to page 135:*
"The Log of Christopher Columbus."

Sign 8   Discuss the reading with your traveling partner.

Reading Question of the Day

Answering Text Questions

This strategy helps focus your students' attention on specific information they will cover during a class reading activity. Begin your class with a "Question of the Day" and have students write it on the front of a large index card.

While your students read their text, have them note information related to the question on the back of the index card as well as the page and paragraph number where they discovered the information. You might have them place a Post-it® note in the book to indicate the section.

Schedule a five-minute writing session at the end of class when students will use the information from the back of the index card to write a paragraph that answers the Question of the Day. Collect the responses and read some (or all) anonymously. Have the class determine whether each response adequately answers the Question of the Day.

Cubing

This strategy uses a large cube as a visual guide to consider multiple dimensions of a text, concept, or issue. Select six related criteria for your students to discuss after reading a text and write each on a square piece of index card. Then tape the six pieces together to create a three-dimensional cube. Have a student roll the cube and respond to the item showing on the top side.

Narrative text components:
- Who?
- What?
- Where?
- When?
- Why?
- How do I feel?

Expository text components (emphasizing using critical thinking to discuss or analyze a concept):
- Describe it: Describe the color, shape, and size, or describe the issue/topic.
- Compare it: Tell what it is similar to or different from (use the phrase, "It's sort of like…").
- Associate it: Tell how it is made, what it is composed of, or how you would break the problem/issue into smaller parts.
- Apply it: Tell how it can be used or how it helped to understand other topics/issues.
- Argue for or against it: Take a stand and support your position, using phrases such as "I am for this because . . . ," "This works because . . . ," or "I agree with _____ because. . . ."

You might also use the cubing strategy to stimulate consideration of various components in preparation for a writing assignment.

Generating Questions

Think about how young children learn about the world. They explore and ask multiple questions. They want to know everything: "Why is this green? Why isn't the flower open? Why are some clouds white?"

> The research shows that children who struggle as readers tend not to ask questions at any time as they read — before, during, or after. It confirms what I've seen so many times in classrooms, particularly with upper elementary and middle school kids. They are inert as they read. They read — or I should say they submit to the text — never questioning its content, style, or the intent of the author" (Keene & Zimmerman, 1997, p. 21).

Reading should provide another form of exploration for students. By asking questions as they read, they engage the text and increase their understanding. Research indicates that proficient readers ask themselves questions about the text's content, structure, and language before, during and after reading. They ask questions for different purposes: to clarify their understanding, to make predictions and to consider choices and opinions made by the author.

When students begin to ask their own questions, their comprehension improves for a variety of reasons. Primarily, they are processing the text more actively. To generate questions, students become aware of whether or not they can answer the questions and how well they understand what they are reading. They use decision-making to determine the type of questions to ask, which helps them focus on the structure, content, and relationship of information within the text.

Help your students learn to ask themselves questions that require them to integrate information from different segments of the text. Some of the strategies in this section incorporate mnemonics to help students remember the steps and other techniques are less structured. When selecting the strategy to teach your students, consider their age and skill level as well as the content they will be reading.

Rather than introducing the concept of generating questions with a statement such as, "Today we'll talk about asking questions," it is more efficient to focus on questions that spontaneously occur in our own minds as we read. Using the Think-Aloud technique, model the process your students will use to think about and generate their own real questions.

A variation of the QAR technique is to create a chart to keep track of the questions students generate before, during, and after reading. The chart below, as suggested by Keene (Keene & Zimmerman, 1997, p. 113) helps to classify questions based on their purpose.

Questions based on . . .	Before Reading	During Reading	After Reading
answers in the text			
answers I must find by thinking about the book and my own experience.			
no certain answers			
clarifying meaning			
what will happen next			
the author's intent			
the author's style			
the author's format			

Two-Column Q & A

Generating Questions

This strategy helps students answer as well as generate questions. It works best with expository text. Have students create a two-column graphic organizer, such as the one on the right. The left-hand column contains questions provided by you, questions from the end of the chapter, or questions the students generate based on section headings in the text. As students read, they record the answer to each question in the right-hand column. Also have students record the location of each answer within the text (page and paragraph number). This component provides an available reference for follow-up, writing, or studying.

Key Question	Answer
	Reference:
	Reference
	Reference
	Reference

142 *The Source for Reading Comprehension Strategies*

KWL

Use the KWL strategy with students at any grade level to help them take charge of their learning and pursue additional knowledge. KWL is especially valuable with expository text but can be used with narrative text, especially if it contains concepts and specific information. The KWL strategy involves three basic steps that correspond to the three letters (several forms of a KWL organizer are on pages A-16 – A-18 of the Appendix on the CD):
1. **K** for Know — what I already know
2. **W** for Want — what I want to know
3. **L** for Learned — what I learned (from my reading)

Follow the KWL activity with a whole group discussion, emphasizing that reading content material serves several purposes. Many students realize that content reading involves finding out what the author thinks is important about the topic. However, expository reading also needs to engage your students and encourage them to identify questions they want to know so they will search for the answers.

KWLH

A KWLH chart is particularly valuable for older students. Begin by creating a KWL chart (or use a copy of one from page A-19 of the Appendix on the CD) and then add a fourth column: "H" for How (How will I find this information?). This column encourages students to think about how and where they will find further resources about the topic, especially to complete unanswered questions generated in the "W" (Want to know) step.

RAP

Your students know the word *rap* as referring to a music or movement style. Hook into that prior knowledge by linking a a visual reminder of a character singing and dancing with the steps for the RAP strategy.

Read the material.
Ask yourself questions.
Paraphrase the information.

RAP is a mnemonic strategy that encourages students to use self-questioning techniques. The steps remind them to question themselves and paraphrase what they have read. The letters stand for:
1. **R** — Read the material.
2. **A** — Ask yourself questions as you read.
3. **P** — Paraphrase the information in your own words.

Skim, RAP, Map

Extend the RAP strategy with a combination strategy: **Skim** (skim the material and look for clues, such as headings, diagrams, and charts), **RAP** (read, ask yourself questions, and paraphrase), and **Map** (create a mind map to organize the information, either by section or for the whole chapter). This combination strategy integrates the importance of previewing, or skimming, before beginning to read.

Chapter 7

RCRC

Generating Questions

RCRC is a mnemonic strategy that encourages students to focus on small chunks of the material and continually ask themselves questions about their understanding as they move through the text. There are four steps to RCRC:

1. **R** – **R**ead a small part of the material.
2. **C** – **C**over the material.
3. **R** – **R**etell yourself what you read (review or paraphrase).
4. **C** – **C**heck to determine if you remember the material correctly by comparing your recall to the actual material.

SQ3R

Generating Questions

This mnemonic strategy is beneficial for older students, as it is slightly more complex than RAP and RCRC. SQ3R encourages students to generate questions while they also chunk material and review information. Have your students follow these five steps:

1. **Survey** — Survey the text to get an overview of the content. Look at the introduction, headings, chapter titles, boldfaced type, graphics, and conclusion.
2. **Question** — While surveying the text, identify what you expect to learn. Write specific questions that focus on main topics and begin with Who?, What?, When?, Where?, and Why?
3. **Read** — Read the text actively. Visualize the author's message, take notes, or highlight the information. Make note of charts and illustrations the author provides to clarify information.
4. **Recite** — Talk aloud to provide a different learning modality. Recall what you have read, talking to yourself or to a partner. Record and say key phrases and facts needed for each of the questions you generated previously.
5. **Review** — Review the information by transforming it: avoid mere repetition of the same phrases. Graphically organize the material, paraphrase it, and/or summarize it.

Initially, you may wish to provide a worksheet or visual frame for the students to use with each step, or have students develop their own.

SQ4R

Generating Questions

SQ4R adds another R step to the SQ3R strategy: Relate. In the Relate step, students consider what they have read and relate the text material to their own prior knowledge (What do I already know about this topic? When have I heard of this topic before?).

Questioning the Author

Generating Questions

This strategy is a text-based instructional format that helps students build a deeper understanding of text by learning to query the author (McLaughlin & Allen, 2002). Students generate questions to determine what the author is trying to communicate in material they are reading.

  The Source for Reading Comprehension Strategies

The basic format involves five questions. Students read a selection of the text (often one or two paragraphs) and then answer the following questions:

1. What is the author trying to tell me?
2. Why is the author telling me that?
3. Does the author express her or his message clearly?
4. How could the author have said things more clearly?
5. What would I say instead?

Use the strategy with the whole group, in small groups, or independently. It is also beneficial to combine QtA (Questioning the Author) questions with strategies such as RCRC, SQ3R, and SQ4R.

Asking Myself Questions While Reading

STOP Page _____

Question _____

_____

Answers/further thoughts _____

_____

How did asking this question help my understanding? _____

_____

_____

Selecting Questions   *Generating Questions*

When students become familiar with the concept of generating questions, enhance their awareness of different kinds of questions and the need to select questions appropriately to match the text and the information they desire to learn. The Read-Aloud Technique (you read a section of text and determine which questions to ask) is a great way to model generating questions for your students.

Give students a worksheet for each question they will be asking (an example is on the left). These directions explain each step:

Before reading
- Decide the number of times you think you should stop for questions.
- Select appropriate stopping places, and indicate page numbers on your worksheet.
  - Visually mark stopping places with a bookmark or a Post-it® note.
- Select questions to ask yourself and record them.
  - Instructor tip: You might post a cue sheet of possible questions to provide suggestions from which students can choose questions they predict will fit the reading passage.

During reading:
- Stop at the indicated spot and answer the relevant question.
- Record your answers on your worksheet.

After reading:
- Return to each worksheet to answer the last question, "How did asking this question help my reading and my understanding?"
  - Instructor tip: This question helps students focus on the metacognitive level.

Here are some questions students might include on their worksheets:
- Why did the author chose that word or phrase?
- Why did the author use that structure?
- Why did the author include _____ (specific information)?
- What does this word, phrase or concept mean?
- What do I predict the result of this section will be?
- Why do I think this result occurred?

When you ask your students to consider additional questions, vary the type of questions you recommend. Here are some category suggestions:
- Questions before, during, or after reading
- Sequencing questions: what happened first, etc.
- Question/answer relationships (QAR)
- Questions related to the structure
- Questions with a single answer (closed questions)
- Questions with multiple answers (open questions)
- Questions related to vocabulary
- Questions that infer or predict

Another technique that helps your students learn to generate questions is to have them predict what type of data chart or visual organizer will best match the information they will read. Examples include a Feature Analysis Chart (page 53) or a Predict-O-gram (pages 105-106). These organizers also provide you with assessment information. When you analyze the questions your students create, you gain important information regarding their level of comprehension, their analytical skills, and their ability to self-question during reading.

Inferential Reasoning

Inferential reasoning is a critical component when reading both narrative and expository text. It is a form of questioning because to infer information, we need to think deeply about the issue(s), use higher order thinking skills, and search for messages. When we infer as we read, we go beyond the literal interpretation and "open a world of meaning deeply connected to our lives . . . . we go beyond the literal and weave our own sense into the words we read" (Keene & Zimmerman, 1997, p. 149).

In framing the strategies for your students, remind them that good readers use the words and pictures, along with things from their own lives, to think about what is probably true in story. When we put these parts together, we infer. Inferences are critical to helping us better understand the story.

Being able to infer information is a critical skill for students to develop, especially because as students move through the grades, our school curricula place greater demand on them for inferential analysis. In order to infer, students must organize pieces of data and conclude something about a component that may be missing or not explicitly stated. A solid foundation for inferential reasoning begins by developing categorizing skills. To determine similarities and differences, students must consider the parts and infer relationships between them. The following components of active reading all require inferential reasoning:
- Critical analysis of the text
- A mental or expressed argument with the author
- Active skepticism regarding the message in the text
- Recognition of propaganda and efforts at persuasion
- Predictions regarding the text
  - Basing a prediction on what is stated but adding an informed guess about what is to come
- Reasonable judgment or conclusion
  - Based on the facts or information available, forming a conclusion after considering the text in relation to beliefs, knowledge, and experience

Inferring with Pictures
Inferential Reasoning

This activity is fun for all ages, but it is especially useful with students as they begin to learn about making inferences. Select a high interest picture and cover a component within it. Ask questions that encourage students to guess (infer) what is covered. Your questions will depend upon the picture's content. For example, you might show a picture of children at a birthday party and cover the part of the picture that shows the cake with candles. Here are some questions you might ask:

- What do you think is under this blank box? What cues led you to that opinion?
- What do you think is going to happen to (this child)? What cues led you to that opinion?
- What do you think will happen now? What cues led you to that opinion?
- What will (the child) do next? What cues led you to that opinion?
- What do you think the other people are saying? What cues led you to that opinion?

Emphasize that there is no right or wrong answer, as long as the student is able to justify a rationale for selecting that answer. As students improve in their understanding of the concept, use more complex pictures and progress to those that contain content that is more academic.

Another use of the strategy is to show students a picture that relates to a story they will be reading, such as the picture on the front of a book. Use guided questioning to encourage them to predict what they think will be in the story.

Inferring with Category Organizer
Inferential Reasoning

Present students with a graphic organizer that identifies these categories: *setting, characters, problem, solution,* and *ending*. Read the title of a new story to your students, and, if desired, briefly discuss the cover illustration. Give students a list of 7-10 key words/phrases from the story. Ensure that your students are able to read the words and know their approximate meanings. There is no need to discuss the words in depth at this point.

Guide students to use their thinking and inferring skills to decide where the words might fit into the story based on the categories on the organizer. Students might place each word in any of the five columns, but they may not repeat a word in more than one column.

After students enter each word into a column, they create their own short story. This short story is an inference of the upcoming story they will read, based on partial facts. Have students share their completed stories.

Help students understand that the stories they have created are predictions about the story they will read. After reading the story, discuss the students' short stories to determine how each related to the actual story. Ensure students that there are no right or wrong answers — predictions are guesses that are based on partial facts. Once students have all the facts (the actual story), they will have more information.

Rationale Reminder

Teaching strategies for the sake of teaching strategies is not the goal. Being able to make connections, ask questions, or visualize is not what matters most. The only reason to teach kids how to be strategic is to help them become more thoughtful about their reading (Tovani, 2004).

Reflections

1. Think about how you formulate questions to ask your students.

    a. What similarities do they have with the three levels discussed on page 127 of this chapter?

    _____

    _____

    _____

    b. What might you do to enhance your own questioning technique? _____

    _____

    _____

    _____

    c. Make a list of some questions corresponding to each level in the table (on page 127) as related to an area of your current curriculum.

    _____

    _____

    _____

    _____

    _____

    _____

2. Select one of the strategies from the General Questions section and create a lesson plan component using that strategy as related to an area of your current curriculum.

    _____

    _____

    _____

    _____

    _____

    _____

    _____

    _____

3. Select some graphic organizer formats appropriate to your students and curriculum. Create a chart organizing these by category.

CHAPTER 8

SUMMARIZING STRATEGIES

A summary is a brief statement that contains the essential ideas of a longer passage or selection. In order to understand what we are reading, it is critical to identify key concepts and distinguish important information from details that are less important. We need to generalize from examples or repeated information and ignore irrelevant details. When we successfully identify and restate the main ideas during reading, we are also effectively monitoring and checking our comprehension.

Training poor readers to reconstruct the gist after reading small segments of text may, in fact, "mimic certain monitoring strategies normally involved in reading" (Jenkins et al., 1987, p. 55).

Instruction in summarization skills helps readers improve their skills for identifying the main idea, recognizing related ideas, integrating ideas, and generalizing from text, while also improving recall. Consequently, summarization strategies are a critical component of multiple strategy reading comprehension instruction. Developing summarization skills might be very difficult for some students, and it is generally a skill that needs to be explicitly taught at all grade levels.

Evidence Base

The strategies in this section incorporate components identified by the NRP as having a solid evidence base and match the mandates of NCLB and Reading First. Studies supporting these techniques are referenced in Appendix A, Chapter 3 of *Vocabulary Instruction Methods: A Summary Of Vocabulary Instruction Methods* (National Reading Panel, 1999, 3-33 to 3-35). A large number of strategy categories relate to summarization skills because summarizing encompasses several other subskills. Here are the evidence-based strategies in this chapter:

- Summarization
- Cooperative learning
- Listening actively
- Mnemonics
- Prior knowledge
- Question generation
- Vocabulary-comprehension relationship
- Comprehension monitoring
- Graphic organizers
- Mental imagery
- Multiple strategies
- Question answering
- Text structure

When to Teach Summarization Skills

Students in grade five and above generally have metacognitive awareness that allows them to discriminate essential from nonessential information. They are able to integrate skills and generalize information to create an effective summary. Many studies revealed beneficial results when training students in upper elementary and middle school to use specific strategic procedures to identify important information. Procedures used included questioning techniques (having students ask themselves "Who or what is the passage about?" and "What is happening?"); identifying the function of details and how they differ from main ideas; producing restatements of important ideas; and constructing graphic organizers to represent the ideas (Borkowski, Weyhing, & Carr, 1988; Graves, 1988; Jenkins at al., 1987; Malone & Mastropieri, 1992; Weisberg & Balajthy, 1990).

It is important not to delay instruction in summarization skills until students mature in their metacognitive awareness skills. Students benefit from beginning to learn about and identify key points as soon as they start learning about connected text and stories. Instruction at this level needs to be concrete, uses manipulatives, and is integrated with listening, rather than reading, activities. As children progress in

> Concrete and manipulative activities help young students learn basic prerequisites for summarizing.

reading skills and learn about story grammar elements, they can use frames to identify and record the various elements as they read. When students use such techniques, they improve their ability to answer comprehension questions and recall important story information (Carmine & Kinder, 1985; Carraker, 2005; Idol, 1987; Idoll & Croll, 1987; Nolte & Singer, 1985).

Concrete and manipulative activities help young students learn basic prerequisites for summarizing. It is also beneficial to help them simultaneously enhance their skills in mental imagery because visual pictures help the information "hang together." These concrete strategies will help students develop critical prerequisite abilities that will later enable them to summarize more complex text.

Concrete strategies are easier to present with narrative text than with text containing abstract ideas and intricate relationships between ideas and information. Because of this fact and weakly developed metacognitive awareness in younger students, some researchers such as Pressley (1989), suggest that summarization might not be a promising approach for students in fifth grade and below. Their reasoning is that young students find it hard to distinguish important from less important information. This author concurs that younger students may struggle to make these distinctions, but observation also suggests that it is even more critical to begin with basic summary skill development in the early grades, but to do so emphasizing concrete and manipulative strategies.

The Importance of Summarizing

Summarizing is a complex activity that involves paraphrasing and reorganizing information as well as distinguishing main ideas from supporting details. Identifying main ideas and summarizing text passages are skills that are particularly difficult for struggling readers. A contributing component to that difficulty is that many times main ideas are not directly stated and the reader must infer from disconnected facts or ideas. Identifying key ideas and reconstructing the gist of the passage while reading are important skills for improving the comprehension of readers who tend to struggle to distinguish information that is essential from personally relevant details. Here are some benefits of training students in summarization skills:

- Greater awareness of the way text is structured
- Greater awareness of how ideas are related
- Increased attention to text
- Increased effort in understanding the text

General Strategies

Cooperative Learning

Cooperative learning strategies are an excellent format to use to help students develop summarization skills. When students instruct one another or interact while using reading strategies, they consolidate their learning of the strategies, and by engaging in intellectual discussion, they increase their comprehension. This procedure develops independent learning and frees the teacher for other activities. Furthermore, students gain more control over their learning and experience effective social interaction with peers.

Cooperative learning or peer tutoring can be developed in group reading situations where students work together to learn and use reading comprehension strategies as a part of a natural reading program. There is evidence that the skills developed generalize well: cooperative learning produces reliable and replicable near transfer.

Think Aloud

The Think-Aloud strategy (see page 130) provides support necessary for learners to develop more sophisticated interpretations and techniques for summarization skill. As students develop familiarity with the strategies, skills, and processes necessary for summarization, they need less guidance and become increasingly more independent. For example, you might provide guiding questions from the perspective of various stances as the students learn to think more deeply about their reading. As the students begin to ask their own questions, increase the complexity of your guiding questions or remove the guides completely. Here are some sample questions based on the poem "Taught Me Purple" by Evelyn Tooley Hunt ("My mother taught me purple; Although she never wore it . . . My mother reached for beauty; And for its lack she died; Who knew so much of duty; She could not teach me pride." [Hunt, 1992]):

- Why couldn't her mother teach her pride?
- What does the author mean in the line, "who knew so much of duty?"
- Why does the poet use the color purple?

Begin by having the students read aloud in pairs or groups. The reader stops reading whenever a thought, question, or concern occurs to him. The group then discusses that issue. As students become comfortable with the technique, you might use it with any of the summarization strategies in this chapter to effectively model the necessary "how-to" processes.

Reciprocal Teaching

The Reciprocal Teaching technique was originally developed by Palincsar and Brown (1986) and elaborated upon by Marzano, Norford, Paynter, Pickering, and Gaddy (2001).

Reciprocal Teaching helps students better comprehend expository text and practice the skills needed for efficient summarization. The technique involves students in an interactive manner as they enhance their understanding of the text at a deeper level.

"Reciprocal Teaching is an instructional activity that takes place in the form of the dialog between teachers and students regarding segments of the text. The dialog is structured by the use of four strategies, and the teacher and students take turns assuming the role of the teacher in leading the style" (Palincsar, 1991).

A wide variety of student populations benefit from Reciprocal Teaching. Poor decoders use the procedure as a read-along activity, second-language learners use it to practice developing skills, nonreaders learn it as a listening comprehension activity, and normally achieving or above average students profit from strategy instruction because it allows them to read and understand more challenging texts. Also, students with more experience and confidence help others in their group by stimulating deeper thinking and understanding.

The four activities incorporated into the technique can be used in one of the two following sequences. Initially, model each role for students and provide extensive instruction in each strategy. Have your students practice until they develop familiarity with that role before combining the strategies into the total technique.

1. Questioning		1. Summarizing
2. Clarifying	**OR**	2. Questioning
3. Summarizing		3. Clarifying
4. Predicting		4. Predicting

The instructor and students initially take turns leading the dialog about sections of the text. Eventually, the students take all of the roles while working in small groups. Each student in the group takes on one of four roles above, and when more than one student has the same role, they work together. As students increase in their familiarity with each role, they may work in groups of four, with a single student having responsibility for each role. Here are the responsibilities for each role:

Questioning
- The role of the questioner is to pose questions about the text to the group and the group responds. The goal is to identify important information in the passage.
  - ✔ Question generating reinforces the summarizing skill. To generate questions, students first identify what information is significant enough to provide the substance for questioning. They then organize information in question form and test themselves to determine if they can answer their own questions.
  - ✔ Question generating is a flexible strategy because students can be encouraged to generate questions at many levels.

Clarifying
- The clarifier facilitates the group discussion and guides members to look for answers in the text.
- The clarifier clarifies any confusing content in the paragraph and may point out the confusion(s) or ask other students to find them.
  - ✔ Clarifying is a particularly important activity when including students who struggle with comprehension. Such students might believe that the purpose of reading is saying the words correctly; they may not realize when the passage does not make sense.
  - ✔ When students are asked to clarify, their attention is focused on the fact that there may be many reasons why text is difficult to understand, such as new vocabulary, unclear reference words, or unfamiliar/difficult concepts.
  - ✔ As they clarify, students learn to be alert to the effects of obstacles to comprehension and to take the necessary steps to restore meaning.

Summarizing
- The summarizer provides a summary of the text up to that point in the reading and summarizes the main idea in individual paragraphs.
- Other students can add to the summary as they discuss the passage.
  - ✔ Summarizing allows students to identify and integrate the most important information about the passage.
  - ✔ Instruct students to summarize across sentences, paragraphs, or the passage as a whole.
  - ✔ When students first begin the reciprocal teaching procedure, they generally focus on a single sentence or paragraph. As they become more proficient, guide them to integrate at the paragraph in passage level.

Predicting
- The predictor makes predictions about what she thinks will happen next.
- The predictor asks others in her group for predictions about what will happen next in the text. Students hypothesize what the author will discuss next.
  - ✔ Students must activate their relevant background knowledge about the topic to successfully predict what will happen next. Predicting also creates opportunity for the students to link the new knowledge they will encounter in the text with the knowledge they already possess.
  - ✔ Predictions help students focus on a purpose for reading: to confirm or disprove their hypotheses.
  - ✔ The predicting strategy helps students learn about the importance of text structure. As they make predictions, students discover that that headings, subheadings, and questions embedded in the text are valuable for anticipating what might occur next.

Prerequisite Skills

Summarization requires substantial metacognitive awareness. When we summarize, we must identify key concepts and distinguish important from less important information. Inferential skill is also involved because we need to generalize from examples or from repetitions while ignoring irrelevant details. To achieve the goal of efficient summarizing, students need to accomplish some prerequisite skills: retelling a story efficiently, paraphrasing information adequately, and drawing well-organized conclusions.

Retelling
Prerequisite Skills

Retelling is a powerful comprehension strategy that you can also use to determine your students' understanding of a passage. For example, student difficulties in processing the linguistic structure of text might be evident when retelling an informational passage: their retelling is less organized and less informative than their peers (Carlisle, 1999). When retelling, students need to identify, clarify, and organize their thinking as they interpret the meaning of the passage. Research confirms that student retelling results in increased understanding of story structure, oral language development, and reading comprehension. Retelling also emphasizes key components of literary elements and genres.

Here are the key concepts involved in retelling
1. Developing an understanding of story structure, oral language, and reading comprehension
2. Examining key components of literary elements and genres
3. Becoming aware of the developmental and instructional steps that lead to written retelling
4. Learning to scaffold comprehension with oral retelling and story props

➤ *Retelling Activity for Younger Students (K-1)*

The following sequence of steps illustrates the concept of retelling "The Three Little Pigs" with young students:

1. Read the story to the students and discuss the illustrations.

2. Read the story again and have students assist by "huffing and puffing," using hand gestures, and/or using different voice tones.

3. Accordian fold a large, white sheet of construction paper into five sections:
   - Point to the first section and discuss what happened first, point to the second section and discuss what happened next, and repeat with the third and fourth sections.

4. Provide each student with a large piece of paper folded as described in the previous step. Explain to your students that they will each make a book to retell the story. Create your own accordion book as the students make theirs and discuss the colors of straw, sticks, and bricks. You might also discuss what a pig looks like and have students provide suggestions on how to represent other objects.
   - Discuss what happened first and have the students draw a picture to represent that event on the the first section of their accordion book. Repeat by asking what happened second, third, and fourth, and having students draw pictures to represent those sections.

5. The students now have a sequence of four pictures to represent the story as it progresses from its beginning toward its conclusion.
   - Section 1: The mother pig says goodbye to her three children
   - Section 2: The first pig builds its house of straw
   - Section 3: The second pig builds its house of sticks
   - Section 4: The third pig builds its house of bricks

6. Discuss how the story ends. Then have your students draw a wolf in the fifth section of the accordion. On the back side of the accordian, have everyone draw a large picture to illustrate the ending of the story.

7. Have a "Story Retelling Time." Have students move their seats to create an audience. Show your students how you use the accordian sections as prompts to retell the story, part by part. After you have modeled the technique have students take turns using their accordian books to retell the story. Encourage the audience to help when part of the story is forgotten, and make sure everyone applauds all efforts.

8. When the students' accordian books and the class activity are completed, encourage students to take their books home and retell the story for their family
   - This is an excellent activity for English-language learners because the students can retell the story in the language most used at home.

9. Follow up the retelling activity by modeling a summary of the story to introduce the concept of summarization.
   - Explain that a summary explains the most important ideas in a story and it usually contains the main idea and two or three important supporting details that explain what the story is all about.
   - *Example summary:* "The Three Little Pigs" is about three pigs and a wolf. The wolf blows down two of the pigs' houses because he wants to eat them but they escape. He doesn't blow down the brick house because it is too strong. He doesn't get to eat the pigs.

➤ *Retelling Activity for Grades 2-4*

Begin the following activity by presenting a shared reading activity: preview the book, discuss key vocabulary, and encourage students to discuss their favorite parts, either after given sections or after the whole story. Help them activate their background knowledge by asking them about another story or experience that is similar. Elicit any questions your students might have about the story. Follow the shared reading activity with a manipulative activity related to the story, such as making stick puppets, sequence cards, or drawing a picture.

On a subsequent day, reread the story without interruption. Follow the reading with additional discussion and highlight anything new. Students might notice information during the second reading that they missed during the first. On another day, explain the concept of retelling. Cover the words in the story and model story retelling to the students.

1. Say to your students, "Story retelling is telling what you remember by looking at the pictures, not reading the words."

2. Provide the following guidelines for retelling stories
   • Begin the story (*Once upon a time, One day, In the summer*).
   • Tell where the story is happening (*in the woods, at the beach, on a farm*).
   • Name the characters (encourage students to use names instead of pronouns).
   • End the story by telling if the problem was solved.

3. Model retelling for a few pages and then have students take turns retelling the story.

As students become more comfortable with retelling, have them use the same technique with their library books and share their retelling with the other students. A wonderful advantage may surface as students begin to seek out a particular library book because a friend was excited about it.

➤ *Retelling Activity for Grades 4 and Up*

Provide students with a story retelling task and rubric containing key elements to include when they retell the story. Explain the activity by saying, "You are a storyteller and you must retell a folk story that you have heard. You must include all of the main elements of the story and you must deliver your story with expression, rhythm, and appropriate gestures." Make sure your students include characters, setting, problem, and solution in their retelling.

Story Beads
You might have students move each bead from one knot (the solid black circles) to another as they retell that part of the story.

Provide students with a concrete manipulative to help them recall the four elements. A manipulative that works well is a string containing four large, colored beads, as shown on the left. You might write or draw a representation for each element on the beads. As a student remembers and discusses each story element, he moves the corresponding bead. For example, as the student discusses the characters, he moves that bead along the string. When he discusses the setting, he moves the next bead. As he discusses the problem and then the solution, he moves the corresponding beads. Using the beads becomes a hook to help the students recall elements and provides a basic structure of the retelling.

As students increase their skills using the retelling technique, create a rubric that contains criteria for including each element, as well as recommendations for enhancing retelling technique. As you explain elements, point out the new element in the rubric for "delivery." Create a scoring system in which each element is worth a given number of points, as in the example below.

Performance Element	High Quality	Acceptable	Needs Attention	Possible Points	Actual Points
Characters	Your retelling describes the character so your classmates have a good idea of what the characters are like.	Your retelling names the characters but does not tell too much about them.	You do not name characters or your retelling is confusing. Think about who is in the story and how they act.	20	
Setting	Your retelling helps others get a clear picture in their head of when and where the story took place.	Your retelling gives some details about where and when the story took place.	Your retelling needs to describe when and where the story took place so the reader can "picture" it.	20	
Problem	Your retelling describes the problem and how it might be solved.	Your retelling includes part of the problem but is incomplete.	Your retelling does not tell what the problem is in the story.	20	
Solution	Your retelling describes what the characters do to solve the problem.	Your retelling includes some story events that lead to the solution. Some are in the correct order.	Your retelling confuses the order of some major events and leaves some others out.	20	
Delivery	You use good rhythm and gestures. There is expression in your voice as you retell the story. Your voice changes for different characters.	Your rhythm and expression are good most of the time. You use some gestures. Your voice changes for most of the characters.	You may improve your delivery by improving your rhythm and expression as you retell your story; use gestures and change your voice for different characters.	20	

Paraphrasing

Prerequisite Skills

Young children (grade 1 through early grade 2) generally learn how to retell a story; however, they do not summarize it or extract the main idea. When they are able to retell a story efficiently, teach them how to paraphrase the information, which is a critical subskill of summarizing. Here are some sample explanations of paraphrasing :

- Rewording something because you want to clarify it
- Expressing the same message using different words and in a shorter format
- Translating or explaining a message in a shorter and simpler way

Many students find the concept of paraphrasing abstract; therefore, it is essential to make the concept as concrete as possible. The following activity begins with an object in a bag. As the students work to guess the object, they develop "detective skills." The next step is for them to transition these detective skills to words using short, concrete passages.

➤ Detective Activities Using an Object in a Bag

Place a simple object in a bag, such as a baseball cap with a logo of a ship on it. Have students ask questions as they pretend to be detectives to determine the object in the bag:

1. Students ask yes/no questions, such as these:
   - Is it something to play with? *no*
   - Is it something to eat? *no*
   - Is it something to wear? *yes*
     - Is it a shirt? *no*
     - Is it a bracelet? *no*
     - Is it any jewelry? *no*
     - Is it a hat? *yes*
   - Record the true facts about the object: *It is something to wear, it is a hat.*
   - In order to find more details about the hat, you might need to provide guiding questions, such as, "You know it's a hat. Now think about going far away. What does that make you think of that goes with the hat. Think about that as you ask more questions."

2 Students ask additional questions:
   - Do you need to wear it when you go away? *sometimes*
   - Does it have some kind of picture on it? *yes*
   - Is it a picture of some place far away? *no*
   - Is it a picture of an airplane? *no*
   - Is it a picture of a boat? *yes*

Transition to Words

Once students have been successful detectives for several different objects, help them transition into using words to summarize their thoughts. A frame, such as the one on the right, helps identify key components: the subject and a key point (or facts).

- *Subject:* hat with a logo of a boat or ship on it
- *Key points:* something to wear, has a picture, the picture is of a boat
- *Summary Statement:* hat to wear; picture of boat on it
- *Summary Sentence:* This is a hat to wear, and it has a picture of a boat on it.

Summary Statement = Subject + Key Point

Subject _____

Key Points _____
_____
_____

Summary Statement _____
_____

Summary Sentence _____
_____
_____

Next, read a short passage aloud, such as the one below. Begin with a listening task to help students focus on the process without having to worry about accurately reading the words.

> Butterflies are beautiful, flying insects with large, scaly wings. Like all insects, they have six jointed legs, three body parts, a pair of antennae, compound eyes, and an exoskeleton. The three body parts are the head, thorax (chest), and abdomen (tail end).

- *Subject:* butterflies
- *Key points:* insects, flies, large wings, body has three parts
- *Summary Statement:* Butterflies are insects; fly; large wings, body has three parts.
- *Summary Sentence:* Butterflies are flying insects with large wings and have three body parts.

Conclusions

Drawing conclusions is a skill related to making inferences. It is a process of arriving at the ultimate meaning of something: what is important, why it is important, how one event influences another, and how one event or aspect leads to another. When students read, it is not sufficient to merely collect the facts. They must think about what those facts mean to them.

Present the following activities to your students to help them enhance their inferential analysis skills while also teaching them to draw a conclusion based on particular criteria: general sense, examples, antonyms, or contrasts. Begin practicing these skills in a single sentence before moving to a paragraph.

Using General Sense to Draw a Conclusion   *Conclusions*

You might imply the meaning of a word or passage by considering the general sense of the context. Here's an example sentence and some follow-up strategies:

Murderers are usually *incarcerated* for longer periods of time than robbers.

- To consider a conclusion, ask yourself related questions:
  - What usually happens to people found guilty of murder and what usually happens to people found guilty of robbery?
  - What does *incarcerated* mean?
- Interpretation:
  - Murderers are punished for a longer period of time than robbers.
  - *Incarcerated* means that the person is locked up in jail or prison.
- Conclusion:
  - Murdering is much more serious than robbery.

Using Examples to Draw a Conclusion   *Conclusions*

You might imply the meaning of the word or passage by considering the examples given. Here's an example sentence and some follow-up strategies:

Those who enjoy belonging to clubs, going to parties, and inviting friends to their homes often are *gregarious*.

- To consider a conclusion, ask yourself a related question:
  - What word or words describe people who belong to clubs, go to parties a lot, and often invite friends over to their homes for dinner?
- Interpretation:
  - *Gregarious* people like to be with other people and do things together.
- Conclusion:
  - *Gregarious* people are social and enjoy the company of others.

Using Antonyms to Draw a Conclusion
Conclusions

You might imply the meaning of the word or passage by considering antonyms presented in the sentence or passage. Antonyms are words that have opposite meanings, such as *happy/sad* or *big/little*. This is a particularly useful strategy when two parts of the passage are connected with a word such as *but* or *however*. Here's an example sentence and some follow-up strategies:

Ben is *fearless*, but his brother Jim is *timorous*.

- To consider a conclusion, ask yourself a related question:
  - If Ben is fearless and Jim is very different from Ben with regard to fear, then what word describes Jim?
- Interpretation:
  - *Fearless* means "not having fear," so Ben is *brave*. Jim is probably fearful, timid, or afraid.
- Conclusion:
  - The two brothers differ in their bravery: one is very brave and the other is fearful.

Using Contrasts to Draw a Conclusion
Conclusions

You might imply the meaning of the word or passage by considering any contrasts presented. Again, this strategy is useful when two parts of the passage are connected with a word such as *but* or *however*. Here's an example sentence and some follow-up strategies:

Dad gave *credence* to my story, but Mom's reaction was total disbelief.

- To consider a conclusion, ask yourself a related question:
  - If Mom's reaction was disbelief and Dad's reaction was very different from Mom's, what was Dad's reaction?
- Interpretation:
  - Mom did not believe the incident. If Dad had a different reaction, he believed the incident. *Credence* means "belief."
- Conclusion:
  - The two parents differed substantially in their reaction: Dad believed the story, but Mom did not.

Using a Frame to Define a Word
Conclusions

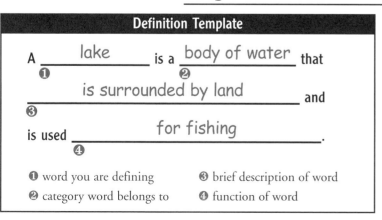

Definition Template

A ___lake___ is a ___body of water___ that
① ②
___is surrounded by land___ and
③
is used ___for fishing___.
④

❶ word you are defining   ❸ brief description of word
❷ category word belongs to   ❹ function of word

Creating a definition for a word often takes the form of drawing a conclusion. The student needs to accumulate the basic facts and integrate them into a cohesive whole. A frame provides students with a template and gives them a format or structure to use. The template, such as the one the left, works well with nouns. Including graphics such as clip art or using software such as Kidspiration® or Inspiration® to create the frame helps make the activity more concrete for students.

Summarizing: Narrative Text

The 5 W's

Activities that lead to development of summarizing with narrative text include the previously discussed frame for key point (page 157), the preliminary conclusion activities (pages 158-159), and the 5 W's activity earlier explained as a listening task (Chapter 5, pages 88-89). A conclusion is basically the answer to the "Why?" question: students need to identify why the most important event took place.

When working with the Listening 5 W's activity, students initially placed five cards vertically that each correspond to a Wh- question on the left side of their working area in this order: Who?, What?, When?, Where?, and Why? The same procedure is used when performing the activity with a reading passage. As students read, or after they complete a reading the passage, they answer each question. As they answer each question, they moving the corresponding card to the opposite side of the work area. The kinesthetic movement reinforces their focus on that particular element. Use the 5 W's to summarize text in the same way but arrange the cards in three sections, in this order: 1. Who?, 2. When?, Where?, and 3. What? Why?

Students attempt each group of questions at a time rather than a single question. The cards provide a framework for developing a succinct summary that contains three distinct sections. An example frame can be found on page A-21 of the Appendix on the CD.

Frames

A frame is a concrete way to help your students summarize using the important components of narrative. You will find guidelines for developing summarizing frames on page A-43 of the Appendix of the CD. The main goal is to emphasize the critical importance of being active when reading for these components and to encourage students to use an active strategy.

You might provide older students who efficiently use the 5 W's strategy in their summarizing with more advanced cues. Give them with a list of the components of narrative text as well as some starting prompts and important criteria (examples are below).

Components	Prompts	Important Criteria for Good Summaries
• Character	• The story takes place . . .	• Key people and/or items
• Setting	• First, next, then, finally . . .	• Key places
• Problem	• The main point was . . .	• Key words and synonyms
• Event	• A problem occurs when . . .	• Key ideas and concepts
• Resolution	• This part was about . . .	
	• The most important ideas are . . .	
	• Overall, this was about . . .	

Narrative Summaries with Longer Stories

Remind students of the basic criteria for narrative summaries:
- Narrative text tells a story.
- A summary is a brief description.
- The narrative summary tells what happened in the story in your own words.

Guide students through a process of developing questions that leads to a summary format:
1. Tell students to perform these activities as they read:
   - Make notes (or draw picture cues) of things you felt were important.
   - Brainstorm questions that would help you know what the book is about.

2. After students finish reading, ask if they asked themselves questions about the characters. Guide them to ask questions, such as these:
   - Who are the main characters? What did they do? Where did they go? Which of those questions would be best to ask first?

3. Explain the concept of a story's setting and guide students to ask themselves these questions:
   - Ask yourself, "What is the setting of the story?" Write that question and leave room for an answer. (pause) The setting is where the story takes place.
   - Another part of the setting is the time period in which the story happens. Ask yourself, "When did the action take place?" Write that question and leave room for an answer.
   - Sometimes authors do not tell us directly about the setting or time period, and we have to look for clues to help us: either text clues (words used in the story) or visual clues (pictures from the story).

4. Focus on the action in a story and characters' reactions:
   - The story begins to get interesting with the action. Ask yourself, "What started the action in the story?" Following the action helps us learn about the story's plot.
   - How characters react to the action usually involves emotions. Emotions tell us how someone or something feels. We can usually tell how someone feels in a variety of ways:
     - Have students brainstorm a brief list (3-4 items) of ways that they have expressed their emotions in different situations. Afterwards, discuss their lists and ask if they included any of these items: words, facial expressions, giving gifts, turning away, arguing, slamming a door (or other specific action), crying, laughing, etc.
     - Have students ask themselves, "How did the characters in the story express their feelings?" (Have students refer to the list they made in the previous step for cues.)
   - Characters often try to accomplish something in a story or work toward a goal. Ask yourself, "How did the characters decide to accomplish the goal(s)?" (Have students write the question and an answer.)

5. Focusing on the ending.
   - Think about the ending of the story. Ask yourself, "What do we always want to know when we are reading a book?" (Have students record their answers.)
   - One thing we always want to know is how the book ends and whether the action was resolved. Ask yourself, "What were the consequences of what happened in the story's action?" and "Are the consequences the ending or what happened because of the goals the characters set?"

After the steps are complete, have the students use their answers to write a summary of the story. Or, you might have students draw pictures for each story element and use those as cues to present a verbal summary. Model the difference between retelling the whole story and stating a summary.

Summarizing: Expository Text

Activities that lead to development of this skill include the frame for key point (page 157) and the preliminary conclusion activities (pages 158-159). While the format of expository texts may vary, the basic questions students need to answer include identifying the subject, information provided about the subject, the main idea, and supporting details. Additional criteria will relate more specifically to the format of the expository text, such as sequential information or cause/effect issues. To draw a conclusion about the topic, students need to identify the facts that support the key point or main idea and write a summary statement (see the Key Point format on page 157).

After completion of the summary statement, students create a conclusion or summary sentence and ask themselves questions such as these:

- Does my conclusion tie in smoothly with the body of the passage?
- Does my conclusion summarize the main points?
- Does my conclusion remind me of the basic theme of the passage?

Here are some additional questions students need to ask when writing a summary:

- Is my ending striking enough to leave a strong impression?
- Does my ending maintain a tone consistent with the rest of the passage?

Remind students about the important criteria for good summaries as listed above, such as key people or items, key places, key words, and key concepts.

Key Elements

Keene and Zimmerman (1997, pp. 184-185) identify some key ideas related to how proficient readers synthesize information during and after reading. These concepts apply directly to the process of efficient summarization and represent a goal for all students.

- Proficient readers maintain a cognitive synthesis as they read. They monitor the overall meaning, important concepts, and themes in the text as they read and are aware of the way text elements work together to create overall meaning and theme.
- Proficient readers are aware of text elements and patterns as they read fiction and nonfiction. They understand that this awareness helps them predict and understand the overall meanings or themes.
- As they read, proficient readers attend more directly to character, setting, conflict, sequence of events, resolution, and theme in fiction, and to text patterns such as description, chronological, cause and effect, comparison/contrast, and problem/solution in nonfiction.
- Proficient readers actively revise their cognitive syntheses as they read. New information is assimilated into the reader's evolving ideas about the text.
- Proficient readers are able to express — through a variety of means — a synthesis of what they have read. The synthesis includes ideas and themes relevant to the overall meaning from the text and is cogently presented.
- Proficient readers purposefully use synthesis to better understand what they have read. Syntheses are frequently an amalgam of all comprehension strategies used by proficient readers.

Specific Summarizing Strategies

Quick Writes

Students can use this simple activity with either expository or narrative text. The goal is for them to capture ideas quickly and make them available for further discussion. Rather than focusing on taking specific notes about all the details, students quickly write their thoughts, questions, and concerns as they read. Their goal is to collect ideas. Depending upon the material, you might have students draw the mental image they are developing as they read. As a scaffold, create study guides to help structure the Quick Write task.

After reading a passage, have students use their Quick Writes for discussion with their peers or as a guide in writing a summary statement.

Stretch to Sketch

Use the Stretch to Sketch strategy (Harste, Burke, & Woodward, 1984) with almost any narrative or expository text. This strategy helps students relate the passages they read to their background experiences. Rather than using words to communicate, students use drawings. Sometimes, drawing their interpretations helps students generate new insights or meanings, or they discover something new regarding their feelings about the text or the relationships among the characters. Stretch to Sketch is especially useful with readers who tend to focus on isolated words, sentences, or pages instead of the overall meaning and structure of the text.

Have your students follow these steps:

1. Read the selected passage or text and then put the text away.

2. Sketch your ideas about the text. Here are some ideas:
   - What the text is about
   - What the text means to you personally
   - The picture you had in you head while reading
   - A major concept learn from the text

3. Write a short explanation of your sketch. You might include these types of statements:
   - Insights into the author's language that sparked certain images
   - Parts of the text that were most clear
   - An especially important or exciting event

4. Share your sketches and explanations in small groups.

5. Your group chooses one sketch to share with the whole class.

If you are using content material, it might be useful to provide students with copies of the passage in a text-only format (eliminating pictures, drawings, and graphs). Having the text often encourages careful rereading, and the students can then compare their sketches with the material originally paired with the content. In such situations, discuss the issue of needing to read charts and diagrams with content materials, and how the charts and diagrams fit with the running text.

Frames

Using frames provides a very powerful summarizing strategy that enhances students' learning and understanding. The frame provides a series of questions that students use to help them develop an accurate summary of the text. Pages A-43-44 of the Appendix on the CD contain a detailed table that lists important elements and example questions for various types of reading passages.

Other Graphic Organizers

The CD contains other graphic organizers that are particularly useful for summarization tasks, such as the Summary Organizer (page A-31) and the Sum It Up Organizer (page A-33). Others are on pages A-25, A-26, A-28, A-29, and A-32.

Card Pyramids for Expository Summaries

Summarization requires students to think about what they have read and to identify the most important information. Using index cards to build a Card Pyramid is a great way to concretely show your students how to identify parts of a story. The first thing students must do is to identify the subject of the passage (what it is about). Sometimes the subject is a word that is repeated frequently; other times the subject is the title or topic sentence. Knowing the subject will help your students identify the main idea, which is the subject plus what the passage says about the subject; the supporting ideas, and the details.

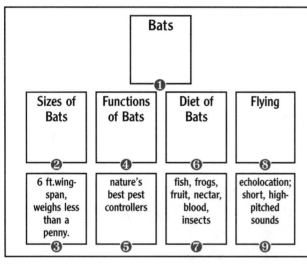

Bats

Bats are the most endangered land mammal in North America. They are the only mammal that can fly, and they are considered nature's best pest controllers. The largest bat has a wingspan of almost six feet. The smallest bat weighs less than a penny.

Some bats eat fish, frogs, fruit, nectar, and blood. Other bats eat insects. The insect-eating bats use echolocation to find and catch their food. Echolocation is a type of sensory perception that helps the bat detect obstacles and communicate with others. The bat sends out a series of short, high-pitched sounds that travel away from it and bounce off of objects and surfaces in its path. The echo returns to the bat, which is how the bat determines what is in its path.

You will need several index cards for this activity. Have your students follow these directions to build a Card Pyramid:

1. Write the subject on a card and place it at the top of your work surface.

2. Write each supporting idea on a separate card and place them in a row below the subject. Place a blank card below each.

3. Arrange your cards (for subject and supporting ideas) as shown in the example above. The numbers correspond to the sequence of the story. Have your students number their cards and lay them out as shown in the diagram.

4. As you read (or reread) the passage, identify details for each of the supporting ideas and write the details for the supporting idea on the appropriate card place them in the bottom row.

Have students use the cards from the Card Pyramid activity to structure an oral or written summary. Make sure students number the cards as shown above and then place them in a pile in the correct numerical order. Your students then take turns using their cards, in order, as cues to orally summarize the passage. When writing a written summary, help students understand that a summary is brief and that as they write, they must make decisions about what is important enough to include in a written summary and what can be left out. The cards from the pyramid will help them frame their thoughts.

Logographs
Specific Summarizing Strategies

This strategy works well with expository text that contains a large number of concepts. It involves presenting concept diagrams, or logographs, using simple illustrations or clip art that your students use as stimuli for summary statements.

Students use each logograph as a cue for an important concept and write a summary statement about that idea. By using their own words to explain the concept, they are interacting with the concepts and hooking into the material. A logograph can be a single illustration or a grouping of pictures to represent a more complex concept. For example, imagine students are studying about the Renaissance. Present a series of five illustrations: a portrait of Henry VIII, a book with "Poetry" on the cover, a sailing ship, a music note, and six pictures of brides. A student summary might be, "Henry VIII wrote poetry, built up the English Navy, wrote music, and had six wives."

Logographs are an effective way for students to take notes while reading, especially when dealing with difficult text. After reading the selection, the students use the logographs and their summary statements to summarize the complete passage, either orally or in writing.

Beach Ball Summary Review
Specific Summarizing Strategies

Writing questions about text directly on a beach ball is a fun way for students to review the basic elements of a passage or text prior to creating a summary. You might also use a beach or Koosh ball to review content at the end of a lesson or unit. Here are three ways to use this strategy (you can use any type of ball for options 2 and 3):

1. Write a question about the text in each section of a beach ball using permanent marker. Then spray the ball with hair spray (to prevent smudging). Toss the ball to a student. The student who receives the ball answers the question that is facing him. Sample questions:
   - What is the title and who was the author?
   - What is the setting?
   - How did it end?
   - Who are the main characters?
   - What happened in the story?
   - What was your favorite part?

2. Toss a plain beach ball or Koosh ball to a student and have her complete one of these statements about the passage:
   - My favorite part was _____.
   - The main characters were _____.
   - In the middle, _____.
   - The setting was _____.
   - In the beginning, _____.
   - At the end, _____.

3. Toss a beach or Koosh ball to a student and ask him a specific question based on the passage:
   - Who is the author?
   - What is the main idea of this article?
   - What is a good title for the selection?
   - What do we know about the author?
   - Name a supporting detail.
   - What did you learn?

Reflections

1. Explain three important reasons to teach summarizing skills to your students.

   ❶ _____

   _____

   _____

   ❷ _____

   _____

   _____

   ❸ _____

   _____

   _____

2. Select one of the following techniques and develop a sequence of specific steps/activities to use with a given aspect of your curriculum with your students.

   - Reciprocal Teaching
   - Paraphrasing
   - Stretch to Sketch
   - Retelling
   - The 5 W's

   _____

   _____

   _____

   _____

   _____

   _____

   _____

   _____

CHAPTER 9

TRANSFER AND METACOGNITION

> Being strategic is much more than knowing the individual strategies. When faced with a reading comprehension problem, a good strategy user will coordinate strategies and shift strategies as it is appropriate to do so. They will constantly alter, adjust, modify, and test until they construct meaning and the problem is solved" (National Reading Panel, 1999, p. 4-47).

Students must actively read and attend to the processes they use to become skilled. Good readers automatically use a variety of reading strategies. Poor readers do not. To help students become automatic strategy users, we need to increase their metacognitive knowledge and awareness. As teachers and therapists, we are competent in applying a series of "Wh-" questions to our instruction: we know when to apply what strategy and with which particular students. But our approaches do not always guarantee that our students progress to becoming independent, integrated strategic readers. To help them do so requires instructional distinctions that go well beyond the individual techniques and strategies illustrated throughout this book. We need to ensure that our students acquire and use strategies in a way that demonstrates that they understand that strategies are plans for constructing meaning rather then rote procedures for students to follow.

Our students need to be aware of and able to integrate metacognitive skills in a way that allows them to transfer the strategies we teach them into their independent reading activities. We can help them make that transfer by remaining constantly aware of the complexity involved in teaching students to be strategic. We must make creative adaptations to deal with that complexity.

Traditionally, we plan, teach, test, and then grade our students. While that procedure may be efficient for tasks that require learning of facts, it is not an efficient way to teach strategies, especially when we want students to flexibly use those strategies. A more efficient procedure for teaching processes such as strategy flexibility, is illustrated in the flowchart. This procedure involves constant observation, checking, re-analysis, and monitoring.

It is important to teach strategies, but teaching alone is not sufficient. We must integrate metacognitive awareness and metacognitive skills into all instruction so that students transfer and generalize what we teach and become active, independent readers. Multiple strategy instruction is the best way to increase your students' reading comprehension skills.

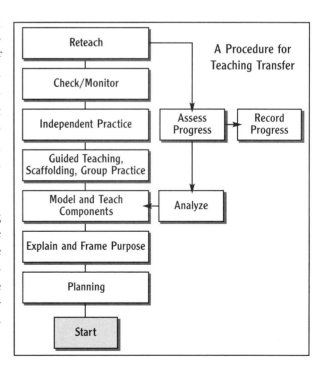

Evidence Base

There is a great deal of evidence supporting the efficacy of integrating metacognitive awareness and skills into strategy teaching. The NRP states, "Multiple strategy instruction represents an evolution in the field from the study of individual strategies to their flexible and multiple use. This method has considerable scientific support for its effectiveness as a treatment, and it is the most promising for use in classroom instruction" (National Reading Panel, 1999, p. 4-46). The evidence supports the use of combinations of reading strategies in natural learning situations. "These findings build on empirical validation of strategies alone and attest to their use in the classroom contexts" (p. 4-46). "Methods which utilize teacher modeling and scaffolding, such as reciprocal teaching, have demonstrated substantial transfer in independent student use" (Rosenshine & Meister, 1996).

> The best way to pursue meaning is through conscious, controlled use of strategies.

A common result of students becoming more flexible in using multiple strategies is that they more effectively comprehend what they read. As their understanding increases, they are motivated to continue to read and as a consequence, tend to read more. More reading yields a greater amount of practice, which continues to build skills. These motivational and reading practice effects are important to the overall success of metacognitive training and multiple strategy instruction. Furthermore, "multiple strategy instruction that is flexible as to which strategies are used and when they are taught over the course of the reading session provide a natural basis on which teachers and readers can interact over texts" (National Reading Panel, 1999, p. 4-46).

Defining Metacognition

Metacognition is having knowledge (cognition) and having understanding, control over, and appropriate use of the knowledge. It involves conscious awareness and conscious control of one's learning. Metacognition increases active involvement because it gives students more control over and use of the information. It is essential for transfer of skills.

Knowledge proceeds control: our students must first become aware of the structures of text, the components of the task, and their own characteristics as learners. Then they will be able to strategically control the learning process to optimize the influence of these factors (Ambruster, 1983).

Proficient readers must be metacognitive: they must be aware of their own comprehension. Sometimes comprehension and strategy use is automatic, but sometimes this is purposeful. With this purposeful awareness, students are then able to begin to use strategies relevant to the reading task as they determine meaning and importance, ask questions, infer concepts, and integrate background knowledge with the text. When we automatically monitor our comprehension and use strategies without overt awareness of doing so, our processes are cognitive but may not necessarily be metacognitive. Our strategies become metacognitive when we monitor and control the strategies as we consciously think about which ones might help us best in the particular reading task.

Metacognition can be defined as "thinking about thinking." Good readers use metacognitive strategies to think about and have control over their reading. Before reading, they might clarify their purpose for reading and preview the text. During reading, they might monitor their understanding, adjust their reading speed to fit the difficulty of the text, and "fix up" any comprehension problems they have. After reading, they check their understanding of what they read (Armbruster, Lehr, & Osborn, 2003, p. 49).

Comprehension strategies can be internal strategies that involve how a student thinks about the task or process, or they can be more concrete and comprise activities a student does on paper. A student who has metacognitive awareness during the reading task will make conscious choices of which strategy or strategies best fit a particular part of the task. The student will also be flexible in using strategies and switch strategies as the need arises. Here are examples of some internal/thinking and concrete/paper strategies.

Examples of strategies "in your head"	Examples of strategies "on paper"
Visualizing	Taking notes
Making predictions	Using a highlighter
Generating questions	Drawing graphs
Identifying main ideas and details	Drawing pictures
Recognizing sequence	Underlining ideas in the text
Using and relating to background knowledge and personal experiences	Creating a chart to illustrate comparisons or relationships
Comparing and contrasting	Making diagrams or other visual organizers
Identifying cause and effect	Creating visual organizers
Summarizing	Brainstorming ideas about the text
Drawing conclusions	Making predictions to be verified after reading
Rereading	

The process of metacognitive awareness has two primary components: knowledge and self-regulation (Carlisle, 2002, p. 62). To help increase students' understanding of the components, use the information below to compare and contrast the characteristics appropriate for your students' age and skill level.

Two Primary Components of Metacognitive Awareness	
Knowledge	**Self-regulation**
1. Knowledge of potential useful strategies 2. Understanding when and why to apply potential useful strategies 3. Recognition of similarities between the current task and situations when a given strategy was helpful in the past 4. Awareness of our own skills and limitations 5. Appreciation of the demands of the task 6. Understanding the relationship between strategy use and comprehension efficiency 7. Awareness that reading is a complex activity that may require many distinct, but related, strategies to accomplish efficiency	1. Monitoring ourselves during the reading process 2. Controlling our actions during the process of reading 3. Maintaining awareness of how well we are or are not understanding as we read 4. Taking appropriate steps to correct any problems and comprehension 5. Altering our strategies in response to various factors in the task • Factors: text difficulty, reduced familiarity with topic, lapses in concentration, gaps in memory • Alterations: reread, slow down, pay closer attention, use context, take a break

One way to help students understand and keep track of learned strategies is to provide a chart like the one below (Keene & Zimmerman, 1997) that identifies metacognitive strategies used by proficient readers. You might show your students the whole table and highlight strategies already familiar to them. Another option is to present only those strategies familiar to the students and add additional strategies to the chart as the students learn them.

Metacognitive Strategies of Proficient Readers		
Strategy	Why the strategy is useful	I demonstrate use of the strategy by asking or telling myself . . .
Activating prior knowledge	• Helps recall • Establishes connections	That reminds me of . . . It made me think of . . . I read another book where . . . This is different from . . .
Determining the most important ideas	• Helps focus • Identifies the main issue(s)	The most important ideas are . . . So far, I have learned that . . . Based on my knowledge of . . .
Asking myself questions and asking question of the authors and the text as I read	• Helps clarify • Enables monitoring of understanding • Increases level of active involvement with the text	I wonder . . . I was confused when . . . Why . . .
Creating visual, auditory, or other sensory connections	• Helps deepen understanding • Helps clarify connections among ideas	I visualized . . . I could see (hear taste, etc.) . . . I could picture . . .
Drawing inferences	• Helps make critical judgments • Helps make unique interpretations • Helps identify interaction among components	I'm guessing that . . . I predict . . . It would be better if . . . I really liked how . . . If I were the main character . . . What I didn't like was . . .
Using fix-up strategies when comprehension breaks down	• Aids in independent reading	I tried these fix-up strategies . . . I reread that part because . . . A part I had trouble with was . . .
Retelling or synthesizing	• Helps to understand more clearly • Helps recall the components	Now that I understand that . . . I have learned that . . . This gives me an idea . . .

In 1992, Pearson et al., proposed that the reading comprehension curriculum for grades K-12 be composed of the 6 most valuable cognitive strategies that will enable students to activate greater metacognitive awareness while reading. These proposed elements remain as critical for today's students:

1. Students activate relevant, prior knowledge before, during, and after reading text.

2. Students determine the most important ideas and themes in a text and ask questions of themselves, the authors, and the text as they read, using these questions to clarify and focus their reading.

3. Students create visual and other sensory images from text during and after reading.

4. Students draw inferences from the text. Drawing inferences includes using prior knowledge and textual information to draw conclusions, make critical judgments, and form unique interpretations. Inferences can occur in the form of conclusions, predictions, or new ideas.

5. Students retell and synthesize what they have read, with the goal of greater understanding. This understanding involves attending to the most important information and to the clarity of the synthesis itself.

6. Students use a variety of fix-up strategies to repair comprehension when it breaks down.

The Importance of Attributions

Teaching students how to use strategies is a fairly obvious aspect leading to metacognition. However, there are other aspects that are less obvious and these can, and often do, interfere with how well a student develops flexible and automatic use of the strategies. Many students, especially learning disabled students, make attributions to themselves that tend to be dysfunctional. They might say, "I'm stupid," "I can't do this," or "This is way too hard." These kinds of attributions can defeat what otherwise might be effective comprehension instruction. Consequently, our teaching of comprehension must involve helping all students make more positive, functional attributions, which will lead to more efficient and successful transfer (Deschler & Schumaker, 1988; Lovett, 2000; Lovett, 2005).

Lovett (2000) states that "executive processing and self-regulatory strategies are important in the context of understanding children's transfer and generalization failures during reading acquisition and reading remediation. Strategy acquisition, application, and self-monitoring are critical to any learning that will extend beyond what is specifically taught." In her PHAST (Phonological and Strategy Training) studies, Lovett combined direct and dialog-based instructional methods. She states, "the importance of strategy instruction and the promotion of a flexible approach to word identification and text reading challenges cannot be overemphasized in our approach to remediating developmental reading problems at every level of severity" (p. 360).

Connections

One valuable strategy is to recognize the commonality between metacognition and mind-body practices. Activities involving conscious breathing and stretching, quiet inward focus, concentration, or conscious habits of thinking about our thinking processes, all require that we control our own minds and brains. Our students need to understand that they have control over the most important and complex device they will ever encounter: their own minds and brains (Geyer, 2005).

Our central nervous system is adaptable and positively affected by mindful breathing, stretching, and moving, as well as by adapting mental habits of mindful perception and metacognitive reflection (Geyer, 2005).

Ask your students to slow down, take perspective of the situation, and attend inwardly. As they learn to focus, reflect, and respond with flexible awareness, they will enhance their overall concentration and efficiency. Maintaining this state of focus is a skill that will assist your students in dealing with the demands of a challenging and changing world.

Another useful approach is to consider the factors that contribute to motivation, which simultaneously relates to our brain's learning efficiency. As you can see in the graphic below, there are six main factors contributing to motivation for highest brain efficiency (Fitzgerald, 2005).

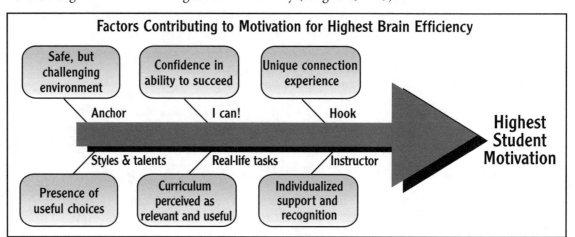

These factors help anchor your students' styles and talents with positive affirmations as they deal with real-life tasks and make connections to their own background experiences. Simultaneously, the instructor provides feedback and recognition. All of these factors form a synergy that increases the likelihood for high student motivation and openness to metacognitive flexibility.

Self-Dialog

Self-talk is a powerful method to help students recall a series of steps and combine them with positive attributions. One example is to coordinate four steps into a "game plan" for students to use. This plan integrates metacognition with positive attributions using these four steps: Choose, Use, Check, and Score or Rechoose (Lovett, 2005, p. 86).

1. **Choose:** My game plan is to first use _____ (*strategy*) and then _____ (*strategy*).

2. **Use:** I am doing _____ (*strategy*) and _____ (*strategy*).

3. **Check:** I am stopping and thinking about whether I'm using my strategies properly. Is it working? If yes, I will keep on going.

4. **Score or Rechoose:**

   a. If successful, I tell myself, "I scored! I used _____ (*strategy*) and _____ (*strategy*) to do _____ (*specific reading task*) and the strategies worked.

   b. If the strategy was not successful, I will begin again at step 1 and choose another strategy to try.

> **S**tructured self-talk provides a vehicle for effective strategy application in a way that a student can internalize for continued self-direction.

The PHAST studies (Lovett, 2005) depend on structured dialog to guide students and to facilitate both successful application of the strategy and future independent execution of it. Following are two sample dialogs for using the rhyming strategy to decode a word. Each concludes with a self-congratulatory statement: a very deliberate aspect designed to retrain your students' attributions and help them appreciate that success depends on whether a particular strategy was appropriate to the task. This type of dialog provides a vehicle for effective strategy application in a way that a student can internalize for continued self-direction.

- **Dialog 1: New Word —** *train*

"I don't know this word but I will use the rhyming strategy to help me figure it out. The spelling pattern is *a-i-n*. The key word with that spelling pattern is *rain*. So, if I know *rain*, I know *train*. I did it. I figured out this word!"

- **Dialog 2: New Word —** *thunderstruck*

"First, I'll mark the vowels and then look for spelling patterns I know. I will underline *u-n*, *e-r*, and *u-c-k*. I'll use the keywords *fun*, *her*, and *luck* to help me read this word. So if I know *fun*, this is *thun*. If I know *her*, this is *der*. If I know *luck*, this is *struck*. Now I blend the parts together — *thun der struck . . . thunderstruck*. I used rhyming and it worked!"

As in the following sample dialog, Lovett's technique can be applied to comprehension strategies to enable students to internalize continued self-direction and positive attribution.

- **Dialog 3: Reading Comprehension**

Passage: A scallop is a bivalve because it has two shells hinged at the base. The marine snail is a univalve. It has only one shell. Bivalves and univalves move by gliding, digging, or swimming with the aid of their strong, muscular feet.

New Words: *univalve* and *bivalve*

Choose:	"I've never seen these words before. They're big. I'll look for word parts and see if any of those word parts are familiar.
Use:	"Univalve has two word parts: *uni-* and *valve*. Each of these parts is familiar. Bivalve also has two word parts and both seem familiar: *bi* and *valve*.
Check:	"This was the right strategy to choose. I know *valve* because I have valves on my trumpet. The valves control the flow of air. Maybe a valve can also control the flow of the water. And, I remember the unicycle at the circus: it was like a bicycle with only one wheel. A bicycle has two wheels. So I guess *uni-* means "one" and *bi-* means "two."
Score or Re-choose:	I scored! I looked at the word parts and realized that they were familiar. It was just that when the parts were together that the words looked so big. Now I know I do understand those words: *univalve* means "having one valve" and *bivalve* means "having two valves." When I reread the passage, I realize that the scallop has two valves because it has two shells and that the marine snail has only one valve and only one shell. Yes! I understand this passage.

Inconsistencies Challenge

Challenge your students to find an inconsistent detail or misplaced phrase in each of several brief paragraphs. This type of challenge has two primary benefits:
- It discourages students from merely reading the words and seeking the concrete meaning of a text.
- It encourages students to read more carefully and to make connections with the text and its meaning.

Here are some sample passages for younger students that contain inconsistencies from the fable of "The Lion and the Mouse":

- **Passage 1**
  Once when the lion was asleep, a little mouse began running up and down over his body. This soon woke up the lion and he placed his big paw on top of the little mouse. Little mouse was frightened. "Pardon me, O King. Forgive me this time!" cried the little mouse. "If you forgive me this time, I shall never forget it. Who knows, but I may be able to do you a favor one of these days." The lion was very tickled at the idea of a mouse being able to help him. He saw an elephant at the zoo, lifted up his paw, and let the little mouse go.

  Inconsistent phrase: "He saw an elephant at the zoo"

- **Passage 2**
  Sometime later, some hunters trapped the Lion in a hidden trap. They wanted to take him alive to the King so they tied him to a tree while they went searching for a wagon to carry him. The ropes were strong and very tight. The lion roared and roared and ate some grass. The mouse recognized the Lion's roar and came to gnaw the rope with his teeth. As he set the big lion free, he told him, "Wasn't I right? Little friends can prove to be great friends."

  Inconsistent phrase: "ate some grass" because the lion was tied up tightly

- **Passage 3**
  Later, some hunters trapped the lion in a hidden trap. They wanted to take him alive to the King and so they tied him to a tree while they went searching for a motorcycle to use to carry him to the castle. The ropes were strong and very tight. The lion roared and roared. The mouse recognized the lion's roar and came to gnaw the rope with his teeth. As he set the big lion free, he told him, "Wasn't I right? Little friends can prove to be great friends."

  Inconsistent phrase: "a motorcycle to use to carry him to the castle"

For Older Students

This activity differs from the one based on the previous passage, because you do not inform the students in advance that there will be an inconsistent phrase within the passage. Furthermore, the inconsistency is more subtle and may not be recognized by all students. Following the passage are six steps to use with students in guiding them to be more critical readers

- **Passage 4**
  Thomas Alva Edison was one of the greatest inventors of the 19th century. He is most famous for inventing the light bulb in 1879. He also developed the world's first electric light-powered station in 1882.

  He was born in the village of Milan, Ohio, on February 11, 1847. His family later moved to Port Huron, Michigan. He went to school for only three months when he was seven. It is warm in the summer. After that, his mother taught him at home. Thomas loved to read. At 12 years old, he became a train-boy, selling magazines and candy on the Grand Trunk Railroad. He spent all his money on books and equipment for his experiments.

At the age of 15, Edison became manager of the telegraph office. His first invention helped improve the telegraph, an early method for sending messages over electric wires. At 21, Edison produced his first major invention, a stock ticker for printing stock-exchange quotes. He was paid $40,000 for this invention. He took this money and opened a manufacturing shop and a small laboratory in Newark, New Jersey. Later, he gave up manufacturing and moved his laboratory to Menlo Park, New Jersey. At this laboratory, he directed other inventors.

During the rest of his life, Edison and his laboratory invented the phonograph, film for the movie industry, and the alkaline battery. By the time he died at West Orange, New Jersey, on October 18, 1931, he had created over 1,000 inventions.

Inconsistent phrase: "It is warm in the summer."

Step	Procedure	Strategy
	Finding an Inconsistent Phrase	
Step 1	• Introduce the topic by talking about inventors and inventions. • Record student responses for the group to see. • Guide the discussion to Thomas Edison. • Encourage students to tell you what they know about Edison.	Frame/hook Activate background knowledge
Step 2	• Tell students you want them to read a passage about Thomas Edison. • Explain that the purpose for reading is to learn additional information about Edison. • Have students read only the first two paragraphs. *Options:* group reading, passage on overhead, silent reading	Establish purpose Read first 2 paragraphs
Step 3	• Elicit your students' response to the purpose: to gather additional information about Thomas Edison. • Ask, "What additional information did you gather from the reading?" • Ask, "What reactions do you have about what you read?" • If someone comments on the inconsistent element in the second paragraph ("It is warm in summer"), discuss why it did not fit. Ask these questions: 　■ How did you detect the inconsistency? 　■ What did you do when you discovered it? 　■ Compliment the students who discovered the inconsistency. • If no one recognizes the inconsistency, ask increasingly direct questions: 　■ Was this passage easy or hard to read? 　■ Did you understand everything you read? 　■ Was there anything that didn't make sense? 　■ Did all of the information fit?	Stimulate reactions Encourage discussion Guided questions
Step 4	• Ask, "What is the purpose for reading the rest of the text?" • In addition to learning additional information about Edison, guide students to identify the purpose of trying to find any other information that doesn't fit. • Have students read the remaining two paragraphs.	Re-establish purpose for reading
Step 5	• After reading, ask students if they detected any other inconsistencies. (There are none.) • Resolve any differences of opinion by revisiting the text. • Ask, "What two purposes did you have for reading this passage?" (to get information about Edison and to find an inconsistency)	Discuss text
Step 6	• Discuss whether or not students read the second two paragraphs in a way that was different from how they read the first two paragraphs. • Point out that good readers always think about whether the text is making sense while they are reading.	Integration of procedures

Effective Strategy Instruction

Effective strategy instruction, especially for reading comprehension, is explicit and direct. After you have framed the activity, explain why your students should use the strategy. Tell your students why the strategy helps them comprehend what they are reading and explain when it is useful to apply the strategy.

> Strategic readers apply strategies methodically and adjust their use of strategies as required or suggested by the text they are reading.

When presenting the strategy, demonstrate how each step is done, rather than just telling the students what to do. For example, you might use Think-Aloud to model a part of the strategy and include techniques for solving the task cognitively. Encourage your students to use a Three-Part Reading Model (see below) and focus on isolating the strategies you'll use before, while, and after you read. Use scaffolding to gradually move students from copying what you are doing to having them perform the strategy independently.

Here are four steps to accomplish effective transfer of strategy instruction:
1. *Teacher Modeling:* Explain the strategy and why it is useful. Demonstrate the strategy and use Think-Aloud to model your mental processes used during reading
2. *Guided Practice* (to gradually give more responsibility to students after explicit modeling): Practice the strategy with students in large groups, small groups, and then as pairs.
   • When students practice the strategy in small groups, scaffold independence with feedback and discussion.
   • Have students share their thinking processes
   • Provide regular feedback to students (from you and from their peers)
3. *Independent Practice:* Students try the strategy on their own while you provide regular feedback (also encourage peers to provide feedback).
4. *Application of Strategy to Real Reading Situation*s (a critical step for encouraging generalization): Apply the strategy to longer text, more difficult text, and to new genres, formats, and situations.

Three-Part Reading Model

You can introduce a Three-Part Reading Model to help your students become more strategic readers. Strategic readers apply strategies methodically and adjust their use of strategies as required or suggested by the text they reading. This is in contrast to students who read and apply strategies automatically or mechanically because they have merely learned a rote set of steps. Here are the components of the Three-Part Reading Model:

1. Before Reading
   • Activate prior knowledge and previous experiences: students connect what they are ready know and what they are learning and enhance their familiarity with concepts or ideas they will encounter
   • *Examples:* brainstorming, predicting, browsing/skimming, monitoring strategies
2. During Reading
   • Use students' prior knowledge to understand the text
   • Enhance active reading
   • *Examples:* adjust reading rate, predict, ask questions, monitor comprehension, monitor vocabulary, summarize, visualize, use fix-up strategies, use visual organizers

3. After Reading
- Expand students' prior knowledge
- Help students create new understandings
- Enhance students' recall
- *Examples:* confirming and adjusting predictions, visualizing, creating visual organizers, retelling and summarizing, completing charts such as KWL or KWLH, taking notes, reflecting (through writing, talking, dancing, drawing), discussing and synthesizing

It is critical to help students transfer a variety of reading strategies into their everyday and independent use. They need to learn how to apply multiple strategies so that they can overcome challenges presented when they read content specific tasks. Help students appreciate the complex processes involved in reading and explain that they simultaneously learn to be flexible in their reading as they monitor their understanding and synthesize the message(s).

Many students benefit from having a concrete flowchart of the Three-Part Reading Model available as they prepare to read and progress through the reading task. Provide space on the chart for students to record their reactions or processes as they move through the task. Use the flowchart in the Appendix on the CD (pages A-45–47) as a model for creating your own.

Using Multiple Strategies

As students increase their awareness of the importance of using multiple strategies flexibly and fluidly as they read, they also enhance their interaction with the text and increase their independent reading skills and efficiency. To arrive at this level, your students need to understand the purpose of each strategy, when to select a specific strategy, and how genre and text structure impact the strategy they select. The following two activities illustrate ways to remind students graphically of the various strategies available.

The Clock   *Using Multiple Strategies*

1. Select six strategies for your initial focus. Write each on the face of a large clock
2. Display the clock graphic (as shown below) and review the six strategies.
3. Explain to your students how each strategy's location on the clock is a reminder to think about that strategy while reading. (This is episodic memory — using location to help trigger recall.)
4. Practice Step 3 by asking your students questions such as these:
   - What strategy do you think of when you think of 2:00?
   - What strategy do you think of when you think of 8:00?
5. Explain location memory to your students: how thinking of a certain location can remind them of something. Use these examples:
   - Say, "Imagine our classroom is a very large clock. The front of the room is 12:00. Directly across the room, at the back, is 6:00. In the center of the left wall is 3:00 and 9:00 is directly across from it."

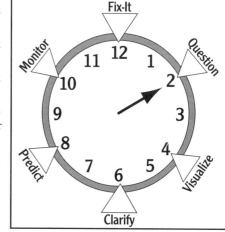

- Place cards strategically around the room to indicate the "time" at each location. Remove those visual cues as students are able to visualize the locations.
- Once the students understand the location of the four "anchor" times, identify the other "on the hour" times.

6. Place a card with a given strategy at each of the time locations on the room clock that corresponds to the large clock graphic you displayed in Step 2. Then have the students use each location to trigger a specific strategy, as in these examples:
   - As students read, have them look at 2:00 and apply that strategy. (*questioning*)
   - Have them look at 6:00 and use that strategy. (*clarifying*)

The Clock technique helps students remember strategies as they are reading simply by glancing at a given location in the room. They use the location to trigger recall of the name of the strategy. As students become more skilled in this technique, you can expand the number of strategies to fill each hour of the clock.

The Map

Using Multiple Strategies

Explain to students that when they know where they are going, they can get there easily. Show your students the map on the right and explain how they can easily get from home to school directly because they know what route you want. (Trace a route on the map.) Explain that the more often we take a route, the more familiar and easier it becomes.

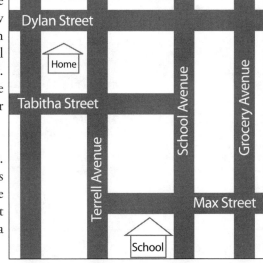

Then ask your students to imagine they are lost. Explain that they might have to try several routes or streets before getting to their destination. Use the map to show how someone might get lost going from home to school and end up taking a longer route by making wrong turns.

Introduce an analogy to your students by saying, "Reading and using multiple reading comprehension strategies is a lot like trying to get somewhere. If we know what we are reading and we understand the text, then we know the route or strategy we might want to use. We can go directly to our destination and progress through the text with clarity and understanding. However, if we are lost and reading something that is difficult, we might need to use many different routes or reading strategies before we arrive at our destination. We need many strategies to help us understand what we are reading just as we can take many routes to get to the same destination."

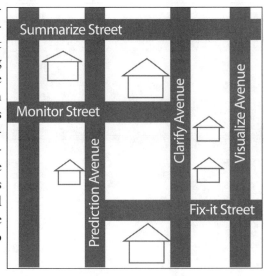

Guidelines

As you read this book, you might ask, "There are so many strategies, where do I start?" The answer to that question is, "Start simple!" Here are some tips for selecting and teaching strategies:
- Select one, two, but no more than three, new strategies to try or to change.
- Practice these strategies until they become easy and automatic. (Practice past perfection.)
- Try another strategy or change only after the first one is working consistently.
- Continuously monitor how you are doing, as well as how your students are doing.

Comprehension instruction is best when it focuses on a few well-taught, well-learned strategies. Although we can now point to a litany of effective techniques, that does not mean that using a litany of techniques will be effective" (Duke & Pearson, 2002).

You might want to develop a list for each area of strategies. Indicate strategies you feel would be most appropriate for your students and your content areas. Then prioritize the strategies on the list to indicate which ones are the most critical to teach initially.

Summary

Our knowledge of what works in teaching reading has come to us through science. Shaywitz states, "This new information can be put to use to provide a sensible and successful approach to teaching children to read — children without any reading difficulties, children who are at risk for reading problems, and children who are already known to be dyslexic" (Shaywitz, 2003, p. 174).

It is an exciting time for us as educators because, for the first time ever, there is an evidence-based guide that explains what works in teaching children to read. It is an outgrowth of a grassroots concern that "while a substantial number of children were failing to learn to read, little was available to help parents and teachers make important choices among different approaches to reading instruction" (Shaywitz, 2003, p. 174).

Subsequent research has illuminated the critical importance of integrating metacognitive awareness skills when teaching the components of reading, with the goal of students becoming strategic, independent readers. This volume strives to provide strategies based on what science has taught us about how to teach our students to read most effectively.

Have fun, read strategically, and teach your students to read strategically!

References

Advanced Study Of The Teaching Of Secondary School Reading. Internet workshop, L517. http://www.indiana.edu/~1517/monitoring.html

Ambruster, B. B. et al. (1983). The role of metacognition and learning to read: a developmental perspective. *Reading Education Report No. 40*. Urbana IL: Center for the study of reading (ED 228 617).

Anglin, J.M. (1993). Vocabulary development: A morphological analysis. *Monographs of the Society for Research in Child Development*, 58 (10, Serial No. 238).

Armbruster, B. B., Lehr, F., and Osborn, J. (2003) for Center for the Improvement of Early Reading Achievement (CIERA). *Put reading first: The research building blocks for teaching children to read*. Washington, DC: National Institutes for Literacy.

Baldwin, Ford and Readence, (1981). Teaching word connotations: An alternative strategy. *Reading World, 21* (2), 103-108.

Baumann, J. F., Seifert-Kessell, N., and Jones, L. A. (1992). Effect of think-aloud instruction on elementary students' comprehension monitoring abilities. *Journal of Reading Behavior, 24*(2), 143-172.

Beck, I. L., McKeown, M. G., and Kucan, L. (2003). Taking delight in words: Using oral language to build young children's vocabulary. *American Educator, 27*(1), 36-41, 45-48.

Beck, I. L., McKeown, M. G., and Kucan, L. (2002). *Bringing words to life: Robust vocabulary instruction*. New York: The Guilford Press.

Beck, I. L., McKeown, M.G., Hamilton, R.L., and Kucan, L. (1997). *Questioning the author: An approach for enhancing student engagement with text*. Newark, DE: International Reading Association.

Bell, N. (1991). *Visualizing and verbalizing for language comprehension and thinking* (revised Ed.). Paso Robles, CA: Academy of Reading Publications.

Berninger, V. and Richards, T. (2002). *Brain literacy for educators and psychologists*. Orlando, FL: Academic Press (Harcourt, Inc.).

Biemiller, A. (2004). Teaching vocabulary in the primary grades. In J. F. Baumann and E. J. Kame'enui (Eds.), *Vocabulary instruction: Research to practice* (pp. 28-40). New York: Guilford.

Borkowski, J. G. and Burke, J. E. (1996). Theories, models, and measurements of executive functioning: An information processing perspective. In G. R. Lyon. and N. A. Krasnegor (Eds.), *Attention, memory, and executive functioning*. Maryland: Brookes Publishing Co.

Brown, J. I. (1947). Reading and vocabulary: 14 master words. In M. J. Herzberg (Ed.), *Word study, 1-4*. Springfield, MA: G & C Merriam.

Brown, R., Pressley, M., Van Meter, P., and Schuder, T. (1996). A quasi-experimental validation of transactional strategies instruction with low-achieving second-grade readers. *Journal of Educational Psychology, 88* (1), 18-37.

Burgess, T. W. (2003). *Old mother west wind*. New York: Henry Holt & Co.

Butterfield, E.C. & Albertson, L. R. (1995). On making cognitive theory more general and developmentally pertinent. In F. Weinert & W. Schneider (Eds.), *Research on Memory Development* (pp. 73-99). Hillsdale,NJ: Lawrence Erlbaum Associates.

Caccamise, D. and Snyder, L. (2005). Theory and pedagogical practices of text comprehension. *Topics In Language Disorders*, 25 (1), 5 to 20.

180   *The Source for Reading Comprehension Strategies*

Carlisle, J. F. (1999). Free recall as a test of reading comprehension for students with learning disabilities. *Learning Disability Quarterly, 22*, 11-22.

Carlisle, J. F. and Rice, M. S. (2002). *Improving reading comprehension: Research-based principles and practices.* Timonium Maryland: York Press.

Carmine, D., and Kinder, B. D. (1985). Teaching low performing students to apply generative and schema strategies to narrative and expository material. *Remedial and Special Education, 6*, 20-30.

Carraker, S. (2005, July). Comprehension: the ultimate goal of reading. Presentation S15 at Research to Practice: Advances in Reading Literacy Symposium, Washington, DC.

Casalis, J., Cole, P., & Sopo, D. (2004). Morphological awareness and developmental dyslexia. *Annals of Dyslexia, 54* (1), 114-138.

Clark, J. M. and Paivio, A. (1991). Dual coding theory and education. *Educational Psychology Review*, September.

Conn, T. (2005, March). Curriculum LINCS: A program from the strategies intervention model by Donald Deshler et al. Presentation at New York Branch IDA Conference.

Corson, D. (1985). *The lexical bar.* Oxford: Pergamon Press.

DePorter, B., Reardon, M., and Singer-Nourie, S. (1999). *Quantum teaching: orchestrating student success.* Boston: Allyn and Bacon.

Deschler, D. D. & Schumaker, J. B. (1988). An instructional model for teaching students how to learn. In J. L. Graden, J. E. Zins, and M. J. Curtis (Eds.), *Alternative educational delivery systems: enhancing instructional options for all students* (pp. 391-411). Washington, DC: National Association of School Psychologists.

Duffy, G. G. (1993). Rethinking strategy instruction: Four teachers' development and their low achievers' understandings. *Elementary School Journal, 93*(3), 231-247.

Duke, N. K. and Pearson, P. D. (2002). Effective practices for developing reading comprehension. In J. Samuels and A. Farstrup (Eds.), *What research has to say about reading instruction* (3rd Ed.). Newark, DE: International Reading Association.

Eagan, T. (1997). *Burnt toast on Davenport Street.* Boston: Houghton Mifflin.

Fitzgerald, R. (2005, April). A system: Using brain research and data for teaching success. Presentation at Learning And The Brain – Rewiring The Brain: Using Brain Plasticity To Enhance Learning And Treat Learning Disorders Conference sponsored by Public Information Resources, Inc.

Fletcher, J. (2004, November). Research-based education and intervention – What we need to know. Symposium at IDA 55th Annual Conference. Session Chair: Sylvia O. Richardson, MD. Philadelphia, PA.

Foorman, B. R. and Torgesen, J. (2001). Critical elements of classroom in small-group instruction to promote reading success in all children. *Learning Disabilities Research and Practice, 16*, 203-212.

Gersten, R., Fuchs, L.S., Williams, J. P., and Baker, S. (2001). Teaching reading comprehension strategies to students with learning disabilities: A review of the research. *Review of Educational Research, 71*, 279-320.

Geyer, G. (2005, April). The neuroscience of innate wisdom: Using metacognition, mediation, and mind-body practices for enhancing student attention, emotional balance, and personal awareness. Presentation at Learning And The Brain – Rewiring The Brain: Using Brain Plasticity To Enhance Learning And Treat Learning Disorders Conference sponsored by Public Information Resources, Inc.

Gunning, T. (1996). *Creating reading instruction for all children.* Boston: Allyn and Bacon.

Hammer, P. (1979). What is the use of cognates? Washington, DC: US Department of Health, Education and Welfare. ERIC document reproduction service number ED 180202.

References

Harste, J., Woodward, V., and Burke, C. (1984). *Language stories and literacy lessons.* Portsmouth, NH: Heineman.

Helfeldt, J. P. and Henk, W. A. (1990). Reciprocal questioning: Answer relationships – an instructional technique for at-risk readers. *Journal of Reading, 33,* 509-514.

Henry, M. (2003). *Unlocking literacy: Effective decoding & spelling instruction.* Baltimore, MD. Brookes Publishing.

Henry, M. K. (2003). *Unlocking literacy: effective decoding and spelling instruction.* Baltimore, MD: Brookes Publishing Co.

Hirsch, E.D. (2003). reading comprehension requires knowledge of words and the world: Scientific insights into the fourth-grade slump in the nation's stagnant comprehension scores. *American Educator, Spring,* 10-45.

Hunt, E. T. (1992) Taught me purple. In J. N. Beatty and W. L. McBride (Eds), *Literature and language* (p 321). Evanston Illinois: McDougal, Littel, (original work published 1964).

Idol, L. (1987). Group story mapping: A comprehension strategy for both skilled and unskilled readers. *Journal of Learning Disabilities, 20,* 196-205.

Idol, L. and Croll, V. J. (1987). Story mapping training as a means of improving reading comprehension. *Learning Disability Quarterly, 10,* 214-29.

Jackson, H. H. (1959). September. In L. Untermeyer (Ed.), *The golden treasury of poetry.* Racine, WI: Western Publishing Co.

Jenkins, J. R., and O'Connor, R. E. (2002). Early identification and intervention for Young children with reading/learning disabilities. In R. Bradley, L. Danielson, and D. P. Hallahan (Eds.), *Identification of learning disabilities: Research to practice* (pp. 99-184). Mahwah, NJ: Lawrence Erlbaum Associates.

Jenkins, J. R., Heliotis, J. D., Stein, M. L., and Haynes, M. C. (1987). Improving reading comprehension by using paragraph restatements. *Exceptional Children, 54,* 54-9.

Jensen, E. (2003). *Tools for engagement: Managing emotional states for learner success.* San Diego, CA: The Brain Store.

Keene, E. O. and Zimmerman, S. (1997). *Mosaic of thought: Teaching comprehension in a readers' workshop.* Portsmouth, NH: Heinemann.

Kindler, A. L. (2002). *Survey Of the states' limited English proficient students and available educational programs and services: 2000-2001 summary report.* Washington, DC: National Clearinghouse For English-Language Acquisition and Language Instruction Educational Programs

Kintsch, E. (2005). Comprehension theory as a guide for the design of thoughtful questions. *Topics in Language Disorders, 25*(1), 51-64.

Kintsch, W. (1998). *Comprehension: A paradigm for comprehension.* New York: Cambridge University Press.

Kintsch, W. and Kintsch, E. (2005). Comprehension. In S. G. Paris & S. A. Stahl (Eds.), *Current issues on reading comprehension and assessment* (pp. 71-92). Mahwah, NJ: Erlbaum.

Kos, R. (1991). Persistence of reading difficulties: The voices of four middle school students. *American Educational Research Journal, 28,* 875-895.

Kuhn, M. R. and Stahl, S.A. (2004). *Fluency: A review of developmental and remedial practices.* Washington, DC: U.S. Department of Education.

Lakoff, G. and Johnson, M. (1980). *Fifty-six metaphors we live by.* Chicago: University of Chicago Press.

Langer, J. A. (2001). Beating the odds: Teaching middle and high school students to read and write well. *American Education Research Journal, 38*(4), 837-880.

Lederer, R. (1990). *The play of words.* New York: Simon & Schuster.

Lenski, L. (1955). *People from Skipping Village*. New York: J. B. Lippincott.

Levine, M. D. (1998). *Developmental variation and learning disorders*. Cambridge, MA: Educators Publishing Service.

Levine, M. D. (2001). *Educational care: A system for understanding and helping children with learning differences at home and school* (2nd Ed.). Cambridge, MA: Educators Publishing Service.

Lovett, M. W., Lacerenza, L., and Borden, S. L. (2000). Putting struggling readers on the PHAST track: A program to integrate phonological and strategy-based remedial reading instruction and maximize outcomes. *Journal Of Learning Disabilities, 33* (5), 458-476.

Lovett, M. W., Lacerenza, L., Murphy, D., Steinbach, K. A., DePalma, M., and Frijters, J. C. (2005). The importance of multi-component interventions for children and adolescents as struggling readers. In *Research-based education and intervention: What we need to know*, S. O. Richardson and J. W. Gilger (Eds.). Baltimore, MD: International Dyslexia Association.

Lyon, G. R. (2001, March). Testimony to the House Committee on Education and The Workforce, Subcommittee on Education Reform, Washington, DC.

Lyon, G. R. (2004). Closing comments from Chapter 1 of this book. In P. McCardle and V. Chhabra (Eds.), *The voice of evidence in reading research*. Baltimore MD: Brookes Publishing Co.

Lyon, G. R. (2004, November). Evolution of evidence-based education. Session T23 Presentation at IDA 55th Annual Conference, Philadelphia, PA.

Marzano, R. J., Norford, J. S., Paynter, D. E., Pickering, D. J., and Gaddy, B. B. (2001). *A handbook for classroom instruction that works*. Alexandria, VA: Association for Supervision and Curriculum.

McCardle, P. and Chhabra, V. (Eds.). (2004). *The voice of evidence in reading research*. Baltimore MD: Brookes Publishing Co.

McGraw-Hill. (2002). *McGraw-Hill social studies series* (grade 5): *Making a new nation*. New York: McGraw-Hill.

McLaughlin, M., & Allen, M. B. (2002). *Guided comprehension: A teaching model for grades 3-8*. Newark, DE: International Reading Association.

Meek, M. (1983). *Achieving literacy: Longitudinal studies of adolescents learning to read*. London: Routledge & Kegan Paul.

Moats, L. C. (2000). *Speech to print: language essentials for teachers*. Baltimore MD: Brookes Publishing Co.

Moore, D. W., Bean, T., Birdyshaw, D., and Rycik, J. (1999). Adolescent literacy. A position paper for the Commission on Adolescent Literacy of the International Reading Association, Newark, DE.

Mora, J. K. (2005). Spanish/English Cognates. Retrieved December, 29, 2005, from San Diego State University, Mora Modules: http://coe.sdsu.edu/people/jmora/MoraModules/SpEngCognates.htm.

Nagy, W. (1985). Vocabulary instruction: Implications of the new research. Paper presented at the Convention of the National Council of teachers of English, Philadelphia.

Nagy, W. E. and Andersson, R. C. (1984). The number of words and printed school English. *Reading Research Quarterly*, 19, 304-330.

Nagy, W. E., Berninger, V., and Abbot, R. (2005). Contributions of morphology beyond phonology to literacy outcomes of the upper elementary and middle school students. *Journal of Educational Psychology*.

Nagy, W., Anderson, R., and Herman, P. (1986). The influence of word and text properties on learning from context. Urbana, IL: University of Illinois, Center for the Study of Reading. Eric Document Reproduction Service Number ED 266443.

References

Nagy, W. (2005, July). Morphological contributions to literacy. Presentation at Teaching Teachers and Teaching Students: A Developmental Approach to Prevention & Treatment of Dyslexia Symposium at Research To Practice: Advances in Reading and Literacy Conference, Washington, DC. Symposium chair, Virginia Berninger, Ph.D.

National Reading Panel. (1999). *Teaching children to read: an evidence-based assessment of the scientific research literature on reading and its implications for reading instruction* (reports of the subgroups). Rockville, MD: National Institute of Child, Health, and Human Development.

Nelson, P. A. (2005). Teaching tips: Could you and your students use a poetry getaway? *The Reading Teacher. Vol 58*(5).

Nolte, R. Y. and Singer, H. (1985). Active comprehension: Teaching a process of reading comprehension and its effects on reading achievement. *The Reading Teacher, 38*, 24-31.

Paivio, A. (1971). *Imagery and verbal processes.* New York: Holt, Reinhardt, and Winston. (Reprinted [1979]. Hillsdale, NJ: Lawrence Erlbaum Associates.)

Paivio, A. (1986). *Mental Representations: a Dual Coding Approach.* New York: Oxford University Press.

Palincsar, A.S. and Brown, A. L. (1986). Interactive teaching to promote independent learning from text. *The Reading Teacher, 39*, 771-77.

Palincsar, A. S., and Brown, A. L. (1985). Reciprocal teaching: Activities to promote read(ing) with your mind. In T.L. Harris & E.J. Cooper (Eds.), *Reading, thinking and concept development: Strategies for the classroom.* New York: The College Board.

Palincsar, A. S., and Klenk, L. J. (1991). Dialogues promoting reading comprehension. In B. Means, C. Chelemer, and M. S. Knapp (Eds.), *Teaching advanced skills to at-risk students.* San Francisco: Jossey-Bass.

Parish, P. (1963). *Amelia Bedelia: I can read picture book.* New York: HarperCollins.

Pasternak, R. H. (2004). A tribute to G. Reid Lyon. In P. McCardle, and V. Chhabra (Eds.), *The voice of evidence in reading research.* Baltimore MD: Brookes Publishing Co.

Payne, R. K. (1998). *A framework for understanding poverty.* Highlands, TX: RFT Publishing Co.

Pearson, P. D., Roehler, L. R., Dole, J. A., and Duffy, G. G. (1992). Developing expertise in reading comprehension. In J. Samuels and A. Farstrup (Eds.), *What research has to say about reading instruction* (2nd Ed.) Newark, DE: International Reading Association.

Prelutsky, J. (2002). *The frogs wore red suspenders.* New York: Greenwillow Books.

Ramsden, M. (2001). *The user's self-training manual: The essential reference for real English spelling.* Self-published; Available from the author at http://www.realspelling.com/.

Raphael, T. E. (1984). Teaching learners about sources of information for answering comprehension questions. *Journal of Reading, 27*(4), 303-311.

Richards, R. (2001). *The source for learning and memory.* East Moline, IL: LinguiSystems, Inc.

Richek, M. A. (2001). *Vocabulary strategies that boost students' reading comprehension* [Video]. Chicago: Northeastern Illinois University

Rosenshine, B., Meister, C., and Chapman, S. (Eds. & Trans.). (1996). Teaching students to generate questions: *A review of the intervention studies. Review of Educational Research, 66*(2), 181-221. Cambridge, MA: Harvard University Press.

Ruddell, M. R. (2001). *Teaching content reading and writing* (3rd Ed.). New York: John Wiley.

Ruddell, R. B., Ruddell, M. R., and Singer, H. (Eds.). (1994). *Theoretical Models and Processes of Reading* (4th Ed.). Newark, DE: International Reading Association.

Sackett, D. (1992). Evidence-based working group quoted by Shaywitz, S. (2004, November) in Evolution of evidence-based education. Session at IDA 55th Annual Conference. Philadelphia PA. Session Chair: Sally Shaywitz.

Sadoski, M. (1983). An Exploratory Study of the relationship between reported imagery and the comprehension and recall of a story. *Reading Research Quarterly, 19-1*, 110-123.

Sadoski, M. (1985). The natural use of imagery in story comprehension and recall: Replication and extension. *Reading Research Quarterly, Fall.*

Sadoski, M., Goetz, E. T., and Kangister, S. (1988). Imagination in story response: Relationships between imagery, affect, and structural importance. *Reading Research Quarterly, Summer.*

Sadoski, M., Goetz, E. T., Olivarez, A., Lee, S., and Roberts, N. M. (1990). Imagination in story reading: The role of imagery, verbal recall, story analysis and processing levels. *Journal of Reading Behavior.*

Sandak, R. (2005, July). The role of brain research in the prediction and treatment of dyslexia. Presentation at Research to Practice: Advances in Reading and Literacy Symposium. Washington, DC. Session chair: Kenneth Pugh.

Shaywitz, S. (2003). *Overcoming dyslexia: A new and complete science-based program for reading problems at any level.* New York: Alfred A. Knopf.

Shaywitz, S. (2004, November). Evolution of evidence-based education. Presentation at IDA 55th Annual Conference, Philadelphia PA. Session Chair: Sally Shaywitz

Shearer, B. A., Ruddell, M. R., & Vogt, M.E. (2001). Successful middle school intervention: Negotiated strategies and individual choice. In J. V. Hoffmann, D. L. Schallert, C. M. Fairbanks, J. Worthy, and B. Maloch (Eds), *National Reading Conference Yearbook, 50* (pp. 558-571). Chicago: National Reading Conference.

Shwa-Alt.Notations (sic). Retrieved December 28, 2005 from http://victorian.fortunecity.com/vangogh/555/

Snow, C. (Chair, RAND Reading Study Group). (2001, January). Reading for understanding: Towards an R&D program in reading comprehension. Prepared for the Office of Educational Research and Improvement (OERI). Washington, DC: U.S. Department of Education.

Snow, C., Burns, M. S., and Griffin, P. (Eds). (1998). *Preventing reading disabilities in young children.* Washington DC: National Academies Press.

Sousa, D. (2001). *How the brain learns* (2nd ed.). Thousand Oaks, CA: Corwin Press, Inc.

Spiro, R. J. (1980). Constructive processes in prose comprehension and recall. In *Theoretical issues in reading comprehension* (pp. 245-78), R. J. Spiro, B. C. Bruce, and W. E. Brewer (Eds.). Hillsdale, NJ: Lawrence Erlbaum.

Spiro, R. J., Coulson, R. I., Feltovich, P.J. and Anderson, D. K. (1994). Cognitive flexibility.theory: Advanced knowledge acquisition in ill-structured domains. In R. B. Ruddell, M. R. Ruddell, and H. Stanovich, Keith. (1986). Matthew effects in reading: Some consequences of individual differences in the acquisition of reading. *Reading Research Quarterly, 21*, 360-407.

Tei, E. and Stewart, O. (1985). Effective studying from text. *Forum for Reading, 16*(2), 46 to 55.

Templeton, S., and Pikulski, J. J. (1999). Building the foundations of literacy: The importance of vocabulary and spelling development. Retrieved June 3, 2004, from Eduplace: http://www.eduplace.com/rdg/hmsv/expert/research.html.

References

Torgesen, J. K. (2001). In R. Gersten, L. S. Fuchs, J. P. Williams, and S. Baker. (2001). Teaching reading comprehension strategies to students with learning disabilities: a review of the research. *Review of educational research, 71*, 279-320.)

Torgesen, J. K. (2004). Remedial interventions for students with dyslexia: National goals and current accomplishments. In *Research-based education and intervention: What we need to know.* Baltimore, MD: International Dyslexia Association.

Tovani, C. (2004). *Do I really have to teach reading? Content comprehension, grades 6 to 12.* Portland, ME: Stenhouse Publishers.

U.S. Department of Education. (2002). No Child Left behind Act of 2001, Reading First Legislation. Retrieved from the Department of Education: http://www.Ed.gov/legislation/ESEA02/

van Dijk, T. A. & Kintsch, W. (1983). *Strategies of discourse comprehension.* New York: Academic Press.

Vogt, M. (1989). The convergence between preservice teachers' and in-service teachers' attitudes and practices toward high and low achievers. Unpublished doctoral dissertation, University of California, Berkeley, CA.

Vogt, M. (1997). Intervention strategies for intermediate and middle school students: Three models (that appear) to work. Paper presented at the Research Institute of the Annual Conference of the California Reading Association, Anaheim, CA.

White, T. G., Sowell, J., and Yanagihara, A. (1989). Teaching elementary students to use word-part clues. *The Reading Teacher, 42*, 302-308.

Wolfe, P. and Nevills, P. (2004). *Building the reading brain, PreK-3.* Thousand Oaks, CA: Corwin Press.

Wood, K. D. and Harmon, J. M. (2001). *Strategies for integrating reading and writing in middle and high school classrooms.* Westerville, OH: National Middle School Association.

Internet Resources

Inspiration – http://www.inspiration.com

Kidspiration — http://www.inspiration.com

Slovo Ed Dictionary — Paragon Software: http://palm-dictionaries.penreader.com/index.html

186   *The Source for Reading Comprehension Strategies*

Index

26-06-987654321